The Case of the Red Pills

—*Six Sensational Ming and Qing Dynasty Court Cases*

Written by Liu Jianye
Translated by Liu Jianwei

Foreign Languages Press   Beijing

First Edition   2001

Home Page:
   http://www.flp.com.cn
E-mail Addresses:
   info@flp.com.cn
   sales@flp.com.cn

ISBN 7-119-02050-1
©Foreign Languages Press, Beijing, China, 2001

Published by Foreign Languages Press
24 Baiwanzhuang Road, Beijing 100037, China

Distributed by China International Book Trading Corporation
35 Chegongzhuang Xilu, Beijing 100044, China
P.O. Box 399, Beijing, China

Printed in the People's Republic of China

CONTENTS

CONTENTS

Prologue

A few famous court cases were tried in the Ming and Qing dynasties in China, creating a great stir in society at that time. These cases, some involving the common people and some involving the ruling houses, were very complicated and fraught with twists and turns, some of them remaining uncleared even to this day. Selected in this book are six stories based on six celebrated cases, the details of which are presented to readers in an autoptic style, disclosing some of the hitherto unknown events that took place inside the Forbidden City and outside.

The Wrongs of a
Noble-Hearted Girl

In 1525, the fourth year of Jiajing's reign in the Ming Dynasty, a surprising incident happened in the Imperial Bodyguards Northern Prison, which had been set up to hold "thieves and other law-breakers."

A young female prisoner, Li Yuying, wrote to Emperor Jiajing to complain of an injustice. The case was veiled in mystery and it emerged and died away several times. Eventually, a fair-minded and courageous judge happened to hear it. After he had made great efforts to clear all the obstacles, the truth was revealed and the real criminals were brought to justice. Because the case was heard by the Chinyiwei (Imperial Bodyguards)* first and was only brought to Emperor Jiajing's attention after a long time, it caused a great stir throughout the country. It was considered one of the most sensational cases in the middle years of the Ming Dynasty.

"A stunningly beautiful girl has been sentenced to be hacked to death by the Imperial Bodyguards Northern

---

* Chinyiwei (literally "embroidered uniform guard unit"), the most prestigious and influential of the Imperial Guards (Chinchunwei) in the Ming Dynasty functioned as the personal bodyguards of the Emperor and cooperated with influential eunuchs in maintaining an empire-wide, irregular police and judicial service.

Prison. She is going to be executed in the forthcoming autumn." As the news spread, many people in the prison sighed while some old prison guards even could not hold back their tears.

In the guardroom in a corner of the prison, some guards were drinking, while talking about the beauty and the crime she had committed. A half-drunk young guard, with his blood-shot eyes glaring, asked "What did she do? How could she get such a severe punishment? To be hacked to death!"

An old guard sitting beside him answered in a sorrowful voice, with sympathy: "Adultery. What a pity! She's so young and pretty."

The young guard seemed to be excited by the crime of adultery and got even more drunk. "Adultery? With whom?" he asked, his face glowing. "Who is the man? I met this prisoner a few times. Look at that face, even lady Yang, the favorite of the Tang Dynasty emperor Xuanzong was not that beautiful. What a pity!"

A middle-aged guard with a gloomy face shook his head in disagreement: "Adultery? I don't believe it. Such a graceful girl would never do such an immoral thing. Aren't there too many cases of injustice in the prison? She will, maybe, become one of those ghosts who haunt the prison wailing for justice."

The group seemed to be depressed by these words, and they all fell silent. Today, all the guards in the prison seemed to be anxious about something. After a while, some of the younger guards walked into the corridor and peeked out; then they went to the female wards and whispered to the women guards. The fact of the matter was, they were looking forward to a glimpse of the peerless beauty who was now the talk of the prison.

After noon, Li Yuying was escorted back to the prison by seven or eight female guards, her ankles fettered with heavy shackles. The corridor was packed with made guards who were waiting for a look at the beauty. Even the prisoners pressed their faces against the iron bars, straining their eyes to see her. Li Yuying was about seventeen years old. Although brutal torture made her appear haggard and hardly able to walk, and her dress was in rags, the slender figure, the pretty chin and the lovely mouth still expressed her extraordinary beauty. Especially her bright eyes, although clouded over with sadness and worry, still shone with exceptional youthful elegance. She staggered across the corridor, her head lowered, eyes filled with tears, teeth biting tensely on her lower lip. She seemed to be unconscious of her surroundings as she was led by the guards to the death cell. In her mind still lingered that unbearable scene in the main hall of the yamen forever branded in her memory...

The malicious judge had stared at her with the insatiable eyes, ferociously questioning her about the whole illicit affair. Mortified, she did not make any reply, her head slightly dropping.

Prompted by the judge, two Imperial Body guards brutally forced opened her hands and put the *zanzi* (clamps) between her fingers. In no time at all, extreme pain shot through her body. She let out a shrill scream and then lost consciousness....

The confession statement was spread out before her, and she could vaguely read: "Fornicating shamelessly, humiliating and bullying her mother, privately writing love letters to her lover, corrupting morals...". Her bloody fingerprint appeared distinctly at the bottom....

The judge was announcing coldly: "Li Yuying, adulteress, carried on an illicit affair for a long time, behaved unfilially, and plotted to kill her stepmother... She is hereby sentenced to death by the process of hacking and will be executed in the forthcoming autumn."

Li Yuying did not dare to recall it anymore. Anyhow, all was finished and everything would be over soon. What would it be like being hacked to death? Maybe it was better than undergoing torture. "Let it come, the sooner the better," she thought. "So that I will not stand trial in the main hall of the yamen every day and suffer all the tortures." As she was lost in these thoughts, the door of the female death-row cell was opened with a clanking noise. The dark prison cell looked like the gate to hell. Li Yuying was pulled over to the door and thrown into the cell. Then the door was slammed shut behind her and locked up with heavy chains. The cell was as dark as night, hardly could Li Yuying see anything. The stinking smell of the mildewed hay mat was overpowering. Her fingers that had been squeezed open by the *zanai* swelled terribly. She tried to rub the fingers, but the sharp pain threw her on to the hay.

In this semi-conscious state, the nightmare of what happened one year ago haunted Yuying again as she relived her arrest and delivery to the prison.

It had been a dark midsummer's night. Yuying had done embroidery for almost the whole evening. Just as she laid down in the bed, she heard someone shouting outside: "Get the adulterers!" Several torches appeared from nowhere and the door of her bedroom was pounded and kicked mightedly, making a big racket. Yuying quickly covered herself with some clothes.

6

Hardly had she got out of the bed than the door was forced open. Her stepmother Jiao, her maternal uncle Jiao Rong and two maids forced themselves moisily into the room. The stepmother scrutinized Yuying from head to foot, her eyes like two vicious swords. Jiao Rong stared at Yuying's plump chest lustfully. Yuying was so embarrassed to discover that in her rush she had not tidied her collar and her breasts were slightly visible. Her youthful modesty made her lower her head and quickly pull her clothes in order.

Her stepmother shouted in a rage: "The intrigant has escaped, but the intrigante is still here! Search for evidence!"

Jiao Rong and the maids began to rummage around in the room. But nothing suspicious was found. Jiao Rong looked to her stepmother for help. The women started to search herself. She turned the shabby cloth box over and shook the thin quilt open, but still found nothing she needed. Then she walked to the dressing table in front of the window and opened the girl's make-up box. Inside the box there was no rouge and no jewelry, only a silver hairpin which had been left to Yuying by her own mother. The stepmother opened a small drawer in the make-up box and found several poems written by Yuying to express her melancholy feelings. All the secrets in Yuying's heart were expressed in these poems. Each time when she finished a poem, she hid it in the small drawer inside the make-up box to keep others from seeing it. Now the poems were found by her stepmother. How embarrassing! The woman scanned the poems quickly. Then she seemed to discover some important evidence.

She pointed to one of the poems and asked in a

sharp voice: "'Whisper with sadness, part with grief,' what's the meaning of this? Whom do you whisper to? Aren't you too young to worry about parting? Here is another one: 'The silent wooden door locks the end of the spring.' Obviously you feel lonely because your lover didn't come on time! What excuse do you have?"

Jiao Rong fiddled for a while with the silver hairpin with ill-intentions. Then he whispered to her stepmother while pointing at the inscription on the hairpin: "unshakable resolve." The stepmother became even more outraged after seeing these words.

She flung the hairpin on the ground and shouted at Yuying: "Where did you get this from? Wasn't it given by your lover? (Unshakeable resolve,) My! How deep is this love. Tell me! Who is the man? Or I'll tear up your lips!"

What ridiculous libel! The silver hairpin had been given to Yuying's father, Li Xiong, as a gift by Prince, Cheng. When Yuying's father was young, he had worked at Cheng's mansion. Cheng had thought highly of Li Xiong's honesty and loyalty. So he had the silver hairpin custom-made as a gift for Li Xiong. What an absurd thing to link this hairpin with an intrigant! Overwhelmed by anger and embarrassment, Yuying couldn't say a word. At this moment, a servant called Li Qiang'er came in, holding a man's shoe and said he had found a shoe when searching outside.

"It was left in the woods dozens of meters away from the wall of the yard," Li Qiang'er said. "It looks like it was lost by a man when he jumped over the wall and escaped in a hurry." The stepmother took the shoe and brought it in front of Yuying's face: "You unfilial girl," she said viciously, "You dishonor the family! I always forgave you when you contradicted what I said every day, but now you seduce an intrigant! How do you expect me to face your father! Now, here is all the evidence. I cannot harbor you and cover up all your evil deeds because you are my daughter. Jiao Rong, send her to the Imperial Bodyguards yamen and have her charged with adultery and unfilial conduct. I don't want others to point at me and say I raised a whore!"

The uncle and two servants tied Yuying up and dragged her to the Imperial Bodyguard yamen...

Yuying was awakened by the noise of heavy chains. The cell was as dark as before. Another female prisoner was being escorted out. She was weeping, her clothes torn into rags. Yuying knew she was going to be tried again. How could anyone bear the tortures of beating, hanging, *zanzi*, hammering of bamboo chips into fingernails and branding with a heated iron on bare skin... Privately, she sympathized with these prisoners. She even believed that there was not one real criminal in the prison.

With the help of the damp wall, Yuying struggled to sit up. The wounds all over her body from the tortures remained burningly painful. However, she was very calm inside. "It is only some twenty days before the execution. Then, I will be completely extricated from this pain. Then, my beautiful youth, my knowledge and talent will all be gone. It is said that after people die, they can meet their deceased families in hell. It means that I will be able to see father, mother and lovely little brother Li Chengzu...". Yuying was lost in fantasy, her eyes slightly closed. The smiling faces of her parents appeared before her again. All the good times from when she was young came to mind. Yuying's father Li Xiong had been a *qianhu* (company commander) in the Imperial

9

Bodyguards. At that time, many officials of the Imperial Bodyguards were imperious and despotic. But her father was not one of them. Li Xiong always taught Yuying and her bother and sisters to be polite, honest and kind. Yuying also had a loving mother who had cherished them very much. Unfortunately Yuying's mother died when Yuying's brother was only two years old. However, Yuying could never let go of her mother's deep love.

Li Xiong often had to leave home on official missions. In order to have someone to take care of the children, Li Xiong married Jiao. In the second year of their marriage, Jiao gave birth to a boy named Li Yanu. In order to have Li Xiong's official post inherited by her own son, Jiao began to maltreat Chengzu*

At first, only when Li Xiong was not at home did Jiao beat Chengzu and refuse to give him enough food. The suffering through such cruelty made the ten-year-old boy bony and weak, but the boy never shed tears before his sisters. He didn't want them to be worrying about him. Each time when the sisters touched the bruises in his face and burst into tears, he would comfort them, saying, "It is no big deal. Don't cry, sisters." Once, the vicious stepmother gave the boy no food for three straight days. Chengzu was too starved to move. That evening, Yuying and her sisters secretly saved some rice gruel and brought it to Chengzu. For the first time the small boy couldn't keep back his tears as his eldest sister held him. Tears fell down his bony face like pearls. The sisters and brother clung to one another deep autumn their faces awashed in tears. The cold, deep autumn

---

* In feudal China, only the eldest son had the right to inherit the father's official post.

10

moonlight shone on the four poor children. The only hope was their father. They were looking forward to their father's early return. But for now, they were surrounded by nothing but freezing cold.

An old Chinese saying goes: "Blessings never arrive in pairs, while misfortune never comes singly." Just as the children were suffering under their stepmother's tyranny, their father was killed in a war in Shaanxi Province (in China's northwest). While the children were overwhelmed with grief, their stepmother went fuarther in her maltreatment of Chengzu. She forced him to go to the battlefield which was hundreds of miles away to look for his father's remains. Obviously she wanted to trap the boy in a dilemma rather than to teach him to be filial. Chengzu knew he had no other choice. He prepared a simple pack and went resolutely to Shaanxi. It was a snowy morning when the girls saw their little brother off. Looking at that naive face, the girls' eyes welled with broken-hearted tears. Chengzu knelt down to give his grieved sisters a kowtow and then carrying his simple pack, decisively marched on his way to Shaanxi. In no time, his skinny figure disappeared in the snow.

Not long after Chengzu left, Guiying was sold to a rich family as a maidservant. The other sister, Taoying, meanwhile could not bear the maltreatment and escaped. She tried to hide at their maternal grandmother's, but was pursued and forced back. She was whipped so severely that she nearly died. Since then, the smallest complaint would usually lead to a scolding and whipping. The wounds overlapped all over Taoying's emaciated body. As time passed, Jiao's heart grew harder and harder, and her punishment of the girls became crueler and crueler. The sisters could do nothing to protect themselves but cry in each other's arms. One year later, Chengzu came back home unexpectedly. He carried with him his father's remains instead of the simple luggage.

Their brother's return brought some vitality back to Yuying and her sisters. Chengzu often told his sisters about the hardships on his way to Shaanxi. The sisters often comforted their little brother with the saying: "One who can endure the hardest of all hardships will become the greatest of all men." But this good spell did not last long. Who could imagine how the cruel-hearted stepmother was malevolently plotting to stop Chengzu from taking back the rights of primogeniture from her own son. She tricked Chengzu into drinking a bowl of vegetable soup in which she had put arsenic. The poor boy! He had survived the dangerous jouney to the west, but couldn't survive his stepmother's cold-blooded murderousness. To avoid incrimination, Jiao unscrupulously chopped the body into pieces and had them thrown into the flowing city moat. Then, Jiao framed the case of adultery against Yuying and had her put behind the bars.

After Jiao Rong handed in the so-called criminal evidence against Yuying, Chen Yin, commander of the Imperial Bodyguards, who was in charge of the case, gave credence at once to the accuser's statement. He did not even give Yuying a chance to explain, but blindly tried to force her to confess who the intrigant was. Yuying had kept silent since she had been sent to the Imperial Bodyguards yamen. She knew very clearly that once she entered the Imperial Bodyguard's prison, there was little hope of getting out alive. Poor Yuying, even under such terrible circumstances, she was still concern about the continuity of the family line—she worried that

12

if she told the truth, Jiao would be punished severely, then nobody would raise her three-year-old brother Li Yanu. If Yanu was starved or frozen to death, Li's family would have no inheritors. She would be the criminal in the family. Therefore, for the past year, although Yuying went through all kinds of torture till she had scars strung together like beads, she had never given any confession. Another half a year passed, but without Yuying's confession and without any sign of the intrigant, Chen Yin could not wind up the case. He laid all the blame at Yuying's door so his hatred of her became more and more intense. Eventually, he had to employ the customary tactics. He had Yuying's fingerprint pressed on a confession which had been written up by someone else while Yuying fainted away from the torture. Then the case was closed. Yuying was jailed in the death-row cell, awaiting execution in autumn. In the Imperial Bodyguards prison, unjust cases happened almost every day. So once a case was settled, normally there was little posibility of reversing the verdict.

At that time, in the political infighting among the ruling class, some injustices happened to be used by one faction to gain popularity. Li Yuying fortunately met a chance like this.

Not long after Li Yuying was jailed an intense political struggle started in the highest ruling class. The newly enthroned emperor Jiajing was a cousin of the late emperor Zhengde. After Jiajing came into power, he was desirous of granting the title Huangkao (Deseased Imperial Father) to his father Zhu Youhang, who was known as Prince Xingxian in his lifetime, and granting the title Huangshukao (Deseased Imperial Uncle) to Emperor Zhengde's father Xiaozong. His intention was strongly opposed by some two hundred important officials represented by the Prime Minister of the cabinet, Yang Tinghe. The officials held the opinion that following tradition, the title of Huangkao should be granted to Zhengde's father and that of Huangshufu (Imperial Uncle) to Emperor Jiajing's father. The two sides strongly stood by their own opinions and neither would give in. The dispute lasted for three years without reaching a conclusion. In the third year of his reign, 1524, Emperor Jiajing, with the support of Zhang Cong, an influential scholar, started to vigorously attack the opposition. In July, the controversy came to a head. One day, Yang Tinghe and his supporters, in total 229 officials, knelt at the Zuoshun Gate of the Forbidden City and expostulated in tears with Emperor Jiajing about the unrighteousness of making his father Huangkao. Seeing this, Jiajing flew into a rage. He ordered the arrest of the remonstrating officials. Among the 220 officials arrested, more than 180 were flogged in the audience chamber, 17 flogged to death, and 8 high officials of high prestige were exiled to frontier regions. Prime Minister Yang Tinghe was forced to resign and return to his hometown. This abrupt suppression made everyone in the government jittery. Many officials who had not been implicated in the event showed their uneasiness and dissatisfaction. In order to ease the tension, Emperor Jiajing promulgated many decrees to change the simmering situation. He knew that there had been many injustices in the Imperial Bodyguards prison. Criticisms had been heard from all over the country. Therefore, Emperor Jiajing issued a special imperial edict to the Imperial Bodyguards: "Prisoners should stop being punished in virtue of the hot weather. A supervising eunuch will be sent to hear the injustices in the prison. Prisoners may appeal in cases of injustices."

The purpose of issuing the edict was to gain the good graces of the public and win over more supporters for the government. The Emperor did not really intend to correct all the injustices. But since the imperial edict had been issued, the Imperial Bodyguards had to act accordingly. A vice *qianhu*, Lu Bing, who later was to become the prestigious commander of the Imperial Bodyguards, was designated to act as the judge accepting appeals from the prisoners. He was fully authorized to review the cases.

During the Jiajing reign period, the power and influence of the Imperial Bodyguards had suppassed Dongchang (Eastern Depot).* When Lu Bing was designated as the judge, he was only a fifth-rank official. However, he had revealed his outstanding abilities. He was very capable and experienced at problem-solving and was impartial in hearing cases. He never followed most of the officials in the Imperial Bodyguards who were keen on framing, fabricating rumors and trumping up charges against their enemies. During the one year when he was on the job, he had the courage to speak against those officials who were involved in injustice. He even dared to challenge the wrong judgements of the emperor. Many judicial officials and imperial thought highly of him.

---

* A palace eunuch agency created in 1420 to investigate treasonable offenses of any kind, gradually becoming a kind of imperial secret service head quarters not subject to the contral of any regular governmental organization.

15

The reason that Chen Yin designated Lu Bing as the judge was that he not only intended to convince the public completely, but also vigorously advertise his faithfulness to the Emperor. However, Chen Yin actually were not really ready to correct any injustices. According to his plan, it was enough that Lu Bing just looked around in the prison for several days and then wrote a memorial to the throne, saying: "All the cases were fairly convicted. Former judgements shall be upheld." Unexpectedly, Lu Bing took his task so seriously that he moved to the Northern Prison right after he was designated. He had the imperial edict printed into posters and distributed through the whole prison. He also severely warned that anyone who was found preventing prisoners from acknowledging the Emperor's edict or hindering the appeals would be executed immediately.

Li Yuying also read the imperial edict in her death–row cell. Her frozen heart began to melt. "If I appeal for justice, the case might be corrected," she thought. It is hard to describe a dying person's desire to live when she sees hope for life, let alone someone like Yuying. She was so young and had cherished wonderful expectations for the future. So her desire to live was aroused. However, one year's hard life in the prison had completely made her realize the incredibly dark side of reality. She feared not only that the case could not be corrected, but that she would go through all the tortures once again. Furthermore, she would bear the bad reputation of defaming her stepmother. It would be too late for regrets if this happened. Yuying was so uncertain what the right action was. She racked her brains over it and couldn't sleep for the whole night.

After the edict was announced through the prison, Lu Bing sent some trusted officers to visit the cells one by one to check for any mischief. Anything suspicious was required to be reported to him. When the officers came to Li Yuying, they were deeply impressed by her serene behavior. So they asked repeatedly if there was any injustice that she wanted to complain of. But Yuying frowned in silence, her eyes full of sorrow. This made the officers even more suspicious. Then they ordered the woman guard to persuade Yuying to speak out. Fortunately, the woman guard was very sympathetic to Yuying. The officers' order fitted exactly with her wishes. So she told Yuying everything about Lu Bing's serious and honest attitude toward cases and the current of search for injustices in the prison. She assured Yuying that as long as there was any injustice, it would definitely be corrected by the judge. After this considerate persuasion, Yuying thought of all the torture, her little brother's distressing death and her stepmother's tyranny toward her and her sisters and brother. Eveantually she made up her mind to appeal for justice despite the risk of undergoing again all the physical torture.

In the bleak prison cell, Yuying spread a piece of paper under a dim kerosene lamp. All the torment she had suffered flooded her mind. Her heart was full of grief and indignation. Suppressing her strong emotions, she dipped the writing brush in the ink and began to write ....

Li Yuying's plaint was very soon handed over to Lu Bing. After reading only a few sentences, Lu Bing became deeply moved by her righteous writings. When he finished reading, Lu Bing's acute insight told him there must be something wrong in the former judgment. Because the

17

plaint was addressed directly to the Emperor, Lu Bing
had to send it to the Emperor without any delay. As
soon as he had it copied down for a file, he had it sent to
Emperor Jiajing. In the meantime, Lu Bing ordered all
the files on Li Yuying's case to be transferred to him. He
was going to retry the case himself.

That same day the whole file was prepared and Lu
Bing began to go through it right away. However, he
knitted his brows at the sight of the first page because
on it was signed the name Chen Yin. Chen Yin was the
commander of the Imperial Bodyguards, Lu Bing's
direct superior and a third-rank official in the imperial
court whom the Emperor had a very high opinion of.
"How can I retry a case concluded by Chen Yin?" Lu
Bing hesitated. Lu Bing had been in the Imperial
Bodyguards for years, and was very familiar with Chen
Yin's personality. Chen Yin was very stubborn and
flamboyant. He was always proud of himself for
winding up cases quickly. The last thing that he could
accept was opposition. When he was only a *qianshi*
(assistant commander) of the Imperial Bodyguards, he
was already notorious for his obstinacy. Anyone who had
a different opinion of his case would be later pushed out.
After he was appointed as the commander of the
Imperial Bodyguards, his superior position would not
allow any criticism at all. But Li Yuying's case obviously
had the signs of injustice. Shouldn't the case be heard
again? The new judge was at a loss. Chen Yin's signature
in front of his eyes turned into a noose tightly fettering
his mind. This was just the first case in the prison, and
Lu Bing was already trapped in a dilemma. What should
he do?

Lu Bing pondered for a long time and could not find

a way out. He skimmed through the files. In no time, he discerned many suspicious points that stood out from his years of experience. Li Yuying's file was very simple, only including an accusation from the plaintiff, Jiao, listing the facts of Li Yuying's slighting of her mother and torn adultery with a man, and a testimony from the Li's footman—Li Qiang'er saying that he saw a man jumping over the west wall of the yard that night and sneaking into Yuying's bedroom, and later he found a shoe after chasing the man. The material evidence was very simple, too—two poems written by Yuying, a man's shoe and a silver hairpin carved with the words "unshakable resolve." The handwriting of the poems was very graceful and exactly the same as that in the plaint, which proved that the poems were not forged. Yuying was well educated and propriety-minded. As a girl at the age of thinking about love, writing some poems about her yearning for love did not definitely imply that she was having a sexual physical affair with someone. And furthermore, though Yuying's poems were written in a sad tone, there was nothing frivolous or immoral in them. Taking these as evidence that she was missing her lover was indeed farfetched. The shoe left behind by the fleeing "intrigant" was a new one. There was only a little mud on the sole. It seemed to have been worn for the first time. No information could be obtained from the shoe for the moment. With regard to the hairpin, it was heavy and easily twisted. The malleability meant that it was made of pure silver. The words carved on the front side said "unshakable resolve," which could be understood as a vow between lovers—but it could also be explained in other ways. Besides, no investigation had been made on the source of the silver hairpin. The conclusion of "presented by the intrigant " was only based on the words from Jiao's statement: "I have never seen a hairpin like this in my family." The evidence did not seem good enough to prove that Li Yuying had committed the crime of adultery. And there was no evidence to show Li Yuying's slighting of her stepmother either. Wasn't it too careless and harsh to sentence a young girl to be hacked to death like this? The most puzzling thing was that not a single word of confession from the criminal appeared in the files. The same two sentences were recorded from the trial each time: "No words from the prisoner," and "The prisoner fainted from the torture." The conclusive statement of confession was written by the secretary. Yuying's fingerprint could be seen at the bottom. But who knew how it had been obtained. Lu Bing shook his head unconsciously. His face grew more gloomy. "Should the case be retried? If yes, would it be approved by Commander Chen Yin? Would I ever be able to reverse the conclusion of my boss?" All the question marks flashed in his mind. At last, he decided to see Li Yuying first before he made any decision.

The Imperial Bodyguards court looked more ghastly and terrifying than other courts like those at the Grand Court of Appeal, the Court of Censors and the Board of Punishment. Today, Lu Bing was going to interrogate Li Yuying here. To relieve Yuying's fear, he ordered the removal of the torture instruments, dismissed the torturers, and only had a few junior officers remain in the court. Even so, the gloomy atmosphere and the "silence", "Keep off the hall," and, tiger-shaped boards on both sides of the court still made one's blood run cold. Li Yuying was escorted to the court with heavy shackles by several female guards. For the past year, she had stood trial so many times that the bloodcurdling atmosphere could not frighten her anymore. However, she could clearly feel that today the court was different from before. There was no scary roaring sound and no ferocious torturers. All the prison guards were holding their breath. It looked as if they were afraid of breaking the solemn silence. Dragging her shackled, feet until she was a few yards before the judge, Li Yuying knelt down. As usual, she remained in silence.

Lu Bing's sharp eyes never left her from the moment she appeared. From her slender figure and elegant manner, Lu Bing could see the graceful manner of someone from a noble family.

Lu Bing asked calmly, "Are you Li Yuying?"

Yuying replied, "Yes, I am."

Lu Bing said, "Look up."

Yuying seemed a little bit startled, but she raised her face obediently. Lu Bing looked at her for a good while. The cruel torture had made Yuying's hair a mess and her face haggard. But her extraordinary beauty and elegance were still revealed. Lu Bing sighed to himself: "What an exquisite and beautiful girl! If she hadn't been involved in such a calamity, but sent to the palace instead, she would have become an imperial consort." But it might happen that a pretty girl, seduced by a man, had done something immoral.

Thinking of this, Lu Bing's voice became stern: "You've been sentenced to be hacked to death because you were found having an illicit relationship with a man for a long time and slighting your mother. What do you want to say?"

Yuying said in a shaky voice, "have been wronged,

Your Honor. Please ascertain the facts!"

Lu Bing stared at her: "Are you saying you didn't commit adultery with a man?"

Yuying replied, "I'm just seventeen years old. My stepmother doesn't even let me step out of the door. How could I have had relations with a man?"

Lu Bing stroked his long beard and continued: "If you didn't have an affair, did you ever lose your virginity?"

Yuying flushed crimson with embarrassment. Her head sank deeply toward her chest. "I have been educated by Confucian classics since I was young, and I understand well propriety, righteousness, honesty and sense of shame. As the old saying goes: 'No physical contact between a man and a woman.' A girl should clearly protect her virginity. How would I dare to lose it rashly?"

Lu Bing nodded his head, "Since you say you didn't have an affair with a man and you didn't carelessly lose your virginity, then you should still be a virgin. Right?"

Yuying answered in a shy, low voice: "Yes."

Lu Bing quickly ordered: "Summon the coroner!" Immediately two coroners hurried into the court. Lu Bing said, "Take this woman to the women's prison and check if she is a virgin. The sooner the better." Immediately, the women guards escorted Li Yuying out of the court.

Lu Bing opened Li Yuying's file with no expression on his face. Staring at the signature of Chen Yin, he frowned again. After a while, Li Yuying was brought back. The two coroners respectfully presented the report to Lu Bing, and said: "Your Honor, the examination shows that the prisoner Li Yuying is still a virgin, despite the wounds all over her body."

Lu Bing asked in a stern tone, "Did you do the examination carefully?"

"Your Honor, we know this is very important. So we wrote the report after we each examined her separately."

Lu Bing nodded his satisfaction, and said: "You can go now." The coroners kowtowed and backed out.

Lu Bing felt flabbergasted. "This is ridiculous! How can a woman still be a virgin after having sexual relations with a man for a long time? Yuying was definitely wronged." Lu Bing looked at Yuying affectionately, and said: "Yuying, since you are still a virgin, it is impossible that you were in a sexual relationship. Obviously, there were mistakes in the former judgement. From today, I will have your cangue and shackles removed, but you have to stay in an ordinary cell until the case is completely cleared. What do you think?"

Li Yuying never expected that the injustice could be corrected so easily by Lu Bing. Gratitude welled up in her heart. She gave Lu Bing three grand kowtows, and said: "Your Honor, you are so perceptive of the minutest detail. I will never forget that it is you who saved my life." A guard came to her, removed the cangue from around her neck and the shackles, then assisted her out of the court.

That night, Lu Bing paced up and down in his courtyard in the Northern Prison. The case of Lu Yuying was tumbling about in his mind. It was not difficult for him to over turn this case in accordance with his years of experience. The problem was it had been judged by Chen Yin. "In the plaint, Yuying openly criticized Chen Yin for his incompetence in judging the case. What a bold criticism! How would Chen Yin react

24

upon reading this? I am just a fifth-rank official with my whole future depending on him. How will he view me if I completely deny his judgement?" Actually, all these matters could be dealt with later, the foremost thing that Lu Bing was worried about was that, even though he could sort everything out in the case, Chen Yin could still deny the correct verdict. If so, Chen Yin would send in another judge. It would be very easy for them to dismiss his judgement—the Imperial Bodyguards was good for nothing, but they were very good at covering up any lies Lu Bing clearly knew about all the kinds of cruel tortures conducted in the Imperial Bodyguards prison. He was also aware that the tortures worked so anyone would tell anything necessary. These brutal tortures might befall to the weak girl again. That was not something he to see happen. All these were the reasons that Lu Bing was at a loss. He could not go to sleep. Summer nights are short. When three morning stars appeared in the east sky, Lu Bing made up his mind after a fierce battle in his head. He decided to see Chen Yin after daybreak to ask for a rejudgement of the case.

Chen Yin was over sixty. He did not look as old as his age. Owing to good care, he was still ruddy-cheeked. His grey hair and beard were tidily combed. His two shewd eyes were always inscrutable to others. His slightly overweight body with his square face displayed undescribable dignity. Chen Yin seldom gave long speeches. He acted exactly the same as usual when he listened to Lu Bing's report today. Although Lu Bing spoke in a rather excited tone, Chen Yin did not let out one sound. He did not even once nod. Later, he simply closed his eyes, which puzzled Lu Bing very much because he was not sure if he had fallen into asleep. In fact, Chen Yin had not missed one word. He was vexed by Lu Bing's serious attitude toward his task, especially by Lu Bing's request to rejudge a case that he had closed. But Chen Yin kept his temper under control because of his dignified status. So he intended to stop Lu Bing with such a frigid manner. He wished that Lu Bing would go with the flow. However, Lu Bing was an outspoken person, and did not even think to spend some time figuring out what his boss' intentions were. He reported everything about the case to Chen Yin.

Chen Yin did not open his eyes until Lu Bing had finished his report. Staring at Lu Bing resentfully for a while, Chen Yin spoke slowly: "I know very well about the case. Both the material evidence and the human testimony were obtained. The prisoner herself had also pressed her finger print on the confession statement. There has been no injustice. You are an official in the Imperial Bodyguards. As a young man, remember not to be too impetuous and aggressive, and don't try to please the public with claptrap. Otherwise you'll be unworthy of my expectations."

Lu Bing replied in a modest tone, "I will remember your teachings for ever. But Li Yuying was sentenced to be hacked to death for the crime of adultery. In the meantime she is still a virgin. How can the public be persuaded by the conviction?"

Chen Yin interrupted him impatiently: "What is your explanation for the intrigant's shoe? And what about the silver hairpin carved with 'unshakeable resolve'? Li Yuying was frivolous. She could be seduced by a dissolute man. It is quite reasonable. Even though they might not really have done it, it is still an affair corrupting public morals. Hacking her to death to improve social morality what's wrong with that?"

Lu Bing said, "But so far, there is no trace of the intrigant. And it is still a puzzle where the silver hairpin came from. There are too many suspicious points in this case. I'm afraid that your reputation could be destroyed by this small case. That is why I'm trying to sort out all the details."

Chen Yin became more impatient. He frowned at Lu Bing. "Didn't I want to find the intrigant? Didn't I want to find out the source of the hairpin? But the girl never said one word since she was sent in here. Once torture was imposed, she fainted away. How could I find out about the intrigant? It is true the intrigant hasn't been found, but the material evidence is there. Unless all the evidence can be repudiated completely—otherwise..."

Lu Bing followed immediately: "May I take the liberty to say that so long as you agree to hear the case again, I will clear every suspicious point. If I fail, I am willing to be deprived of my rank and punished."

Chen Yin let out a scornful laugh: "Plead for the people, what a good official! The problem is the case has been reported to the imperial court. In two days, the memorial will be sent to the Emperor to read over. If you can clear the case in two days, there is a chance to withdraw the original report. Otherwise... you'd better forget it."

Lu Bing saw there was some leeway in those words. He immediately stood up and said: "I promise to clear the case in two days. I beg your approval, sir!"

Chen Yin shook his head in reluctance: "All right, I'll give you two days. But you have to understand if you can't sort out all the details in two days or there are no injustices in the case, don't ask for my forgiveness."

Lu Bing answered quickly: "Yes, sir". Chen Yin stood up, gave Lu Bing an angry stare, and then walked out of the room with much displeasure.

Lu Bing was very clear on the risk in demanding that the case be retried. But he did not expect Chen Yin to only give him two days to finish it. From the intimidating words, "Don't ask for my forgiveness," Lu Bing realized that if he could not clear up the case, what he would lose was not only his official position. He was taking more and more risks.

Lu Bing did not dare to waste a minute. As soon as Lu Bing returned to the Northern prison, he summoned Li Yuying right away and found out everything about Jiao's murder of Li Chengzu and the source of the hairpin. To save time, while he sent someone to the mansion of prince Cheng to look for proof, Lu Bing himself went to the Li house to investigate in person.

Lu Bing was just about to start off when he was informed that another official named Zhu Huanan who was a *qianshi* in the Imperial Bodyguards had been sent by Chen Yin to accompany him in investigating the case. *Qianshi* was a fourth-rank official, one rank higher than Lu Bing. It was quite clear that the purpose was to tie up Lu Bing. Lu Bing's heart became heavy, but he had to pretend to be very delighted and greeted Zhu with great respect. Zhu Huanan was a valiant military officer and knew nothing except to obey the orders of Chen Yin. He came under the order of "supervising" Lu Bing, in another word, "specially to look for." He urged an immediate start after he knew that Lu Bing was going to visit the Lis' house. Lu Bing then prepared another sedan-chair for Zhu without delay and, they left for the Lis' house which was outside of the Guangan Gate.

Jiao was only twenty-three years old and rather good-looking. But there was too much zest in her talk, which showed her to be a little frivolous. Jiao Rong was Jiao's twenty-one-year-old brother. He was rat-eyed and buck-headed, and didn't look like a righteous man. After Lu Bing and Zhu Huanan were seated, Lu Bing summoned Li Qiang'er for inquiry. Li Qiang'er was much older than Jiao and very short in stature. He spoke with a stutter. He stammered out the whole course of events surrounding the discovery of the adultery that night: After midnight, when he was going to the backyard to get something he had seen a man sneaking into Yuying's bedroom. After a short while, the light in Yuying's room went out. He rushed to Jiao Rong's room to tell him. Together with Jiao Rong and another two maids, they went to catch the intrigant. But when they broke into the room, he had fled. Li Qiang'er guessed that the intrigant had jumped over the wall, so he also jumped over the wall to trace him. In the woods dozens of meters away, he had found the shoe left behind, but the intrigant himself had disappeared.

Lu Bing immediately asked Li Qiang'er from where he had jumped over the wall. Li Qiang'er led them to the west wall and said, his hand pointing at a part of the wall: "Right here." Lu Bing looked carefully at the wall and found that it was too high for Li Qiang'er to climb up. Li Qiang'er read Lu Bing's mind, and explained at once: "There were two big stones there before. It was easy to climb up. But after that night our hostess had them moved away. She feared that someone would jump in again."

Zhu Huanan nodded and said to Lu Bing, "His words are believable."

Lu Bing said nothing. Instead, he asked for a ladder, climbed up and looked out. Right outside the wall was a dry gutter. It seemed that there had been no water in it for years, only a very thick layer of soft dirt and some rubbish that had been discarded by the villagers. A dense grove could be seen some dozens of meters away.

Zhu Huanan, standing on another ladder said, "There was no place to hide outside the wall, so the intrigant ran directly to the woods. That's quite reasonable."

Lu Bing still did not say a word. He told the officers to invite all the neighbors for questioning. Then he came down from the ladder.

He asked Li Qiang'er: "So, it was you who saw the intrigant sneak into the room. Did you see what he looked like?"

Li Qiang'er answered, "It was very dark, I couldn't see clearly. And, I was behind him, I could only see his back. But he looked like a big guy. He seemed strongly built from the back." Lu Bing nodded. At that moment, all the neighbors arrived. It Strangely, Lu Bing did not start with the case. Instead, he chatted with them about the harvest of the last two years. The neighbors all said that the harvest was not good. There had been floods last summer. It had been cloudy from June and had very often rained heavily. The ditches along the roads had been full of water, not just the fields. But this year, there was a terrible drought. Not a single drop of rain had fallen yet. The crops were all withered. Lu Bing comforted them sympathetically: "I will ask for an exemption from taxes for you."

After chatting for a good while, Lu Bing started to nonchalantly ask about the Li family and Yuying. The neighbors all said that the Lis used to be a family possessing courtesy and righteousness. They had not expected that the young girl would seduce an intrigant.

Zhang Bao, a peasant who lived to the north told him, "I saw something concerning the adultery earlier. During autumn two years ago, I always found the gate of the Li house was not securely closed at night. A lot of times at midnight, I saw a man come in and out furtively. And each time, he was holding something in his arms."

Li Shuan, who also lived to the north, provided another clue: "It's strange that for a period last fall, something drove my dog crazy. It ran to the Li courtyard all the time. One day I followed him to the Li house and found several dogs sniffing around a big scholartree. The soil under the tree was loose. I guessed that the intrigant had brought too much liquor and meat. They couldn't finish it all, so he had buried the leftovers under the tree."

Lu Bing did not look like he was listening to the story very carefully. His eyes were focusing on a big bronze mirror in front of the door. The mirror was rubbed to shining. Zhu Huanan was looking at the mirror as well.

He said to Lu Bing, "How shiny the mirror is!"

This roused Lu Bing from his meditation, and he responded perfunctorily, "Yeah, it's good, good..."

Jiao came forward, smiling: "If Your Honor likes the mirror, please have it moved to your house."

Lu Bing shook his head and laughed. "How can I take your treasure?" Then he turned to Zhu Huanan: "Do you have anything to ask, Your Excellency?"

Zhu spread his hands: "I am just a monitor. If you have finished with your questions, then me too." Lu Bing then thanked the neighbors and said to Jiao, "You are kindly reqested to come to the Imperial Bodyguards yamen for the final verdict tomorrow morning." Then he called his group to return.

Just as they arrived at the yamen, Lu Bing immediately called two intimate officers to his side and whispered to them for a minute. The two then left in a hurry.

Zhu Huanan said to Lu Bing, "You see, the case is very clear now. If I hadn't gone with you to investigate, I wouldn't have known that Li Yuying was involved in an affair two years ago."

Lu Bing laughing, replied: "You really have a shrewd mind. The case might be wound up tomorrow. You must be tired. Please go back and have a good rest. I'm not going to work on the case this afternoon. We will wrap up the case tomorrow morning in court. What do you think, Your Excellency?"

Zhu Huanan said, "Very well. I will definitely come tomorrow morning."

It was after Lu Bing had seen Zhu Huanan off that he summoned the officer who had been to Prince Cheng's mansion to look for the source of the hairpin. The officers reported the situation at the Prince Cheng mansion. Prince Cheng himself met the officer. When Prince Cheng saw the silver hairpin, he recognized it at once, saying it had been presented to his former bodyguard Li Xiong as a gift. He also said that Li Xiong had been a hereditary *baihu* (platoon commander) of the Imperial Bodyguards who had been very careful and loyal when he worked in the prince Cheng mansion. So he had recommended Li Xiong for the position of *qianhu* with his personal guarantee. In order to verify that the hairpin had really come from the Cheng mansion, Prince Cheng wrote a testimony himself. Now the source of the silver hairpin was very clear. Lu Bing felt more confident in handling the case.

The next morning, the yamen of the Northern Prison was packed with people. Runners filled the hall. All kinds of torture instruments were placed on both sides of the court. Lu Bing and Zhu Huanan came up to the court accompanied by a group of officers. Lu Bing humbly invited Zhu Huanan to be the judge. Zhu declined politely. Lu Bing did not try to force him further, then seated himself on the judge's chair then called the court to order. The court became quiet soon after the runners shouted for order. Lu Bing ordered: "Bring in Li Yuying."

Li Yuying was escorted in and knelt in the middle of the court. She had changed into clean clothes and the shackles had been taken off. Though she had not recovered from the torture wounds completely, she did not appear as haggard as before. Her graceful figure drew all the eyes in the court.

Zhu Huanan was about to shout at Li Yuying but was stopped by Lu Bing with a gesture. Lu Bing spoke to Li Yuying kindly: "Your injustice has been cleared. I pronounce you innocent before the court. After the criminals who defamed you and murdered your brother are brought to justice, you may go home..." The unexpected declaration dumbfounded Zhu who couldn't say a word.

After these words, Lu Bing put on a grave expression, his eyes flashing with a kind of loathing. He struck the table and shouted command: "Bring forward Jiao and Jiao Rong!"

A minute later, Jiao and Jiao Rong were dragged into the court. Only minutes ago Jiao, still thinking she was the accuser, had tried to engage in conversation with the officers outside the court. Suddenly she heard a shout and found herself dragged into the courtroom. She was completely at a loss. She knelt there and looked around, having no idea what was going on. Lu Bing struck the wooden block on the table, and demanded in a severe voice: "Jiao, Jiao Rong, tell the court how you murdered Li Chengzu and defamed Li Yuying."

Jiao pretended to be puzzled: "I came to listen to the judgment against the accused by your order. What are these charges all about?"

Lu Bing said severely: "According to the investigation, Li Yuying is innocent. There is solid evidence that Li Chengzu was savagely murdered by you and Jiao Rong. And there is also evidence that you framed Li Yuying. Do you want to see the evidence one by one?" Jiao and Jiao Rong together cried out their protests.

Lu Bing laughed scornfully. "Bring Li Qiang'er up!"

In no time, Li Qiang'er was escorted into the court. Lu Bing sternly called him to account: "Li Qiang'er, you accepted Jiao's bribe to frame Li Yuying. What do you have to say about this?"

Li Qiang'er cast a sidelong glance at Jiao, and said: "Your Honor, everything I have said is the truth. Why am I charged with framing?"

Lu Bing threw the shoe which had been picked up by Li Qiang'er at him, and asked: "Is this the shoe lost by the intrigant and picked up by you?"

Li Qiang'er took a look at the shoe, and said, "Yes, it is."

Lu Bing sneered, and continued: "You said the intrigant was a big man. Do you think such a small shoe could fit him?"

Li Qiang'er was struck dumb by the question and did not dare to let out another sound. Lu Bing continued: "Yesterday, when I did the investigation at the Li house, I was told by the neighbors that there had been a flood last year. All the ditches and depressions had been filled with rainwater. The ditch outside the west wall of your yard is in a low-lying area. It had to have been filled when it rained. If the intrigant had climbed out over the wall and jumped into the ditch as you described, he would have had to somehow step in water and mud. Then there should be mud on his shoes. How come is this shoe is so clean? Did the intrigant fly over the ditch?"

Li Qiang'er had become soaked in a cold sweat and could not force out one word in response. "With all this evidence you still won't confess?" reproached Lu Bing. "Put him to torture" At once, a blood-stained torture instrument was pushed out. Li Qiang'er was so frightened that his face lost all its color. He knelt down and made one kowtow after another, begging: "Forgive me, Your Honor! I confess, I confess!"

Lu Bing roared coldly: "Speak!" Trembling with fear, Li Qiang'er told the real story.

In fact, the whole thing had been directed by Jiao. Jiao Rong had had intentions toward Yuying and had been unwilling to frame her at first. It was Jiao who had forced him to send Yuying to the Imperial Bodyguards yamen. Afterwards, Li Qiang'er had been awarded with two hundred taels of silver. Not long after that, the news spread that Yuying had acquiesced to the accusation against her. The three scoundrels had been cheering that their plans had been accomplished perfectly. But none of them had expected that Lu Bing would uncover the loopholes.

Lu Bing ordered Li Qiang'er to be put into prison, and turned to Jiao and Jiao Rong: "You two still won't confess to the murder of Li Chengzu?"

Jiao answered in a shaky voice: "I am wrongfully accused."

Lu Bing said to the runners: "Bring the bloody clothes."

Two runners came up and threw some pieces of rotted, bloody clothes before them. At a sight of this, Jiao was terrified out of her wits. Jiao Rong was also pinned to the ground paralyzed with fear. This radical turn of events puzzled Zhu Huanan.

Severely, Lu Bing demanded of Jiao and Jiao Rong: "Do you refuse to admit your crime until you undergo great torture?"

Jiao did not dare to disavow any longer. She confessed: "Don't use instruments, Your Honor, I will confess. It's true that Li Chengzu was poisoned by Jiao Rong and me."

"What kind of poison did you use?"

60 "Arsenic."

"Who provided the poison?"

"Jiao Rong bought it from the apothecary in the city."

"What did you do with the body?" "I chopped it into pieces, which Jiao Rong then took out at night and scattered into the moat. The bloody clothes and the head were not so easy to destroy, so I buried them under the scholar tree in the courtyard."

"Is what you say the truth?"

"I swear, Your Honour."

Lu Bing then turned to Jiao Rong: "Jiao Rong, what else do you have to add?"

"I know my crime. But everything was planned by my sister. I was only the accessory."

The quick wrapping up of the case was truly dazzling to be hold. The officers and runners in and outside the court all gasped in admiration. Now Lu Bing relaxed a little. He ordered the confession to be finger printed by Jiao and Jiao Rong. Thus, a weighty lawsuit was cleared by Lu Bing in less than two days.

After Jiao and Jiao Rong were put in cangues and shackles, and escorted out of the court, Lu Bing turned to Li Yuying who was kneeling to the side: "Yuying, you can go home now. I have had your sister Li Taoying tracked down and returned. She is now waiting for you outside of the court. You suffered a lot in the prison for the past year. Now you are granted two hundred taels of silver to start a living with. Your plaint to the Emperor has been respectfully read. An imperial edict has been issued, ordering the Imperial Bodyguards to clear the case. Now the truth has been revealed. You can thank the Emperor by Kowtowing towards the imperial edict."

Tears were covering Li Yuying's face. Full of respect and gratitude, she made three kowtows toward the edict. Then she was accompanied by the women guards out of the court to meet her sister. Lu Bing held his hands to make an obeisance toward Zhu Huanan and then shouted to the court: "Case dismissed!" The court returned to silence after a few minutes.

Zhu Huanan stood up quickly when he saw Lu Bing coming toward him to help him, but didn't start walking.

He asked Lu Bing sincerely in a scholarly tone: "Your Excellency, how did you find out Jiao was the murderer? And how did you obtain the blood-stained clothes? I will be puzzled for the rest of my life if you don't tell me the details."

Lu Bing smiled. "The information all came from the investigation at the Li house. Zhang Bao said that in the autumn of the year before last, a man came out of the Li house every midnight, each time holding a bag. Zhang Bao thought the man was Li Yuying's lover. But I figured out that this was the time that Li Chengzu had been murdered. Carrying bags out at midnight—this had to be destroying the traces by discarding the body. And I reasoned the man might be Jiao Rong. Meanwhile, I reckoned it was impossible to throw the bloody clothes into the river. They had to be buried somewhere. Then Li Shuan said his dog ran constantly to the Li house and barked under the scholar tree. Dogs have a keen sense of smell. They can make out the smell of blood. Thus the bloody clothes could be buried under the scholar tree. While Li Shuan was talking, I stared at the bronze mirror, because I could see Jiao's face in it. Li Shuan had no particular intention when speaking, but Jiao read her own meaning into it. I found that she looked very nervous and kept stealing glances at me. She thought she was at my back and I couldn't see her, so she took out her handkerchief to wipe her brow. I thus believed she definitely had something to do with Li Chengzu's death. After we came back, I secretly sent two shrewd and capable officers to keep Jiao and her brother under surveillance. They did not dare to remove the blood-stained clothes. This morning, after they had left for the yamen, the two officers entered the yard and dug out the blood-stained pieces of clothing. All these things had been done before the court session had opened. That's why I was so confident at the hearing."

Zhu Huanan finally came to full understanding. He held his thumb up in admiration: "You can rival Judge Bao*. I will put in a good word for you in front of Commander Chen and recommend they promote you to more important positions."

Zhu Huanan staggered away clumsily. Lu Bing turned around and looked at the empty court. He sighed to himself: "The injustice has been over turned. But how can I dispel the grudge in Commander Chen's mind?"

---

* A very famous judge in the Song Dynasty

The Mystery of a Roadside
Female Corpse

In the middle period of the Ming Dynasty, the place around Gulou (Drum Tower) was the most prosperous commercial area in Beijing. There was a street extending west from Gulou called Xixie Street, which wound along Shichahai and led to Jishuitan. Jishuitan was a huge lake, on which was covered with the leaves of blooming lotus in summer. The view was gorgeous. On both sides of Xixie Street stood a lot of taverns, theaters, shops and an exquisite tower called "Lake View Tower." Looking out from the tower, the vast expanse of green water rolled and stretched into the far distance. The lotus pond with beautiful arch bridges across it here and there and, exquisite airy pavilions and set off by the distant green mountains presented a really splendid picture. That was why many prominent officials and eminent personages visited it often. At the same time, a lot of pedlars gathered there selling snacks, such as lotus-seed congee, seedpod of lotus, fresh waterchestnut, and so on and so forth. Their daily income was quite considerable.

Half way down the street, there was a small alley in which lived a family with the family name of Zhang. They made a famous snack in Beijing, called Four-Fruit-Ice. The recipe of it had been passed down in the family through generations. It was made of fresh lotus seeds, lotus root slices, rice and arrowhead. At first, they were made into a paste, and then mixed with ice. It tasted sweet with a touch of bitterness, leaving a lasting and pleasing aftertaste with those who had it. With the deliberate improvement on the recipe by several generations of the family, Four-Fruit-Ice had become one of the most popular snacks around Shichahai. At this moment, the head of the household was named Zhang Zhu. Aged twenty-six, he was honest, naive and kind. The neighbors respected him a lot because of the pecuniary assistance he offered them. He was not yet married. His father had passed away. His mother was almost sixty. Mother and son worked very hard and earned their living making family-recipe Four-Ice-Fruit. In summer, the fresh seedpods of lotus and arrowheads had to be picked up before the sun rose and when the dew was still on them. Then they should be immediately cleaned and preserved in sugar. By the time the sun was up, the fruits had already been well preserved. The natural fragrance was still apparent. The Four-Ice-Fruit made by them was very special and appealed to people. Therefore, every morning just after fourth watch, Zhang Zhu would carry a big bamboo basket and hurry to Shichahai to collect fresh seedpods and arrowheads.

This morning, Zhang Zhu got up a bit late. He did not feel very well. Though he did not have to go picking fruit, he had been used to getting up early. He struggled up, took the basket and left the house. In summer, after 5 o'lock, everything could be distinguished in the dawn light. The alley was very quiet, no passersby. A thick milky haze was floating above the ground, the air was extremely fresh, mixed with the fragrance of lotus. Taking deep breaths of the cool and refreshing air, Zhang Zhu found his discomfort was alleviated a lot.

The moon was dancing the last music in the lake before the sun touched the leaves. To collect more fruit, Zhang Zhu walked briskly toward the lake. Suddenly, he found a dark blur lying in the middle of the lane dozens of steps away. What was that? Zhang Zhu slowed down but could not help approaching it slowly in curiosity. It was not until he was a few steps from it that Zhang Zhu recognized that it was a woman in plain silk clothes of coarse quality. He was a bit shocked. And then he hurried up to her. Zhang Zhu was always ready to help others. The first thing one thought of when he saw a person lying on the ground was that he might be ill. But when he helped the woman up, he found her body was rather rigid. As his hand carelessly touched her chest, he was frightened because her chest was soaked with something sticky, like blood. He pulled back his hand at once. The body fell to the ground heavily. Zhang Zhu felt a coldness creeping through his whole body and his eyes tingling. He slowly backed off from the body, turned around and ran home trembling, leaving his basket behind.

At day break, the clatter of horses' hoofs broke the dawn's silence. Several riders appeared by the lake of Shichahai. They all wore pyramid-shaped hats and dark green suits with the kind of rumpled indifference that instantly marked them as *fanyi* (runners) of Dongchang (Eastern Depot) to anyone who had the slightest knowledge of such things. Dongchang was a kind of a criminal investigation bureau during the Ming Dynasty. It had been set up in the 18th year of the Yongle Period of Emperor Chengzu's reign (1420). Since its establishment, Dongchang had been veiled in mystery and terror, with all the cases in the court, such as extortion, murder, injustice and such, related directly or indirectly to it. Dongchang was right under the administration of the emperor. It could be put in this way: within the country, no one was beyond the surveillance of Dongchang, except the emperor, of course. The activities of Dongchang were extremely arbitrary and clandestine. They stretched their feelers to every corner of the country.

The runners who appeared by the lake were similar to the police nowadays, they were charge of apprehending thieves and maintaining public order. They came out from Dongchang in the second half of the night and patrolled along Wangfujing Street northwestward. When they came to Shichahai, they turned to the east and trotted by the lake. As they unintentionally passed the alley, they unexpectedly found the corpse. They got off the horses and started to examine the site. The woman was approximately forty-four or forty-five, with fluffy hair, three knife wounds in the chest and to the sides of the chest. Blood was everywhere. There was nothing around the body except a bamboo basket, which was several steps away from the corpse. As they emptied the basket, a sharp sickle and a piece of string were found. The head of the group called the *dibao* (local constable) immediately and expected him to identify the corpse. Then they started to search for clues on the ground. Vaguely, several bloody footsteps could be distinguished extending into depths of the alley.

In a minute, the constable Zhao Yi arrived. Zhao Yi was an old man. He had lived in the alley for many years. As soon as he saw the corpse, he recognized at once that it was Zhang Sunshi who lived at the south end of the alley. As he looked at the basket carefully, he was shocked to see clearly written on it, "Four-Ice-Fruit." Obviously, the basket belonged to Zhang Zhu. Taking another look at the things in the basket, he groaned inwardly for Zhang Zhu: "Well... well, boy, everyone knows you are honest, but how did you get yourself involved in a killing?" But with all the evidence laid before him, he could not lie and cover up. Therefore, when the runners inquired, he answered honestly.

By this time, the news had spread that a woman had been murdered in the alley. More and more curious onlookers gathered. They sighed and shook their heads in sympathy. After a while, a girl of about twenty ran over flurriedly. She had a tall and slender figure and pretty face. Her eyes were full of anxiety and fear. She elbowed through the crowd of people and came to the front. As she caught sight of the dead woman, she fainted without a word.

The constable asked a woman close by to help move her, and reported to the runners: "She is Zhang Sunshi's daughter. The woman also has a son called Zhang Fu. He isn't around at the moment."

The runners talked it over for a few minutes and then said to the constable: "You get some men to lay the corpse in a coffin and inform her son immediately. Ask him to arrange the funeral. We are going to arrest the suspect." Then they followed the footprints.

Zhang Zhu had been scared to death almost by the corpse. His almost recovered illness became worse. Shaking, he pounded open the door and threw himself onto bed. "Oh my..." after only one word, he lost consciousness. His mother was frightened. She had no idea what had happened. As she approached her son to check, she found Zhang Zhu's face as pale as a sheet of paper, his hands in tight fists and his body shaking. Looking at his clothes, she saw the front was smeared with blood. The soles of his new shoes were also stained with blood. The most astonishing thing was that Zhang Zhu's right palm was covered with blood, too. Though she asked again and again what the matter was, Zhang Zhu just could not say one word. He just shook his head, like he was in a nightmare. Zhang's mother could do nothing but to get a basin of water and clean Zhang's hand. She managed to take off the bloody clothes and soaked them in water. The new shoes were completely spoiled with the blood which could not have been cleaned off, so she discarded them on the rubbish pile in the corner of the yard. After she finished, she realized that Zhang Zhu had not had breakfast. So she hurried to the kitchen to make some food. At this moment, someone pounded heavily on the courtyard door. Zhang Zhu's mother was an honest person. She had always abided by the law and acted virtuously. During her fifty-odd years, she had never heard the gate being pounded like this. Her heart started to quiver, a feeling of foreboding flashed through her mind.

Panic-stricken, she put down the eggs then walked to the door and asked in a trembling voice: " Who is it?"

A voice shouted from outside: " Shut up, open the door!"

Zhang's mother sensed that disaster had come to the family. All of a sudden, she thought of the clothes and shoes stained with blood. She realized that these things could be very harmful to her son, so she ran wildly toward the shoes, picked them up, and was going to hide them—But it was too late. The door was broken, the runners rushed at her and snatched them away rudely.

They looked at the shoes, and said scornfully: " So, you were going to destroy the evidence?"

Zhang's mother was scared. She muttered: "No... no..."

The head of the group set Zhang's mother aside and ordered his men to search. These runners had been working in Dongchang for years. They all were very experienced. It did not take them much time to find the bloody clothes in the basin. As they lifted the clothes up from the basin, the water in the basin had been dyed red. Without saying anything, the runners rushed into the room and pulled Zhang Zhu up. Zhang Zhu was still dizzy. He did not even have strength to sit up. A runner pulled out a length of chain, put it around Zhang Zhu's neck and dragged him out of the room. Seeing her son being shackled, Zhang Zhu's mother immediately knelt down before the chief, and begged: " My son is ill, please save him, I'll go with you." One runner saw Zhang's mother blocking their way out, and lifted his leg and kicked her on the left side of her chest. Zhang Zhu's mother fell aside like a piece of wood. Poor woman. How could she stand such a kick at her age. She lost consciousness right away.

The head of the group said in a loud voice: "Let's go." Two runners lifted Zhang Zhu up, threw him on the back of a horse, jumped on their own horses and trotted away.

As the clip-clop faded into the far distance, Zhang Zhu's mother came to. She struggled up on her elbow, looked around and found the yard was empty. The door

on to the street was broken. Things were scattered everywhere. It looked as if the house had been robbed. She called her son's name unconsciously, but heard no reply. Then she suddenly realized that he had been arrested by the Dongchang. When she recalled the past years of how they had depended on each other for survival, and how her honest and kind son had always looked after her so much, a kind of indescribable loneliness penetrated her heart. She could not hold back her tears, but sat on the ground and cried. She wanted to stand up, but found her body limp. She struggled again to get up but again failed. She could not gather one bit of strength. The left side of her chest was agonizingly painful. She could not help groaning, and grieving.

The neighbors came over to see what had happened. They could not understand the day's events. They all knew Zhang Zhu's usual behavior, and could never believe that he had committed murder. However, after they heard the vivid description of those who had been to the scene of the murder, none of them could deny that Zhang Zhu definitely had some connection to the murder. The reason they came over to comfort Zhang Zhu's mother was that they wanted to repay the family for then past help and relief. Some of the neighbors were moved by her grief and started to weep to themselves. They helped Zhang's mother up, carried her to the bed and tried to comfort her. But it seemed that she was deaf to their words. She struggled to sit up, and pushed her way to the wardrobe. She opened it, took out several items of clothes and a thin quilt folded them neatly and made a parcel. She thought of the eggs she had just boiled and staggered to the kitchen, took the eggs out, put them in a bowl and wrapped them in a piece of cloth. She was well aware that no matter who one was, so long as he had been arrested by Dongchang, he would never be discharged easily. What she could do at this time was to send some clothes and food to her son. She thanked the neighbors incoherently, picked up the parcel and her bamboo walking stick, and started on her way to Dongchang.

Unfortunately, she was too late. Right after Zhang Zhu had been taken back to Dongchang, he was interrogated and cruelly tortured. Before Zhang Zhu had been arrested, the son of Zhang Sunshi, Zhang Fu, had hastened to Dongchang and charged Zhang Zhu with murder. The person who was on duty that day was a junior police inspector (*li xing bai hu*) called Li Qing. According to the organization of Dongchang, the highest official was called *zhang yin tai jian* (Seal-holding Eunuch). Under him was a *zhang xing qian hu* (senior police inspector) and two *li xing bai hu*. Usually, seal-holding Eunuch did not stay in Dongchang, and ordinary criminal cases were handled by the police inspectors. The police inspectors were very cruel. Whenever they conducted cases, they always tortured the suspects to confess.

In this case, Li Qing happened to be a friend of Zhang Fu. As soon as he received the plaint from Zhang Fu, he ordered the arrest of Zhang Zhu. Right at this moment, the runners had brought Zhang Zhu back. After he examined the murder evidence, he was completely convinced. Therefore right after Zhang Zhu was escorted into the court, Li Qing tried to force him to confess to the murder. Zhang Zhu was timid, but this case would decide his life. So he called up all his courage to describe the whole course of events, how he had found the corpse and how he was so scared he had run home. But Li Qing would not believe him. He requested for Zhang Zhu to be cruelly tortured. In two hours, Zhang Zhu suffered twice the agonies of *jia gun* (boards for pressing the sides of a person) and once hot irons. Then they punished him with the most brutal tortures, filling his nostrils with peppered water and piercing his fingernails. Poor Zhang Zhu—the tortures almost killed him. When the runners pulled the bamboo splinters from his fingernails, he was breathing weakly. The determination Zhang Zhu was aroused. No matter what tortures were used, he did not give in. Li Qing had heard many many cases, but he had never seen a case like this. He became very tired and bored after several hours of interrogation, so he asked for the case to be transferred to the Ministry of Punishments.

When Zhang Zhu's mother arrived at Dongchang, Zhang Zhu had already been put into the jail of the Ministry of Punishments. In order to find out the whereabouts of her son, she proceeded to the Ministry of Punishments. The yamen of the Punishments was not a good place for commonfolk. When the runners of the yamen saw that Zhang Zhu's mother was a poor woman and she did not have any money to give them, they first looked at her with frowning brows and angry eyes, and then pushed her out of the yamen. The parcel and the eggs were all grabbed and scattered on the ground by the runners. Poor mother, how could she fight against them. Sobbing, she moved away slowly, with the help of the bamboo stick.

The Tang Guan (senior official) who was in charge of cases in the Ministry of Punishments did not dare to delay. He sentenced Zhang Zhu to death right after he received the transferred documents, even though no confession had been obtained, let alone a fingerprint. As usual, since the case had been transferred from Dongchang, it was not necessary to have all the documents completed. Immediately, Zhang Zhu was put in shackles and chains and thrown into the death cell. As soon as the sentencing statement was stamped by the official in charge of the stamp, Zhang Zhu would be executed. However, just as the unjust case was about to become history, an incredible thing happened which gave it a glimmer of hope.

The summer dusk seemed extraordinarily long. Though the sun had set behind the mountains, darkness conquering of the land was delayed. At Shichahai, the orange evening glow reflected on the water. The reddish waves rolled and danced in the breeze. It was the right time for the offspring of the nobility to come to enjoy the coolness. However, Zhang Zhu's mother had no intention of enjoying the scene one bit. She had been sitting under the sophora tree in the yard since she had come back from the Ministry of Punishments. Her eyes were staring in front blankly. Nobody knew what was on her mind. The neighbors were very sympathetic with the old woman who had been traumatized by the sudden disaster. They all came over to talk with her again. Some even brought dinner to her. But Zhang Zhu's mother was numb. It seemed that she did not notice the existence of the crowd. She did not say hello to anybody. After some time, the neighbors left in sighing—only she was left, sitting there like a statue.

At this time, the door was pushed open and a girl in mourning dress ran in. She came to Zhang Zhu's mother and knelt down, in crying: "Aunt Zhang, it is all our fault. We ruined Brother Zhang." Zhang Zhu's mother was lost again. All that had happened had been so unexpected. Who was the good-looking girl with swollen glowing eyes? Why had she come to me wearing such deep mourning dress? Zhang Zhu's mother rubbed her eyes and looked at her carefully. Then she recognized that she was Zhang Xiuping who lived at the south end of the alley. It was her mother who had been killed that morning.

From her puzzled eyes, Xiuping saw her doubts. So she tried to hold back her tears, and said sorrow fully, "It was not Brother Zhang Zhu who killed my mother, it was my own Brother, Zhang Fu."

" Ahh..." Zhang Zhu's mother stared at Xiuping with her eyes widely stretched. But the lovely girl was serious and sincere. Suddenly, a light of hope arose in the old woman's heart. But she was afraid that she had heard wrong, so she asked uncertainly, "Could you say that again?"

Xiuping said firmly, "Zhang Fu killed my ma, not Brother Zhang Zhu." After this, she threw herself into the arms of Zhang Zhu's mother and burst into tears.

Zhang Zhu's mother recovered a bit. She stroked her slim shoulders tenderly and said, " Don't cry, girl, tell me the whole story."

Xiuping sobbed and then step by step told the truth of the whole affair. Zhang Fu was actually a rogue. Recently, he had been lured by several gamblers and become mired in gambling. For several days, he had wallowed in the gambling house and lost all his money. Last night, he had come back home and asked his mother for the treasured family heirloom—a pearl-inlaid jade pendant. He intended to win back the money. His mother earnestly pleaded with him to get rid of the terrible habit after she discovered the truth. Zhang Fu pretended to consent, but he concealed his real thoughts. After his mother had gone to bed, he quietly opened her dressing table and took the jade pendant away. His mother woke up and found the precious heir loom gone. She knew where it was and was furious. She tracked Zhang Fu down and caught him at the entrance of the alley. She held one of his arms and intended to pull him back. But Zhang Fu was a really gambling addict. All he wanted to do was to go back to the gambling house and win back the money. When suddenly all this was blocked by somebody, his frustration exploded. In resentment, he drew out the dagger hidden at his waist and stabbed her in the chest. Zhang Fu had completely lost his senses. He kept on stabbing her in her chest until her body dropped to the ground softly. The poor mother, in such a bizarre way she was thus slaughtered by her own son. When Zhang Fu came back to his senses, he became frightened. He squatted down numbly and shook her shoulder. When he found she was dead, he ran away in a sudden panic.

Xiuping was a diligent girl. She was very good at weaving. She always worked until very late at night. Last night, she did not go to bed until midnight. After a day's hard work, she was pretty tired. She had slept deeply that night and been unaware what had happened. In the morning, she was awoken by the voices of the neighbours. She got up and found her mother was not in. When she heard that an old lady had been killed, she became a little upset. Full of curiosity and panic, she got to the site, then realized that all her worse fears had come true. Her brother was good-for-nothing. Her mother and she had had only each other to depend on. But now that her mother had been murdered, how would she live on? Luckily, the constable was a warmhearted person, who helped her buy a coffin, put her mother in it and move it to her house. Xiuping put on mourning dress and kept vigil beside the coffin. She was so sad that she could not take any food and water for the whole day. At noon, her brother Zhang Fu came back, and on his face there was a kind of evasive look. He did not look sad when he saw his mother's bier. He hurried to his own room after a careless glance at the coffin. Xiuping was puzzled. She followed him to the door and found it was locked from inside. So she peeked from the window. Her brother pulled out a cloth parcel, untied it and took out a piece of clothes covered in of bloodstains. He cut it into small pieces with scissors and then piled them under his bed. Xiuping's heart pounded heavily. She did not dare to let out a peep and came back to her mother's bier quietly. After a short while, Zhang Fu hurried out. Then Xiuping sneaked into his room, took out the cloth parcel and opened it. She found that it was exactly the clothes her brother had worn yesterday. The sleeves were gone. Obviously, they had been taken away by her brother to destroy. Then she recalled that her mother had tried to persuade her brother not to gamble anymore last night. And she recalled that her brother had asked her mother for the pearl-inlaid jade pendant. She went to check her mother's dressing table and found the heirloom was gone. She came to full understanding. It was Zhang Fu who had killed her mother while skating the treasure. But Zhang Zhu had been taken as a scapegoat. That was why Zhang Fu had looked so strange when he came back home. And that was why he was so unconcerned about his mother's death. Thinking of this, Xiuping could not stay still any longer. Deep sorrow and her conscience drove her to come to Zhang Zhu's mother and tell her the truth.

After hearing this, Zhang Zhu's mother calmed down a little. She was so grateful that she sympathized with the young girl's tragic lot. Full of compassion, she held Xiuping. Both women cried in each other's arms for their misfortune.

It was getting late, with a new moon somehow already risen high into the sky, which sky was so clear that it was crowded with thousands of twinkling stars. Several fireflies were dancing about in the yard, dragging their faint light. Zhang Zhu's mother moved Xiuping's tender hand away softly and stood up.

"Where are you going, Aunt?" asked Xiuping.

Zhang Zhu's mother answered, "There are some leftovers in the kitchen. Let me warm them up again for you. You haven't had any food for a whole day, have you?"

Looking at the kindly old lady with white hair, Xiuping thought of her own mother. Weren't they the same? She stopped her immediately and said: " No, Aunt, let me cook something for you."

" No, I... want to accompany my son... together leave this world..." the old lady shook her head mournfully. Xiuping could not bear it any longer, and was moved to exclaim: "No, you can't die, and neither will Brother Zhu. My Brother Zhang Fu shall go to hell. I'm going to the yamen of the Ministry of Punishments to make an entreaty for Brother Zhu tomorrow morning."

Zhang Xiuping did not go back on her promise. After she left Zhang Zhu's mother, she headed direct for the Ministry of Punishments. She got up the cowage to beat the drum in the court for an audience with the judge. The official on duty hurried to the court and found Xiuping testifying about a crime committed by her own brother. This was considered a very significant lead. After careful discussion among the officials in the Ministry of Punishments, it was decided that the case should be heard again and Wei Yingzhao, was appointed as the judge.

Wei Yingzhao was a *jinshi* (Metropolitan Graduate, a degree compared to the academic doctorate in modern times) who had won the status at the beginning of the Jiajing reign period. He had worked at the yamen of the Punishments for twenty years, during which he had witnessed the darkness of the Punishments and experienced being enslaved by the Dongchang and the Imperial Bodyguards. But his loyal and honest character had not been. As he said to his colleagues: "The red brushes in the hands of the officials of the Ministry of Punishments decide the lives of countless commoners. That's why we should act according to the dictates of our conscience." Therefore, he had quite high prestige in the yamen, though his rank was not high. This morning, a notice reached him suddenly, saying that he was appointed as the judge to rehear the murder case of Zhang Zhu. He had heard about the case days before. The story of the murder was already well known in the streets. But why should the case be heard again? He had no idea. As he saw it, Zhang Zhu's family had spent some money and expected the sentence could be alleviated a bit.

But after he looked through all the documents, he really considered the original judgment was too careless. From his experience, he believed that the judge had neglected three points: First of all, in the file there was a sickle which was considered as the legal weapon. But not a single stain of blood could be observed on it—instead, there was only one or two died green waterweeds. Obviously, this sickle was used to cut waterweeds. If the criminal did also use it to kill, the waterweeds on it should have been stained with blood. From this point, a conclusion could be reached that this sickle was not the murder weapon. Secondly, there were some questionable points on the bloody clothes and shoes which were obtained from Zhang Zhu's home. Though the clothes had been soaked in water, it was not difficult to observe that the bloodstains were on the cuffs of the sleeves, and there was no bloodstain in the front. It looked as if the sleeves were smeared with blood. But usually, when a dagger thrust into a body, blood would spurt out from the wound and stain the front of the clothes. And looking at the shoes, only the soles were covered in blood. No doubt, it was because Zhang Zhu had stood in the blood. And this was contradicted with the common knowledge that usually the murderer escapes in panic after killing. It seemed unreasonable for the murderer to wait until the blood was all over the ground and then step in it before leaving. Therefore, the so-called bloody clothes and shoes could not be taken as of criminal evidence. Thirdly, if it was Zhang Zhu who killed the woman, how could he have left the basket saying "Four-Ice-Fruit", at the site? Didn't he know that the basket would be used against him? Even the most idiotic criminal would not do such a stupid thing. As well, he had never had a feud with the murdered woman, making the killing seem still more unreasonable. From these points, it was easy to find that the evidence was not strong enough. Besides, there was the complaint in the file presented by the daughter of the murdered woman. She was accusing her brother Zhang Fu as the murderer. The plaint was well written, the reasoning was clear. And the most important thing was that it was a sister charging the brother. In accordance with the idea of Yingzhao scribe, Zhang Fu's house should be searched immediately to get the bloody clothes from under the bed. Wei Yingzhao shook his head and smiled. He knew that if Zhang Fu was the murderer, he would never hide the criminal evidence under the bed for too long. A search would do no good but to alert Zhang Fu. In order to find out the cause of the case, he decided to do an investigation in casual dress, instead of informing the suspect.

This summer was scorching hot. Rays of the sun shone on the earth like burning needles. Few pedestrians could stand it. They all managed to find some shade to wait until the sun weakened. There were hardly any people in the streets. There were usually a lot of pedlars in Xixie Street along Shichahai, but today they were all driven back home by the scorching sun. At this time, a physician with a Shanxi accent stopped under a big tree. He put out his trade board and started to do business. The physician behaved very queerly. He did not feel pulses while diagnosing, but touched the patients' ears. Then he told the cause of illnesses. Besides this, he had another special talent—he could tell the patient's good and ill fortune for three years while making his diagnosis. He was very accurate.

Therefore, people ignored the heat and bit by bit gathered around. Some wanted medicines and some inquired about illnesses. The physician was very unruffled—no matter how crafty the question was, he would answer patiently and obligingly. He was a brilliant conversationalist. Everybody liked talking with him. People kept on coming and going for the whole afternoon.

But the physician seemed very curious about strange things. As he was talking, he would nonchalantly change the topic of conversation to the murder that had taken place a few days ago. He was quite interested in the murderer Zhang Zhu. He asked people several times about his behavior. When he was told that Zhang Zhu had been law-abiding well: behaved and very kind to people, he would always shake his head in disbelief. At last, an earnest patient got all the neighbors there to back up the truth of his claim. All his neighbors said Zhang Zhu was very kind and none of them believed that he could kill someone. They told the physician that Zhang Zhu went to Shichahai to collect fruit at the fifth watch every morning. On the morning of the incident he was a little bit later than usual. Not long after he left home, he ran back out of breath.

The next-door cobbler Li Zheng said: " I was brushing my teeth in the yard when Zhang Zhu ran back. I heard him knocking hard at the door, saying: 'It's horrible.' I thought Zhang Zhu might have fallen in the lake, so I did not pay much attention. But now I think it might be that Zhang Zhu had kicked the corpse in the dark and ran home scared."

A neighbor called Wang Yun said: "I wouldn't swear to anything else, but I'll never believe that Zhang Zhu killed someone."

The physician replied with a smile: "Maybe you are only brave enough to say this here. If you were summoned to the yamen, would you dare to say it again?"

Wang Yun patted his chest and answered: I'd dare to say this before the Emperor, let alone in the yamen."

Then the physician asked the crowd that who was the actual murderer if not Zhang Zhu. An old patient with the nickname the Wise Man, said: "The one who was killed was a kind woman. She became a widow when she was in her twenties. She did not marry again and brought the two kids up alone. Her daughter Xiuping is a gentle and good-looking girl. She always helps the neighbors with sewing. She never asked for any payment no matter how hard their life is. Everybody knows that. We don't think the mother and daughter have any enemies. But the son Zhang Fu is good for nothing. He idles around every day and doesn't do any decent work. Once he worked a spy for Dongchang for quite some time and ruined lots of people. I'm sure the disaster has something to do with him. He might be the killer. Anyway, who knows?"

The physician asked doubt fully, "How can a son kill his mother for nothing?"

The Wise Man continued: " This guy doesn't engage in honest work. He lives off his ma and sister. His mother always tried to persuade him to be good, but he used to just call his mother "useless old shit." So, you see, he didn't have any affection her. And besides, the mother hated Dongchang spies. If Zhang Fu's secrets were discovered by his mother, who knows what he would do."

At this time, a young man stretched his head out and said: "I find Zhang Fu suspicious. That morning, I saw him throw something into Shichahai."

The physician seemed to realize something. He looked at the young man for a while, and said, "Wait, your pupils are so dark, something must be wrong with you. Come here, let me check." His voice was full of care and worry.

The young man became a bit upset, and replied quickly, "I have felt my stomach swollen for days, I was wondering if I could ask for a diagnosis." The physician pulled the young man to him gently and got his name while touching his ear. The man was called Wang Fuyi. He made a living on planting lotus. After the physician saw several patients, it began to dark. He collected his board and got ready more to leave. But some people were still gathered around and reluctant to leave. The physician had to promise that he would come back again after a few days. Then the crowd began to slowly disperse.

The physician was Wei Yingzhao himself. Through the private investigation, he had managed to get hold of the basic information of the case. After returning to the yamen, he sent two experienced runners to see Wang Fuyi and find out the exact location where Zhang Fu had discarded the object. And to disguise themselves as lotus growers and then he asked them dive into the water to look for the dagger. As suspected, they found one shaped like an ox horn which was used specially by the Dongchang personnel. Then the dagger was examined thoroughly and bloodstain were found on it. Obviously, it was the criminal weapon. Wei did not bat an eyelash. He sent some guys to quietly watch Zhang Fu. At the same time, he brought Zhang Zhu to trial again. Zhang Zhu's mother was summoned too. Zhang Xiuping was asked to court for questioning as well because she happened to be with Zhang Zhu's mother at the time. Xiuping was a smart girl. After she handed over the complaint, she had cut and kept a small piece of the bloody clothes hidden under the bed while Zhang Fu was out. She Provided powerful evidence for the clearing up of the case. To find the pearl-inlaid jade pendant, Wei dispatched some people to look through the pawnshops in the north section of the town. Luckily, they found the receipt for the heirloom in Hengsheng Pawnshop which was inside Deshengmen Gate . The date on it was the third day after Zhang Sunshi had been killed. And the person who had pawned the treasure was called Wu Ba, a famous gambler. So Wei had Wu Ba arrested. From him, Wei obtained the information that the jewel had been sold to him by Zhang Fu for five hundred *liang* of silver right on the afternoon of Zhang Sunshi's murder. By now, the causes and the whole chain of events around the murder were clear.

When all the preparatory work was finished, Wei ordered the immediate arrest of Zhang Fu and tried the case on the same day. Zhang Fu was arrogant as he was escorted to the court. But after Wei Yingzhao put all the evidence before him, he was completely beaten. He broke down and told the truth about the murder. And he also confessed that he had bribed Dongchang's police inspector, Li Qing, with five hundred *liang of* silver after the incident had happened, and got Li Qing to promise to execute Zhang Zhu in twenty days. Wei Yingzhao looked glum after he heard this. He paused for a while, then had Zhang Fu's confession printed. He did not announce the result of the trial, but ordered the criminal to be put into jail and then retreated from the court.

It was getting dark again. Wei Yingzhao had sat at his desk for several hours absorbed in thought. But he could not figure it out. Generally, the case could have been closed this morning. But as Zhang Fu had confessed, Li Qing was involved in it, which made it much more complicated. During the last few days, Dongchang had urged several times that Zhang Zhu be executed. Wei had thought that it was only because Dongchang did not want to lose face. But now, it was clear—it was because Li Qing had accepted bribes. After the trial was finished that morning, the old scribe passed a piece of paper to him privately, on which it was written "Zhang Fu was Li Qing's *da zhuang* [pile driver] be careful!" Just a few words, but they clearly described the covert secret relations between Zhang Fu and Dongchang. At that time, there was an unwritten practice in Dongchang that runners were allowed to hire thugs from the society to collect information. The thugs chosen by Dongchang, always looked for trouble and framed people. In Dongchang, they were named *da zhuang*. But common people scornfully called them *er gou zi* (jackal). Since Zhang Fu was Li Qing's *da zhuang*, they must be people of the same ilk. If Zhang Fu was sentenced to death, Li Qing would feel like a fox mourning for the death of a hare. He would definitely speak up for Zhang Fu. The Emperor never doubted the word of anyone from Dongchang. And on the other side, Wei worried that he was just an official of the fifth rank, so he would never have a chance to speak to the Emperor face to face. If the scale tipped in favor of Dongchang, probably he would be charged with "sheltering a criminal and acting with utter disregard for human life." Then he would lose all standing and reputation. It was because of these worries that Wei Yingzhao did not announce the result of the hearing that morning. In fact, he was not sure how the case should be judged. Since coming back from the court, he had been sitting at his desk weighing the pros and cons. All these questions and doybts spoiled his appetite for lunch. In a daze, he wonder red if there was any way out.

The curtain to the door was gently lifted and his wife Xu, walked in quietly. She sat down in front of Wei, her eyes staring at him full of affection. After a few minutes, she let out a sigh and dropped her eye. Xu was thirty-two years old. She was decorous in appearance and natural and graceful in behavior. And what made her more precious was that she was very strategic and intelligent. Sometimes she even had better ideas than Wei. More importantly, she knew clearly the right thing to do and the principles to follow. She had won a lot of respect from Wei. The reason that Wei did not tell his wife the weight on his mind was that his future, even his life, was tightly tied up with the judgment of this case. He did not want her to be troubled by worries. But he had been staying in the study for almost a day and sighing and groaning all day long. His wife had seen this. She did not like to see her husband like this. So she came in carefully. Wei could not hide it anymore. So he told her the whole story.

Xu, however, showed no hesitation, and said seriously, "This concerns the laws of the country. As an official in the Ministry of Punishments, you ought to punish evil and let justice prevail. If you let two or three lackeys around the Emperor obstruct, you are stooping to compromise, then Zhang Zhu will die quietly and nobody will know his injustice."

"But the case has Dongchang directly involved, so I'm afraid that I'll be in trouble because of this...."

"Don't worry. If you are exiled, I'll be with you wherever you go."

"What if I am put into prison?"

"I will go to the Grand Court of Appeal to protest the injustice."

"If I am sentenced to death?"

"You will die for the country and for the people. That's worthy. I'll bring up the children and teach them to follow your resolve and promote justice."

With these words, Wei Yingzhao did not have any more worries. He hurried back to the Ministry of Punishments and immediately commenced proceedings. In court, he made a categorical announcement: " Zhang Fu slaughtered his mother savagely, the evidence is solid and sufficient. It is hereby announced that Zhang Fu is sentenced to death. It was wrong that Zhang Zhu was arrested for nothing and suffered various tortures. He shall be released in court. Zhang Xiuping placed righteousness above family loyalty and upheld justice. She deserves to be commended in an official announcement."

The crowd was surprised at the sentence. The news spread quickly throughout the capital. Of course, Wei Yingzhao was the focus of the talk. The commoners highly praised his wisdom and courage. For several days after that, there were always some people gathered at the yamen of the Ministry of Punishments for the purpose of having a look at Wei Yingzhao. There were some people who had also suffered injustice among them.

They begged Wei for justice. But no one knew that Wei had offended Dongchang, and disaster would soon befall him.

In the Jiajing reign period, Dongchang had already become well established. Its headquarters were to the north of the Dongan Gate of the Imperial City. The gate of the complex faced south and was always closed, which gave it an awe-inspiring and mysterious air. Across from the small gate on the southwest stood an ancestral temple, in which lay the memorial tablets of the eunuchs who had controlled the seals in Dongchang. In the temple, there was a small but exquisite memorial arch, on which was written "Leave a Reputation Which Will Go Down in Posterity." The arch was bestowed by the Emperor. It manifested his great trust in Dongchang. The eunuchs and runners who worked in Dongchang were very proud of this. About ten meters to the east of the temple, stood an exquisite hall. It was a sitting-room for the Seal-holding Eunuch. There was also a smaller hall on the left which was used to try cases by police inspectors on duty. Today, the smaller hall seemed much more quiet than usual. Li Qing told the guards to stop anybody from bothering him. Even officials who delivered files and documents were kept out. Li Qing was alone in the hall. He walked up and down with his arms clasped behind him. He was vexed and upset. The Ministry of Punishments had sent the findings of the trial for the murder of Zhang Sunshi to Dongchang two days ago. Li Qing was irritated after reading the findings. Just as he was about to reject the file, he heard that Zhang Fu had confessed right in the court that he had sent five hundred *liang* of silver to him as a bribe. This put him in a dilemma: if he rejected the hearing's findings directly, it was no different from telling the public that he·had accepted bribes. If he pretended to be indifferent toward the hearing, it would show that he was upset inside. What should he do? He was at his wits' end.

It was midday. The blazing summer sun penetrated through the carved window and shone on the large desk. Li Qing felt a bit dizzy from the strong light reflecting off his desk. He looked up slowly and caught hold of the picture of Yue Fei* hung in the middle of his front wall. He fixed his eyes on it unmoringly for a good while and in his brain appeared the images of the characters "Perhaps so"** came out from nowhere and grew bigger and bigger in front of him. He was suddenly enlightened. Excited, he pushed the files away and said to himself firmly: "A small mind makes no real man a real man lacks not in venom."

Then he picked up an ink brush and started to quickly write on official document paper which was only for reports to the Emperor. In the report he described a vivid story of how Zhang Zhu had plotted to kill the woman and how Zhang Fu had been wronged. With special attention to the fact that Zhang Xiuping had exposed her own brother, he made up a story how this

---

* A national hero of the Southern Song Dynasty (A.D. 1127-1279).

** When an accusation of treason was laid against Yue Fei and brought before Qin Hui, the prime minister, the latter condemned Yue Fei to death, on the ground that Yue Fei had *perhaps* committed the crime.

was due to Zhang Zhu and Zhang Xiuping having an illicit affair. To end with, he accused Wei Yingzhao of taking three hundred *liang* of silver in bribes from Zhang Zhu, sheltering the real criminal, perverting the law and unjustly killing innocent people. After the memorial was finished, he stamped it with the Dongchang seal without it being polished by the secretary, and asked an intimate runner to send it to the Emperor immediately. He knew very well that nobody was bold enough to detain a memorial presented by Dongchang. Even at midnight, though the Donghua Gate was closed, the memorial could still be inserted in through the crack of the gate and reach the Emperor that day. He also knew that the Emperor never rejected an urgent memorial from Dongchang. Therefore, he reckoned that in two days Wei Yingzhao would be seriously punished and the case would be over-turned.

The confidential report reached the Emperor by that afternoon. The Emperor was only keen on making pills of immortality. He dreamed of staying young for ever. He did not care about state affairs, but he never neglected a confidential report from Dongchang. Emperor Jiajing was completely persuaded by Li Qing. Actually, he had lost his trust in the officials in the Ministry of Punishments long ago and the report triggered his hidden fears again. So he did not hesitate in commenting on the report: "The Ministry of Punishments shall be blamed for the presumptuous decisions made in judging the case. Wei Yingzhao acted with utter disregard for human life. Even death cannot atone for the offense. He shall be put into jail to await the hearing right after the edict is announced. The case shall be transferred to the Censorate. Assistant Censor

Xiong Jia is appointed as the judge to hear the case again. The result shall be reported to the Palace in ten days." He was afraid that the cabinet would stop the edict from being sent, so he asked the Directorate of Ceremonial to send the edict to the Censorate directly.

Xiong Jia was surprised when he received the imperial edict. He was wondering why the Emperor was concerned about such a run-of-the-mill murder case among the common folk. He had heard that the Ministry of Punishments had won over the public because of its wise judgment of the case. He was acquainted with Wei Yingzhao. They had worked together on some big cases before. He was very impressed by Wei's hardworking and meticulously principled nature. But whatever he felt inside, he had to obey the Emperor. He issued an order to arrest Wei Yingzhao and have him sent to the prison of the Royal Imperial Bodyguards and then sent an official communication to extract all the files of the case. But before the files were transferred from the Ministry of Punishments, Wei Yingzhao's wife, Xu, was beating the drum outside the court to protest the injustice. Xiong Jia began to get a sense of the complicatedness of the case. He received the complaint and started to study the files.

The files transferred from the Ministry of Punishments clearly stated that the evidence for Zhang Fu's killing of his own mother was complete and solid. There were no suspicious points. But one look at the charges on Li Qing's confidential report, revealed that they were all nonsense—totally insupportable. For example, Li Qing said that Zhang Xiuping had committed adultery with Zhang Zhu. But after personal investigation, Xiong found that the two had never even

69

met each other before the incident. Another example, Wei was accused of taking bribes of three hundred *liang* in silver. But when they searched Wei's house, they only found less than thirty *liang* of silver. What a clean official he was! The situation was quite obvious. Dongchang's account was pure fabrication. They were framing Wei and the Ministry of Punishments. Of course, it was all because of Wei Yingzhao. He had offended Dongchang. But how could the Emperor believe Dongchang so easily? The case had been completely turned upside down by Dongchang. For the moment Xiong Jia could only rack his brain trying to figure out how to conclude the case.

Xiong felt like he was a balance. On one scale sat the Emperor and Dongchang, on the other scale were Wei Yingzhao and several ordinary commoners. But how could Wei Yingzhao and the commoners fight against the Emperor and Dongchang, though they were innocent and right? Assistant Censor, I have to handle the case justly and impartially," he thought, "but the problem is that that will be against the Emperor's wishes and will kick Dongchang in the butt, with the result..." Xiong battered his brains looking for a solution that would satisfy both sides. But this was a case related to human lives. The settlement would get someone killed, or one could say, sacrificed. There was not a middle way. So? This law enforcement official who was famous for great resolve did not know what to do. He recalled his twenty-odd years of vicissitudes of official life. He recollected the hard journey from being a petty official to becoming a second rank official in the Ministry of Punishments. When he thought about being almost fifty years old and a senior imperial official a few years short of retirement, he really did not want to risk offending the Emperor. Therefore, he made up his mind to write a memorial affirming the proposal from Dongchang.

However, as he put the memorial into the envelope, he thought of Wei's wife, Xu. He thought of the plaintive and resolute expression on her face while she was beating the drum. Again he seemed to see Wei speaking sternly to him out of a sense of justice, as he had said when he was jailed: "How can the imperial law be abrogated so carelessly? How can the law be bent for private gains?" He hesitated again. In his mind he saw the innocent Zhang Zhu tied up and escorted to the execution field and slim Zhang Xiuping put in chains and shackles and thrown into jail; then the triumphant laughing faces of Li Qing and Zhang Fu. He could stand it no longer. He felt guilty for doing this. He felt it was against his character and a profanity against the just and honest beliefs he held in his heart. He felt as if all the people in the capital were pointing at him and cursing.

"I can't," he murmured to himself, "I just can't do this in exchange for the pleasure of the Emperor and Dongchang. He drew the memorial out and put it into the flame of the candle. He watched it slowly consumed by the flame. As the last piece be came ash, there was a slight smile at the corner of his mouth, which arose from relief along with bitterness and disdain for an uncertain future.

Yangxin Dian (Hall of Mental Cultivation) in the Forbidden City used to be the place where Emperor Jiajing dealt with government affairs and met the cabinet officials. But since he had become attracted by making immortality pills, the exterior officials were not allowed in there again. It had been like this for more than ten years. For convenience, he had a stove which was identical to that of the Taoist Patriarch installed in the East Nuan Ge of the hall. And he sat before the stove every day with his legs crossed in the front, muttering incantations, adding firewood and fanning the flames. He looked forward, with great hope, to a day when immortality pills were made. But in fact, he never isolated himself from the mortal world. He kept on the lookout for any signs of disturbance and trouble outside the confines of the Imperial Palace. Extreme desire for power made him distrustful of any officials, except the two spy organizations—Dongchang and the Imperial Bodyguards. Three days ago, he had personally written his comments in red ink on the confidential memorial presented by Li Qing. Since then he had been expecting the memorial from the Censorate. When that day he asked the chief of the Directorate of Ceremonial again about the report from the Censorate the eunuch did find one from Xiong Jia. When Emperor Jiajing saw that the memorial was neatly written, a pleasurable feeling rose from the bottom of his heart. He was surprised at Xiong's efficiency and was pleased that his official valued his edict so much. He took the memorial out, unfolded it and started to read. His face began to change as he read down. More and more signs of anger appeared on his face. When he finished, he was so exasperated that he rolled the memorial into a ball wildly and threw it into the blazing stove. Do you know why? Xiong Jia spoke for the Ministry of Punishments. He insisted on affirming the original judgment by Wei Yingzhao and moreover, he castigated Dongchang for taking bribes, bending the law for their own profit and wronging the innocent. He also advised the Emperor to remove Dongchang's right to interfere in the activities of the three judicial departments. Returning the judicial powers to the three judicial departments was the last thing Emperor Jiajing wanted to hear about. And that was why he was in a fury.

The maids and eunuchs were all terrified. They knelt quietly to the side, waiting for Emperor Jiajing's words. Jiajing's hands were shaking. He had forgotten about his pills of immorality. He shouted at the eunuch in charge of taking down the emperor's words: "Convey my words, Wei Yingzhao is to be dismissed from office and interrogated. Xiong Jia is to be dismissed from office and await my word. "The Supervising Secretaries Lu Can and Liu Xijian in the Ministry of Punishments are appointed as judges to hear the case again. The result must be presented in five days. If anything goes wrong they will be held responsible." The eunuch quickly wrote down all these words, stamped the edict and had it sent to the Ministry of Punishments immediately.

It was already evening when Lu Can and Liu Xijian received the imperial edict. They did not dare to delay a minute. They could not even wait for the arrival of the files and hurried to the Censorate to discuss the case. Lu Can was just past forty. He was also a person of resolve. And he was upright and honest, somewhat like Bao Zheng*. In the yamen of the Ministry of Punishments, he had a very close friendship with Wei Yingzhao. In fact, Wei had talked with him about the case right after

---

* Bao Zheng was a prefect of Kaifeng, capital of the Northern Song Dynasty (960-1126), famous for his impartiality in handling cases.

the rehearing had finished. Therefore, Lu Can knew pretty well what the case was about, although he had not gone over the files. Wei Yingzhao also told him about how torn his mind had been hearing the case and he had given Wei some personal advice. He thought that so long as Wei decided the case impartially according to the law, nobody should blame him. But who could have known that the Emperor would issue two edicts in a few days, ordering the dismissal of Wei from his office and his interrogation him. Then Lu Can started to understand the seriousness of the situation. But he had not expected that the case would fall on to him.

Lu Can clearly understood that the case appeared not that complicated. The Emperor's wish was very clear: he wanted it to be judged as suggested in the confidential report, which had marked Zhang Zhu's name with a red cross to execute him. That was all. Then Zhang Fu would be released and everything would be finished. But that being so, wasn't it true that everything was upside-down? It was not a big case. But after the hearing had been held repeatedly, everybody in the capital was aware of it. If the judgment was to please the Emperor, it would go against the public. He would not only be spat upon and cursed by the people, but condemned by his best friend Wei Yingzhao. That was what made the case so hard.

Right after they were seated, Lu Can spoke his mind. Liu Xijian was already graying around his mustache and beard. He was very circumspect and farseeing. He had accumulated a lot of experience from forty years of working as a law enforcement official in the Ministry of Punishments. He did not express his own opinion at all after Lu Can's words.

Instead, he asked Lu tactfully, "So, your excellency, what way do you think the case should be judged?"

Noticing Liu Xijian's eyes were evasive, Lu thought to himself: "It looks as if he hasn't formed any idea yet. I'd better move him with the righteousness of the cause and persuade him on to my side." So he said sternly: "It is a very clear case. The evidence is sufficient and the criminal has confessed. Wei's judgment was clear and just. It cannot be overturned."

It seemed that Liu did not understand him. He blinked his half-closed, small eyes and asked, "You mean to clearly affirm Wei's judgment?"

Lu was a little irritated. He answered coldly. "That's right."

Liu did not say anything more. But he started to mutter to himself interminably, his eyes slightly closed. Lu could not hear what he was saying, but he could sense that he was figuring what the result would be if the case was handled as Lu proposed. Lu thought his expression was pretty funny. He stared at his face close, awaiting his conclusion.

After quite some time, Liu shook his head and said, "No, no, it's no good. If the case were judged like this, you would draw fire on to yourself."

"So we're going to maintain Dongchang's judgment?" asked Lu, full of unhappiness.

Liu seemed not to hear his words, but carried on with what he saying in a quite low voice,

"Execute Zhang Fu, and it means Dongchang loses the case—Li Qing will never forget it. Surely he will take his revenge sometime later. Release Zhang Zhu, and it means we take the imperial edict as shit—the Emperor will never let us go easily. Look at Xiong Jia, what a high

75

rank and lustrous reputation he had. But so what? Just because he spoke for Wei Yingzhao, he was dismissed from office and is awaiting the Emperor's word. We are just fourth rank officials. What kind of efforts should we make to turn the tide?"

Lu Can felt completely discouraged. Though he had some thoughts on Liu's philosophy, he had to agree with him. All at once, he did not know how to argue against him.

The sound of the watchman's clapper coming from the street told them that it was already the third watch. The two judges looked at each other, but could not find a satisfactory solution. Liu stood up from his chair, walked slowly to the door and opened it. The night breeze mixed with the fragrance of flowers suddenly blew. It was so fresh and cool. Liu did not go back to his chair again. He walked around the room with his arms clasped behind him, his body bent forward. After a while, it seemed that had discovered something.

He lifted his head suddenly and looked at Lu: "I've got it." His eyes were shining.

"Your Excellency has found a way to turn around the bad situation?" Lu approached him and asked.

Liu no longer looked old and weak suddenly. He looked at Lu solemnly and sincere: "Your Excellency, when I received the imperial edict, I already knew my official life could be completed soon after we receive the case. In fact, I understand very well that the public can only be satisfied and comforted if the judgment given by Wei is affirmed. What I worried about was only you! You are just over forty years old. You have a prosperous future. And besides, you possess exceptional talent and are impartial and honest. All this should bring you a brilliant future. If you stand up with me to expose the evils of Li Qing, our fate will be the same as Wei. But it is not worth sacrificing both of us. Therefore, I was racking my brains to find a compromise. But fire and ice can never stay in the same oven at the same time. I just can't find a solution satisfying both sides..." He paused for a while and continued, his eyes sparkling: "Tomorrow, you ask for a leave. I will present a memorial to the Emperor alone in three days to make Wei understood. If the god of heaven has mercy on me, the case may be well settled. But if the Emperor is offended and he charges me, I will be the only one sacrificed. I'm old. My sons and daughters are all working far afield in Sichuan. I don't have to worry about my family being implicated..."

"No!" Lu stopped him before his words were finished, "Your excellency is aged. How can I let you bear all the risks? We'd better do it this way, you ask for sick leave and I'll handle the case by myself. I'd rather take all the responsibility."

Liu was deeply moved by his character of not shrinking from difficulties and dangers. Both of them tried to persuade his counterpart to stay behind. But neither of them succeeded. This argument took about half an hour.

Lu Can said finally, "If so, why don't we submit a joint letter to the Emperor. A letter jointly signed must be more influential than one with a single signature. The Emperor might adopt our sincere proposal."

Liu thought for a while and then did not insist any longer. So they started to draft the memorial to the Emperor.

The Emperor had not expected that Lu Can and Liu Xijian would present their findings of the review just on the day after his edict had been issued. He believed that the reason that they had finished the report in such a short time was that they had understood his wishes very well. The report would decisively overthrow the original verdict of the Ministry of Punishments, he thought. As he unfolded the letter, he took a careful look in particular at the bold signatures at the bottom. But as he read the text of the memorial, he again became exasperated. There was not much description of the process of the case in the report. It only listed all the criminal evidence, which made the case as clear as a sheet of blank paper. At the same time, it described every detail of how Li Qing had taken bribes, how Dongchang had run amok and inspired seething popular discontent. In conclusion, it called for the wicked unit to be severely punished and its powers out for extreme lack of discipline, so as to stabilize the public. Emperor Jiajing felt like his heart was being stabbed with needles. He hated any criticism of either of his favorite organizations. He could not bear such a foolish memorial completely ignorant of the times. He would not forgive them. He spitefully threw the paper into the stove and ordered that Lu Can and Liu Xijian be sent prison. He clearly stated that the officials in the Ministry of Punishments were biased toward each other and in favor of killing innocent people. And he also stated that the judgment given by Wei had to be overturned. Being afraid of further objections against his edict, he ordered it sent to Dongchang first and designated Li Qing to transmit it to the Ministry of Punishment in person. A vice-minister was assigned to be in charge of the case. Li Qing was to monitor it. Though the order had been sent out, Emperor Jiajing had not calmed down from his fit of rage. He even forgot to add firewood to the stove, until a maid screamed that the fire was dying out. He dashed to the room and hurriedly fanned the flames.

The news spread quickly through the capital that, all because of a common murder case, Emperor Jiajing had issued three imperial edicts in ten days and put three officials of the Ministry of Punishment into jail. Everywhere—be it taverns or teahouses, streets or alleys, the topic was the same. Wei Yingzhao, Xiong Jia, Lu Can and Liu Xijian were highly praised. The wish that could be heard the most was that if all the officials in the three judicial departments were like these, there would be no need to worry about the stability of the country. Some merchants and members of the local gentry had food sent to the imprisoned judges to express their admiration. People were continually visiting Xiong Jia every day. To avoid suspicion, Xiong Jia did not greet any of them. People were all watching how the case would end.

The judge in charge of the fourth hearing was "Vice-minister" Xu Zan. He had been working in the Ministry of Punishments for years, but was not noted for any outstanding achievements. It was said that he seldom spoke when hearing cases. Therefore, he left others an impression of hauteur and concealing real feelings. People in the Ministry of Punishments kept him at a respectful distance. There were no bad words about him and no good either. When the edict was handed over to him, a trace of hesitance could be noticed on his face. But he did not refuse. Then he announced that a committee was to be set up consisting of more than twenty people. He had the files sent to the Ministry of Punishments on the same day. On the second day, he summoned Zhang Zhu, Zhang Fu and Zhang Xiuping to the Ministry of Punishments and put them all in jail. Though Li Qing was under orders to monitor the hearing, he was diplomatically prevented from approaching the committee. All this was like the wild beating of gongs and drums before a Beijing opera started. It made people more and more curious about the results of the hearing.

Ten days had passed before people realized it. A cool wind signaled the beginning of autumn. But the results of the hearing were still now here in sight. It was said that Xu Zan had sent more than twenty people to search and investigate around Shichahai and that new evidence had been discovered. But nobody knew who the evidence was favorable to.

In fact, Xu Zan had finished the memorial days ago. The reason that he did not submit it was that he wanted to take the time to watch the attitude of the public. On the day he received the imperial edict, he had told himself that there was no way out unless the case was ended as the Emperor's wished. He had been an official in the capital for many years. He was well aware of the political rules. No one could be promoted continuously unless the emperor was fond of him and he did not offend Dongchang and the Imperial Bodyguards. At present, the situation was quite clear, the Emperor and Dongchang were on one side and Xiong Jia and Wei Yingzhao on the other. No matter how the weights were changed on the scales of the balance, the Emperor and Dongchang were always heavier than their counterparts. Therefore, Xu Zan had made up his mind to judge the case one hundred percent according to the Emperor's intentions. He laughed at Xiong Jia and the others who intended to break a stone with an egg. He shook his head and said to himself that he would never do such a stupid thing. So far, he had kept the case under wraps for a dozen days. He had realized the sentiments of the people. He knew almost all of them were sympathetic with Zhang Zhu and Zhang Xiuping. He knew that the people nursed many grievances against Dongchang, too. But he believed that, if he settled the case according to the Emperor's will—otherwise, his head might be cut off. On the first day of the ninth lunar month, he opened the case to the public.

The outside of the yamen of the Ministry of Punishments was full of people. They all came to listen to the hearing. The doddering mother of Zhang Zhu and Wei's wife, Xu, who was in simple dark dress stood at the front. The atmosphere of the court was not gloomy as usual. Only the twenty-one committee members were allowed to enter. Even the runners scribes on shift in the punishment section were not in the court. The hearing was much simpler. Judge Xu ordered the prisoners brought to court and then announced the sentences. There was even no interrogation. It took less than half an hour to finish the so-called hearing. Of course, the murderer was Zhang Zhu. He was sentenced to execution. The son of the victim, Zhang Fu, was announced innocent and released in the court. He was compensated with five *liang* of silver for wrongful imprisonment. The sister of Zhang Fu, Zhang Xiuping, was to be driven out of the capital after being beaten one hundred times with a bamboo stick for her dubious relationship with Zhang Zhu and framing of her brother. Wei Yingzhao was exiled to Yunnan on charges of taking bribes and biased judging. Li Zhen and Wang

Yun, Zhang Zhu's neighbours, were accused of providing false evidence and were exiled with Wei Yingzhao.

When the announcement was published, the city burst into an uproar. Though the people's talk was a fearful thing, power was more repressive. Innocent Zhang Zhu was escorted to the execution ground and executed. His mother could not stand the grief and rage and drowned herself in the moat. Zhang Xiuping could not stand the insult and hanged herself from the beam of her house.

The late-autumn wind tore the grass and the leaves from the trees and blew them tumbling over and over. In a shabby pavilion outside of Guanganmen Gate, Wei Yingzhao bid a tearful farewell to his colleagues from the Ministry of Punishments. His torn clothes had been changed. Though he had gone through terrible tortures in the jail, he did not look defeated and down. His wife was with him carrying a simple parcel. Wei Yingzhao sprinkled the spirits his colleagues had toasted him with on the ground and bowed deeply to them, full of compassion. Then he wiped the tears from his eyes, walked out of the pavilion and advanced along the winding lane which was almost covered by wild wormwood.

Thus far, a case which had absorbed the attention of the whole city had ended with the triumph of Dongchang. Zhang Zhu had been sacrificed, while Xu Zan had saved his official post. As Emperor Jiajing received the finial report from the Ministry of Punishments, he only said: "What a pity, Zhang Zhu is only in his twenties." And then he returned to his stove to make his pills.

The Attempted Assassination of the Crown Prince

It seemed that spring was very late in coming that year, 1615. It was already early the fifth lunar month when the flower-buds of the peach trees in the Forbidden City began to open. Except for some luxuriantly green bamboo, other plants in the imperial garden still looked yellowish and far from resembling a landscape of late spring. The Dragon Boat Festival was coming. The halls had been festively decorated by the eunuchs of the Directorate of Ceremonial and the inner court Directorate for Imperial Accouterments. Bunches of sweet calamus and wormwood were put at the gate of each hall. Long scrolls with pictures about some traditional legends were hung on the gates of some important halls. The coiling incense smoke spread with the fragrance of sweet calamus and wormwood. Palace maids had all changed into festival dress. At their waist, hung little bags full of realgar and cinnabar. This all created a festive atmosphere.

It was cloudy on the fourth day of the fifth lunar month. The Forbidden City had be come shrouded by dusk before anyone noticed. The Cining Palace, which was the bedchamber of the crown prince Zhu Changluo, appeared very quiet today. The thirty-four-year-old prince had been born with a gloomy character. He had no interest in tomorrow's festival. In the afternoon, he listened to part of a lecture on *Lisao* by the Grand Tutor at Yangxin Hall. It only made him more depressed, so he returned to his residence before the teacher finished the lesson. As the custom, he checked the decorations in the Cining Palace at dusk. But he gave no comment and entered the West Chamber with his hands crossed behind him. The attendants were put at a loss and had no idea what to do with the decorations. Even the chief eunuch in charge of affairs of the Eastern Palace (residence of the crown prince) felt perplexed. He could only order everybody to be more cautious and careful at each post.

It was getting dark. The brass lamps on the two sides of the imperial roads decorated the vast and deep palaces with their dim light. The attendant Li Jian who was on duty guarding the palace gate was leaning against the half-closed gate. He felt a bit uncomfortable and closed his eyes for a rest. Suddenly, a rustle of steps made him. He opened his eyes wide and found a shadow swiftly moved along the wall and seemingly rushing to the gate. The Cining Palace was located deep in the Forbidden City. No outsider was allowed in here. It had to be some scoundrel who had sneaked in. Li Jian was immediately roused.

He shouted to the shadow: "Who is it?"

Hardly had he finished his words when the shadow was coming at him. Li Jian had practiced some gongfu (martial arts) before and escaped easily from the first attack. "Bang!" The date stick in the scoundrel's hands smashed hard on the gate. Before Li Jian could recover from the shock, the stick was swishing toward his head again.

Li Jian shouted loudly, while dodging the stick:

"Assassin! Assassin!" The assassin was sent into a frenzy by Li Jian's shouting. The next three attacks were all aimed at fatal parts of Li Jian's body. The stick moved indescribably fast. Li Jian could not escape the whacks and was beaten heavily to the ground before other guards came. The assassin seemed to have a plan well thought out beforehand. He stopped fighting with Li Jian, and dashed to the main house where the crown prince lived. He broke the door with just one single hit and was about to burst in. At this moment, another guard, Han Benyong, arrived with some twenty guards. In no time, the assassin was surrounded. The assassin found the situation not in his favor. He swung the stick to force the guards back and tried to find a way out. However, the heavy security of the palace made it impossible. Countless guards had appeared from all sides. Although the assassin was a big man, he couldn't fight against so many people. After a short while, he was caught by Han Benyong and some other guards.

It was quite unexpected that someone would be bold enough to try to assassinate the crown prince in the Forbidden City. In great panic, Zhu Changluo ordered to the assassin to be imprisoned at Donghua Gate. He himself went to the Qianqing Palace that very night to report the event to his father, Zhu Yiju, or Emperor Wanli. The Emperor had been born with a lazy and timid character. His heart went pit-pat upon hearing the news. He ordered security in the palace to be reinforced and the assassin transferred to the Imperial City's judiciary for rigorous interrogation.

Liu Tingyuan, the official responsible for the judicial affairs of the Imperial City, heard about the assassination attempt after midnight. He was scared into a cold sweat.

85

It was absolutely beyond his reckoning that somebody could intrude into Cining Palace to do violence! He considered himself lucky that the crown prince was all right. However, as an imperial law official, he had been completely unaware while someone was slipping past their tight security to try to murder the crown prince. This was obviously a negligence of duty for which he would be criticized severely. Therefore, Liu bore a vehement hatred of the assassin and began the interrogation right away.

In the dim interrogation room, the candles were flickering, which added to the frightening atmosphere of the twenty-square-meter room. The assassin was brought into the room, tied up tightly with ropes. Liu Tingyuan looked swiftly at the scoundrel and drew a startled breath. The criminal was very tall and had a strong build, and on his square face appeared a ferocious look. He was dressed like a peasant. His weapon was a date-branch which was very thick and weighed no less than fifteen kilograms. Liu thought to himself, if there had not been some guards who knew some gongfu, the crown prince would probably have died under this stick. Liu was scared by this thought. And the greater his fear grew, the more he became enraged.

He struck the table heavily and shouted at the criminal: "How dare you, you scoundrel! Where did you come from? Why did you break into the palaces with a plan to assassinate the crown prince?"

The man seemed to hear nothing. He kept silent, his head dropping before his chest. Liu Tingyuan got more angry. With the order "Beat!" the waiting eunuchs in charge of torture immediately pushed the assassin to the ground and beat him severely. Under their sticks of those well-trained eunuch-torturers, the assassin was almost beaten to a mess of blood and flesh. He could only repeatedly ask for mercy.

Liu Tingyuan then ordered the beating to be stopped, and roared: "Will you talk or not?"

The assassin's arrogance had completely disappeared. He answered in a shaky voice, "Don't be angry, Your Honor. I'll tell everything. My name is Li. I came from Fangshan County…"

Liu Tingyuan struck the table at once and retorted: "Nonsense! You speak with an accent from east of Beijing. How can you come from the west in Fangshan County? Looks like you won't tell the truth without some great torture. Guys Clamp him!"

The eunuchs responded by throwing the clamping bars in front of the assassin. Now the assassin was really undone. He kowtowed again and again and begged: "Don't! Don't do it again! I'll tell you everything. I am from Jixian County, east of Beijing. My name is Zhang Chai. I work on a farm. I often chant the name of Buddha and do not eat meat. I never did bad things before. Today I entered the palace by mistake and got lost. When I found someone trying to stop me, I was so afraid to be caught that I wanted to kill…"

Liu Tingyuan asked, "How did you enter the Forbidden City and how did you get into the Eastern Palace?" Zhang Chai equivocated for some time and couldn't give a clear answer. His embarrassment showed there might be something difficult for him to speak out about.

Liu Tingyuan's heart was getting heavier. He had been working in the Imperial City for a long time and was quite familiar with the Forbidden City. The

Forbidden City was so well secured that even a cat couldn't sneak in. How could a man as big as Zhang Chai and with a thick stick enter it so easily? Suppose he made it anyway, how could he reach the Cining Palace which was located deep inside the palace grounds, without meeting groups of patrolling guards? It seemed he had walked in some empty places through thin air. From his hesitant attitude, it was obvious that somebody was behind him instigating. Who was this person? Liu Tingyuan also knew that the crown prince was born by the imperial concubine Lady Wang who was a former maid in the palace. So the Emperor was not very much fond of the crown prince. The third prince Zhu Changxun was whom the Emperor adored the most. He had been granted the title Prince of Fu a few years ago. All the court officials knew that the Emperor had the intention of removing the present crown prince and grant the title instead to Zhu Changxun. During the recent months, the prince of Fu's mother Lady Zheng was winning more and more favor from the Emperor. It was said the crown would soon be removed from the oldest prince and given to the third prince. The incomprehensible assassination incident had happened at this key moment. Were there any inside stories…

In the last years of the Ming Dynasty, struggles among the different factions in the imperial court started getting more and more intense. It became common practice for officials, imperial concubines, princes, eunuchs and royal kinsmen to scheme against one another, striving for power and position. Everyone had to think ahead and look back before dealing with anything to avoid making a fatal mistake. Liu Tingyuan knew about this all too well. At this moment, facing the assassin, Liu was quite uncertain what to do. He might have his whole family killed if he pursued this to the end and found the case involved the Emperor and Lady Zheng. Or he might be accused of conniving with the criminal if the assassin had nothing to do with the power struggles. It was a real dilemma. The only solution was to get way and shift the case to someone else. But how?

Liu Tingyuan's mind started wandering as he heard the assassin's farfetched confession. He thought it over and over and finally got an idea which looked reasonable one way or the other. He interrupted Zhang Chai's confession and wrote a memorial to the throne right away, saying: "The assassin Zhang Chai looks idiotic and speaks incoherently. It indicates that he is possible insane. However, observation shows his actions seem crafty. The Imperial City having no specialized judicial bodies, it is hard to uncover the whole truth. Therefore, I hereby ask to have the assassin transferred to specialized judicial bodies for further interrogation." At that time, this memorial could be counted as a typical official document which pushed away responsibility. Defining the insanity of the assassin was for the convenience of the instigator. Insanity would be the best excuse if the Emperor didn't seriously want to go into the incident. Mentioning the craftiness of the assassin would leave himself a way out. If the truth was revealed after all, nobody could criticize his connivance with the criminal because he had already pointed out the assassin was crafty.

Liu Tingyuan's method worked well. The assassination case was shifted to the Ministry of Punishments. Without any delay, three officials, Hu Shixiang, Zhao Huizhen and Lao Yongjia, were designated as the judges to hear the case together. The three officials all had worked with the Ministry of Punishment for a long time and knew very well that a big burden had just been thrown on to them. They could neither push it away nor investigate it to the end. They understood better than Liu Tingyuan that the removal of the present crown prince was just a matter of time. Lady Zheng's family was winning more and more favor from the Emperor. Zheng not only was stunningly beautiful, but could understand Emperor Wanli's changing minds very well. She had become a person whose side Wanli could not leave for a second. Zheng's father and brothers were high-ranking officials in the court. Her son, the Prince of Fu, had grown up in Wanli's arms and was his favorite prince. No one in the imperial court could not succumb to the overwhelming power of this family. Even Prime Minister Fang Congzhe had to take his cue from Lady Zheng. Now Zhang Chai had dared to make an attempt upon the crown prince's life in the palaces. If there had not been someone plotting behind him, he would never have been bold enough to do this. Who was the instigator? Lady Zheng or the Emperor himself. Then the interrogation would finally lead to the Emperor and Lady Zheng. Wasn't it playing with their lives! But could they not investigate the case? No, because the case had shocked the whole country. Many righteous officials had sent in memorials, asking for a complete investigation into the case. If they procrastinated any longer, the officials would together accuse them. Even their minister would not allow this.

Therefore, without seeing the criminal, the three judges got together to work out suitable countermeasures. He Shixiang was the cleverest among the three. In the documents transferred from the Imperial City, he found Liu Tingyuan's memorial that defined Zhang Chai as a madman. It was really the perfect excuse. They could simply push the boat in the direction of the current and cling to Liu's view that Zhang Chai was a madman. Madmen did mad things. He might dare to attack the Emperor, let alone the crown prince. It was quite a reasonable solution that could work everything out.

After the discussion, the three judges acted respectively. As old hands in the Ministry of Punishments, it was no big problem for them to create false statements. The next day when they heard the case, the judges somehow cooperated with one another very well in the court and "got the whole incident about the madman into shape."

According to their report: "Zhang Chai had been making a living selling firewood. Early this year he had offended someone and the firewood he had accumulated with so much effort was set on fire and burned up. Zhang got so mad that his mind was damaged. In the fourth lunar month this year, when he came to Beijing to file a suit, he had met two strangers. They sympathized against injustice and encouraged him to bring his case to Emperor. They told him if he had no written complaint, he could hold a thick stick as a signal so that the people in the Forbidden City would not stop him. Zhang Chai was very eager to take revenge. So he held the stick and sneaked into the Forbidden City through the Donghua Gate. He didn't know the way and mistook the Cining Palace for the Empreor's residence. Therefore the false alarm was made."

There was a clear thread to the case. Zhang Chai's fingerprint was on his confession. The judges considered

91

the conclusion of the case reasonable after discussion. Zhang Chai had hurt eunuchs with a lethal tool in the Forbidden City and frightened the crown prince. The crime was unforgivable and Zhang should be executed at once.

The interrogation of the case was quickly reported to the Ministry of Punishments. Next step, it would be reported to the Emperor. With the Emperor's approval, the case would be closed. It was incredible to see such a shocking case about to end so quickly. Not only were the three judges pleased with themselves, even the Minister of Punishments was surprised and very satisfied. However, before the report was ratified and returned, news spread like wildfire causing a big stir inside and outside the court. Memorials were sent to the Emperor from all sides, criticizing the Ministry of Punishments for not clearly trying this serious case and asking for an investigation into the instigator. The closing of the case was then delayed.

Emperor Wanli lived in the Kunning Palace. He usually got up very late. But after the assassination incident, for several nights he couldn't sleep well. It was not because he was worried about the crown prince, but because his favorite concubine cried every day, urging him to end the case quickly. As a matter of fact, Wanli had known nothing about the inside story before it happened. Afterwards he didn't even associate the assassination attempt with the power struggles. He ordered the Ministry of Punishments to make a full investigation. He meant to look into the incident seriously. But after the case was transferred away, Lady Zheng became upset. She said he should have heard the case himself. A few days later, officials' memorials came one after another, pleading for the pursuit of the culprit of the crime. Now Wanli felt the assassination no longer had nothing to do with his favorite concubine. With this thought, he himself was thrown into a panic. Lady Zheng had become so important in his life. Although the Emperor had thousands of women in his harem and each of them had her own beauty, he considered Zheng the most extraordinary one. Her extreme tenderness and consideration made the Emperor want to give her everything. He once promised her he would grant Zheng's son, the third prince, the title of crown prince. But this idea had been strongly opposed by the court officials. A dozen years later, he had to grant the oldest prince Zhu Changluo the title of crown prince and make Zheng's son, Zhu Changxun, the Prince of Fu. This made the Emperor feel sorry for his favorite concubine. And now, if Zheng was truly behind the assassination plot, she would have no way of surviving after everything was revealed. Then how could he spend the rest of his life without her? Therefore, suddenly it was Wangli who became afraid of the details of the case being uncovered.

That morning the Emperor woke up very early. His first words were: "Has the report on the case arrive?"

The attending eunuch answered, "It arrived last night."

Wangli sat up immediately. He hurriedly threw on some clothing and took up the report at the "dragon table." While reading the report, he became greatly delighted and murmured to himself: "Capable officials, they are really my capable officials!" But when he picked up the writing brush and was about to write his endorsement of the report, he caught sight of the many memorials on the table written by other officials. They appeared to go directly against him—all demanding to seek out who was behind the crime. The memorials pointed out that Zhang Chai must have had somebody cooperating with him inside the Palace, and that there must be an instigator behind him. They thought the intention of the Ministry of Punishments' plan to quickly execute Zhang Chai was obvious: kill him to avoid his betrayal of a secret and cover up for the one responsible for the crime. Some pointed out that Zhang Chai was not insane and he could tell the whole truth under severe torture. They pleaded for the punishing of the instigator and the disciplining of the harem. "Discipline the harem!" Wasn't this directly saying the instigator was in the harem? Wanli was overwhelmed by anger. He really would like to kill some of these bold officials. But of course he knew that killing officials would be no more than adding fuel to the fire. Wanli leaned wearily against his "dragon chair," with no ideas coming to mind. At this moment, the eunuch in charge of taking down the Emperor's words came to the Kunning Palace, waiting for the Emperor's comments on the memorials that had arrived last night. Wanli had no other way except to use the old method of holding all the memorials. He ordered another imperial edict sent to the Ministry of Punishments, for a closer watch on Zhang Chai to keep him from contact with others. There would be severe punishment if something went wrong.

In the fifth lunar month in Beijing was already early summer. The windows in the prison of the Ministry of Punishments were still tightly closed. No wind could enter. The prisoners breathed heavily in the heat. Some prisoners' torture wounds began to fester. They couldn't help groaning loudly in pain. The prison guards whistled their whips and roared at the prisoners to stop their groaning. But the groaning spread again in the prison after just a short silence. In the guardroom, a man in his early forties was bent over at his desk, lost in his mediation, ears covered with his hands. He was Wang Zhicai, an official with the Ministry of Punishments. Although he was just a sixth-rank official, he was experienced and capable in his work. With his straight and righteous character, he was deeply respected by his colleagues. After the assassination attempt, Wang had watched the progress of events calmly. For years, as other righteous officials, he had sympathized with the crown prince who was left in the cold by the Emperor. When the news spread that Wanli intended to get rid of the oldest and adopt the younger, Wang Zhicai worried for the crown prince even more. The assassination attempt shocked the whole country. Wang's sharp mind told him it was Lady Zheng who was the devil behind it. He really hoped that the judges from the Ministry of Punishments could find clues in the case and pursue it to the end until Zheng's ugly plot was revealed to the world. Unexpectedly, Hu Shixiang had done everything in such a slick way that the disturbance had been almost suppressed. Wang felt very indignant about this. But he was not the judge of the case and couldn't interrogate the assassin. In order to reveal the whole truth, Wang decided to investigate the case secretly. An investigation needed contact with the assassin. But recently the guarding of the prison had been reinforced. Zhang Chai's prison cell was particularly well guarded. Even the Ministry officials needed a specially issued pass to enter, let alone other people who came to visit the prisoner.

This created a huge barrier to the investigation.

Wang Zhicai racked his brain and thought out a good plan to get close to Zhang Chai. Although the prison was well guarded, the prisoners needed to eat. If he could obtain the job of managing the prison meals, it would be a lot easier for him to enter the prison. So, he visited The Assistant Minister of Punishments, Zhang Wenda, and easily got the job he needed. During the ten days since he had taken charge, he himself led the prison guards to deliver meals to the prisoners every day. In this way he could observe Zhang Chai secretly. He found that the wounds all over Zhang's body didn't influence his appetite. It seemed that the food in the prison couldn't fill him up. There was another thing which made Wang very excited: Zhang's movements were very swift. He didn't look like a madman at all. This proved Wang Zhicai's former judgment quite right.

Today, Wang Zhicai was going to take a risky action. He wanted to interrogate Zhang Chai at mealtime. Wang was not the designated judge. If he was found interrogating the prisoner, he would be accused for it. And Zhang Chai was an important criminal. If his expected objective couldn't be reached, Wang would get himself punished. Also the time of the interrogation couldn't be too long, or the higher officials might interfere. Finally, the revelation of the truth needed a suitable method of interrogation… Wang sat in the guardroom and thought hard. He went over and over his plan until he decided it was flawless. Then he stood up and ordered the start of the meal.

Mealtime was the most active time in the prison. Today, Wang Zhicai purposely let the cook add a little stewed pork to the simple food. When the food cart was moving from cell to cell, the tempting aroma filled the air. The prisoners hadn't tasted meat or fish for a long time. Their stomachs rumbled with hunger when they smelled the pork. As usual, Wang supervised what food was sent to each prison cell. But today he made a special order not to give food yet to Zhang Chai.

Food reached all the other prison cells. The prisoners ate their food with great relish. However, the door of Zhang Chai's cell was still closed tightly. Nobody came to him. The good smell made his mouth water. Several times Zhang held on to the door and tried to look out, only to find nobody coming to give him his food. The loud eating noises from the others made his stomach rumble. Finally he began to knock on the door and shouted: "My food hasn't been sent!" While he was crying with his last bit of strength, the door suddenly opened. Wang Zhicai walked in with some guards and a secretarial official. The smell of pork came out from the wooden barrel carried by a guard. Zhang Chai's eyesight was locked on the barrel. He murmured to himself: "Pork, pork…" Wang Zhicai's heart began to thump loudly. He was afraid that his well-prepared plan would fail. He understood this moment was like the arrow on the bow—poised to strike. If he couldn't get any new results, he would have to confess to the Ministry the crime of interrogating a criminal privately and would be sent to distant exile.

Wang Zhicai spoke calmly, "Zhang Chai, I want you to speak about the details of the assassination today."

As Zhang heard this, he showed the whites of his eyes: "I entered the Forbidden City to file a suit to the Emperor. Why do you ask me?"

Wang said, "I came here especially to absolve you. I

can manage to set you free if you tell the truth."

Zhang pointed at the barrel, "How about eating first?"

"No. Your food is here. But only after you talk can you eat. You'll strave to death if you don't speak up." The prison guard stirred the pork broth in the barrel with a spoon. The good smell wafted into his face. Wang Zhicai sat down on the ground and gestured for the secretary to sit down too. A guard brought a small table as the secretary produced his writing brush and ink.

Wang said, "Zhang Chai, I know you were tricked into commiting a major crime. As long as you speak out about the whole thing, I will surely give you a light sentence."

Since Zhang Chai had been arrested, all the officials he had met had been wrathful and cruel to him. But this one seemed kind. Zhang remembered yesterday when his food was not enough, this official ordered that an extra bowl of rice be given to him. "And today, he has not only delivered the food to me himself, but also wants to absolve me. He is really a good man," thought Zhang Chai to himself. His vigilance evaporated.

Wang Zhicai had been a county magistrate before. He had a good knowledge of criminal psychology. Now he knew a breach had been nearly opened and began to shoot out vital questions according to his plan. Zhang was eager to eat and also to be exonerated. He then described the whole process of events, although he hummed and hawed sometimes.

98

Zhang Chai, nicknamed Zhang Wu'er was born in Ji County. He made his living by working on the land. This year, spring had come too late and the harvest was going to be very poor. Zhang then thought about finding some work in Beijing. He had a neighbor who he called Uncle Ma. Ma introduced to him a eunuch who was named Li and worked in the Palace. Li said he could find a job in the Palace for Zhang Chai. Ten days ago, Li brought another eunuch to Zhang Chai. This eunuch was unwilling to tell his name. Li told Zhang Chai as long as he did what this eunuch told him to do, he would have enough to live on for the rest of his life. Then Zhang Chai followed the eunuch to Beijing. They lived in a big house where all the people who came were eunuchs. Zhang lived there for several days, eating good food and not doing any work. Before the Dragon Boat Festival, the eunuch who brought him here asked Zhang Chai to kill a man. The man was in his thirties and wore dragon clothes. The eunuch also said Zhang Chai could receive a piece of land after this. Zhang Chai thought it was profitable, so he agreed. The eunuch gave him a thick date stick and took him inside the Palace through a big city gate. They went almost to the door of the intended hall. Zhang Chai was told the man he was to beat was living inside. Then, the hall intrusion incident took place….

The whole course of events became very clear. Wang Zhicai asked further about the place Zhang had lived after he came to Beijing. Zhang said he could only remember it was in the middle of a wide street. He said he knew nothing about other details. Since the interrogation had already taken long time, Wang dare not stay longer. He then asked the secretary to read the confession. Zhang Chai nodded his agreement and pressed his fingerprint on the confession. Wang then said some placating words to Zhang Chai and hurried out of the cell with the others.

After Wang Zhicai returned home, he was still very excited. He hadn't even told his wife about his plan before he had carried it out. He had been ready to lose official rank and be exiled. Today, his plan had succeeded. The situation became quite favorable. He studied Zhang Chai's confession very carefully again and decided there were no loopholes. Despite the hot weather, Wang began to write a disclosure right away. He finished three thousand words at one sitting. The entire process was described clearly. At the end of the disclosure, he emphasized: "The trouble had started inside the Eastern Palace. Zhang Chai was not insane at all. There must be someone instigating from inside the harem. If this case not judged fairly, Providence will not forgive! According to the old rules, the criminal should be tied to Wenhua Hall for an open interrogation by the Three Judicial Offices* whole imperial court. Or all documents should be transferred to the Three Judicial Offices* for a joint interrogation. In this way, the instigator will have no way to escape." After he finished writing, Wang Zhicai stood up and opened the window. An intoxicating fragrance at once filled the room. He found it was already mid-summer. In the courtyard, little yellow flowers were blooming all among the flourishing date trees....

---

* The Censorate, The Ministry of Punishments and the Court of Judicial Review.

Qianqing Palace in the Forbidden City was unusually tranquil today. Servants and maids all walked quietly, afraid of making any sound. Since early morning, Wanli had lost his temper three times. They knew it was because the Emperor was twisting his brain to deal with the assassination case. So all of them were more careful than usual, not even daring to breathe normally. Wanli had received the disclosure written by Wang Zhicai and care of the Assistant Minister of Punishments yesterday. It was really a life threatening document for Lady Zheng! At the same time, he had received a secret report from the spies of Dongchang. The report said Wang's report had spread widely through the capital city. Public opinion in the streets and lanes was severely critical of lady Zheng's intention to murder the crown prince. In a teahouse outside Zhengyang Gate, someone had turned the story of Wang's interrogating Zhang Chai into a song and sang it in public. This upset Wanli even more. The lovely concubine had come to the Kunning Palace yesterday. She had just paid her respects to him quietly then left. Wanli found she was looking very haggard and there were traces of tears on her face. He had more pity for her but no idea about how to comfort her. This morning when he went to Qianqing Palace, he found the memorials about this matter had piled up mountain-high. In some writings, the words "treacherous kinsmen" caught the eye. The spearhead was obviously directed towards Zheng's family. Although the Emperor could hold these memorials in the Palace and give no response what about the public opinion in the streets and lanes? What's to be done if the cabinet send in memorials to press the matter? What if the crown prince came and cried for justice? Wanli was really at a loss what to do.

At this moment, a eunuch of the Directorate of Ceremonial came and reported that all the court officials were gathering outside the Meridian Gate, begging the Emperor to hold court.

Wanli waved his hand agitatedly: "Tell them I'm not feeling well. No court today."

The eunuch asked in a low vice, "What is the reply regarding the assassination case?"

Wanli said unwillingly, "Tell the Ministry of Punishments to gather together the directors of the Thirteen Bureaus* to carry out a joint interrogation."

After the eunuch drew back, Wanli sank helplessly in the "dragon's chair," like a balloon pricked.

According to Wanli's order, the Ministry of Punishments gathered the directors of the Thirteen Bureaus, together with Wang Zhicai and Hu Shixiang who were familiar with the case. They carried out a joint interrogation of Zhang Chai on the twenty-first day of the fifth lunar month. In the severe atmosphere of the court of the Ministry of Punishments, Zhang Chai dared not deny his guilt any longer and confessed to more details of the incident. His Uncle Ma's name was Ma Sandao. The eunuch Li was called Li Shoucai. The eunuch who brought him to Beijing was a palace attendant called Pang Bao who had gone to Ji County to supervise the construction of a smelter. The big house he lived in after arriving in Beijing was located outside the Chaoyang Gate. The host of the house was a palace

---

* Collective reference to the thirteen bureaus, each named after a province, that were the major subordinate units in both the Ministry of Revenue and the Ministry of Punishments.

eunuch called Liu Cheng. When Zhang Chai was questioned on who asked him to do violence in the Palace, he answered without hesitation that it had been Pang Bao and Liu Cheng. He said they told him clearly to beat the "little master." They said to him: "If you kill the little master, you will never worry about earning a living for the rest of your life." At last Zhang Chai was asked about his associates. He admitted there were five people who had come together, including his brother-in-law Kong Dao.

Now the case had come to light completely. Pang Bao and Liu Cheng were Lady Zheng's trusted eunuchs. And "Little master" was how the eunuchs called the crown prince. It was obvious that Lady Zheng instigated her eunuchs to murder the crown prince. In order to have more testimony from witnesses, the Ministry of Punishments suggested that the Court of Judicial Review and the Censorate ask the Emperor's approval to catch Pang Bao and Liu Cheng from the inner Court to verify the facts.

When the news came to the Palace, Lady Zheng could hardly stand. She had racked her brains scheming the assassination plan for several years. But now it had been ruined by Pang Bao and Liu Cheng. Zheng knew what kind of people Pang and Liu were. They appeared outwardly tough, but were cowards inside. Once they were caught by the court, how could they stand the severe question by the Three Judicial Offices? Then, not only would she lose all her standing and reputation, but ruin and shame would also befall her father and brothers. How ghastly to think about the consequences! She thought in circles and decided there was no turning back. The only thing she could do at present was to place hope on Emperor Wanli who adored her most of all. She should try to ask him to mediate in the matter. But Zheng felt it so difficult to make such a request.

While Zheng was worrying, footsteps were heard from outside the room. Then a maid walked in quietly and reported, "The Emperor is here." Lady Zheng felt greatly comforted. She quickly wiped away her tears and applied a little rouge on her face. In no time, she looked beautiful and attractive again. Wanli walked into the chamber. The concubine moved lightly with a graceful demeanor to meet the Emperor. Wanli held her small and milky hands and examined her.

After a while, he sighed, "You've become so thin these past few days, my dear."

Zheng took the chance to throw herself into Wanli's arms and said grieviously, "I'm all right. Even your Majesty is worried about it. Many people in and outside the Palace suspect I wanted to murder the crown prince. They even want to arrest my close eunuchs. Once the lie becomes true... It's doesn't mater if I die, but Your Majesty…"

Crystal tear welled up in her eyes. Zheng's sorrow added to her usual charms. Wanli's heart was full of compassion for her and her dilemma. He came here to unburden his heart. Now he was utterly upset by her crying.

Zheng found Wanli didn't look too good. She quickly stopped crying and held Wanli's arms lightly to lead him to the carved dragon-and-phoenix settee.

Wanli looked carefully at her for a minute and said: "These days, I've been thinking about ways to save you. But after the joint interrogation, the situation took a dramatic turn for the worse. It looks like an interrogation of Pang Bao and Liu Cheng is just a matter of time."

Lady Zheng looked at Wanli with all her tenderness and gingerly asked, "Could Your Majesty give a decree not to allow them to go?"

Wanli shook his head: "Gossip is terrible! There are some officials in the court who complain all day long, not fearful of death. If I don't approve the arrest, it would look like I had a guilty conscience."

This time Zheng was really scared. She knelt down with tearful eyes, pleading for the Emperor's help. Wanli contemplated for some time, then said, "Since things have taken such an ugly turn, it's hard to suppress people's anger just with my words. If the crown prince is willing to come out to mediate, there maybe a chance to turn the situation around. But, the one who creates the trouble should be the one to solve it. You need to go to the crown prince's palace to persuade him. As long as the crown prince agrees to it, I can arrange everything."

Lady Zheng thought to herself there was nothing else she could do. It was easy for her to curry favor with others. And furthermore, she was just a concubine and it wouldn't be losing face if she were to plead with the crown prince. So, Zheng got closer to Wanli and went into the details about what she should say in front of the crown prince. It was late at night when she led Wanli to bed in her chamber.

Zhu Changluo, the crown prince, had been put in humiliating situation. He had not been liked by the Emperor from the time he was very small. He had grown up in lonely and bleak circumstances, shaping his weak and gloomy character. He had been scared to death by Zhang Chai's assassination attempt before the Dragon Boat Festival. These days, he was disturbed by the public opinion from outside. Although the court officials' opinions were in his favor, and he knew Lady Zheng had something to do with the assassination attempt, he felt the memorials had unconsciously pushed him into a position opposing his father. So, even if Zheng was punished, the only thing he would achieve would be his father's enmity. Therefore, the crown prince hoped the court officials would not longer seek for the person responsible for the crime. He would be quite content if the parties involved could reconcile with one another, and no trouble was remained, so that everyone could live in peace.

The crown prince had discussed this with his teachers several times, trying to find a good way that would not only down assuage people's anger but also not offend his father. While he was worrying, from outside of the palace came the announcement: "Lady Zheng is here." Zhu Changluo was confused. How could this woman who had gone against him for twenty years come to see him? The curtain was lifted before he could stand up. In came Lady Zheng followed by a bevy of maids. The crown prince dared not slight the concubine. He got up quickly to greet her.

When Lady Zheng entered the room, the crown prince gestured for his servants to retreat. When there were just two of them left in the room, Zheng suddenly dropped on her Knees before the crown prince. The unexpected act flustered him. He also knelt down and intended to support her up with his hands. Zheng stretched out her slim hands and helped him to his feet. The crown prince's heart could not help admiring her: "What a beauty!" Zheng parted her rosy lips and began to speak softly. She said she had deep respect for the crown prince for these last twenty years. The assassination attempt really had nothing to do with her. But now the unfair talk among the officials and the gossip from the public made it hard for her to explain. She could find no redress for her grievances but to come and speak her mind to him. She asked the crown prince to come out and save her for the sake of the Emperor. As the concubine spoke tears ran down her face and she could hardly finish her words.

Zheng's crying put Zhu Changluo at his wits send. He was a kind person by nature and had all along wanted this troublesome case to end. So he said in earnest tones, "Don't worry, Your ladyship I can surely persuade the court officials in person and ask them not to pursue the so-called instigator."

Hearing this, Zheng was still not put at ease. She pleaded for a written order. The crown prince did not refuse. He sent for the eunuch Wang An, the prince's Reader Companion, to write an order. It said: "Since the assassin Zhang Chai has been arrested, the case can be ended with his execution. The talk about someone being behind the scene is pure imagination. Court officials should not keep looking for an instigator." When the writing was finished, the crown prince let Zheng read it before sending it out with the prince's seal. Now Lady Zheng's tears had turned into smiles. She thanked the crown prince profusely and went back to her palace.

It looked as if the case had come to an end. However, the officials were not satisfied with the crown prince's attitude. Some suspected this was the result of Zheng's putting pressure on the crown prince. They felt even more keenly the injustice on his behalf. Memorials which insisted the pursuit of the culprit continued to come thick and fast to the Palace. Finally, even Prime Minister Fang Congzhe could no longer keep silent. Like other high-ranking officials, he wrote a memorial saying: "Seek the instigator who should not be let off with impunity." This time the imperial court erupted into a major commotion. Emperor Wanli was then forced to wind up the matter himself.

In the middle of the sixth lunar month, an imperial decree suddenly came out from the Forbidden City, announcing that the Emperor was going to meet the court officials at the Cining Palace and hear the assassination case. This was really big news because Emperor Wanli had been tired of dealing with state affairs and not appeared in court for twenty-five years. But now he was coming to court again for the palace murder case. It was clear how important the case was to him. But how would the Emperor end the case? The officials could get no information about it.

On the 18th day of the sixth lunar month in the year 1615, the Cining Palace in the Forbidden City was shrouded in a solemn atmosphere. Prime Minister Fang Congzhe led other court officials into the palace. Wanli was sitting on his throne, the crown prince standing beside him. Three imperial grandsons were gathered here too, standing at the foot of the left stairs. After the officials showed their profound respects to him, the Emperor struck first by blaming their insistence on finding the chief culprit for sowing discord between father and son. The Emperor continued, saying that it was a case of Pang Bao and Liu Cheng using an insane person to murder the crown prince. There was no deeper version of the incident. Since the criminals had been discovered, sentencing them to death would end the matter. There shouldn't be this great fuss over trifles and implicating of others.

Next, the Emperor held the crown prince's hand and said: "The crown prince has always listened to me. I have always liked him very much. If I wanted to remove him, why I wouldn't have issued a decree long ago? Furthermore, the Prince of Fu is now living in Luoyang, far away from Beijing. There is gossip saying I want to get rid of the elder and grant his title to the younger. Can the Prince of Fu fly here without my decree? Today the crown prince has also come here. You can ask him if you have questions on the matter."

Finally, the Emperor pushed the crown prince to face all the court officials, and said to him: "All the court officials are here today. You can say whatever you want. Don't have any misgivings."

The crown prince knew his father wanted him to say something in favor of Lady Zheng. He was willing to do so. First he stated that his father and he had gotten along very well since he was very little. After he was granted the title of crown prince, their relationship became even closer. Then the crown prince emphasized that Zhang Chai was really insane and deserved execution. But it was going too far to look for an instigator for no reason at all. He demanded that the officials not pursue the matter any further. As for Lady Zheng, the crown prince said, she had been on friendly terms with him and he respected her very much. So there was no ground to suspect that she had been plotting behind the scenes. This idea shouldn't be mentioned again. The crown prince's words were very sincere. The officials could say nothing more although they knew this was to reconcile all parties concerned and shelter Zheng. The officials then retreated most respectfully from the palace.

The next day, Zhang Chai was escorted to Xisi to be executed. Two days later, Pang Bao and Liu Cheng were interrogated before the Wenhua Palace. Since Zhang Chai was dead, there were no witnesses. Pang and Liu pushed all the responsibilities away from themselves. Lady Zheng wanted to save their lives, but Wanli felt they could be the seeds of misfortune. So he gave an order to have the two executed.

Therefore, this major case which took place in the Imperial Palace subsided with the two-man performance by Emperor Wanli and his son. The men who were killed had just been scapegoats. The real schemer was protected amidst the complex contradictions. However, the case hadn't come to an end. In the years of Emperor Tianqi (1621-27) and Emperor Chong Zhen (1628-44), "the case of the attempted assassination of the crown prince," and "later the case of the red pills" and "the case of moving the palace" went through several reversals. Many more people died in those reversals.

The Case of the Red Pills

In the 48th year of Emperor Wanli's reign (1620), the seventh, eighth and ninth lunar months were the most depressing months since the establishment of the Ming Dynasty. In middle of the seventh month, Emperor Zhu Yijun who had been on the throne for 48 years passed away. Music was forbidden, as well as merry-making. Both government officials and commoners had to be in deep mourning, truly or artificially. In the Forbidden City, long mourning streamers hung solemnly everywhere. Incense smoke curled up slowly. What a dreary scene! Following traditional practice, the Crown Prince Zhu Changluo had inherited the throne on the first day of the eighth month. But unfortunately, even before the funeral of Emperor Zhu Yijun had come to close, the newly crowned emperor also fell in. And his condition got worse and worse. After holding a consultation on the state of his pulse, prominent imperial physicians dispensed four different strong medicines to keep his condition from deteriorating. But they failed to achieve the hoped-for results. The Emperor became so enraged that he swore at the physicians. Even the President of the Imperial Academy of Medicine was hesitant to say the cause of the illness after he in person also checked the pulse. He just made up some prescriptions to preserve vigor. But no effect at all was noticed after the medicine was taken. On the sixteenth day the news spread out from the palace, that the Emperor could not get out of the bed.

Only half a month after the new emperor had succeeded to the throne, he could no longer handle state affairs. The cabinet members were crazy with anxiety because the memorials to the throne presented by the ministries and provincial governors were hundreds each day, among which many were very urgent. But now since the Emperor was ill, he could not make any decisions. They could only put all the memorials aside and wait. At first, the Prime Minister of the cabinet, Fang Congzhe, was calm and easy. But after several days he became anxious and upset. Before Fang was appointed as the Prime Minister, he had been the Minister of Rites and Grand Academician. During the Wanli reign years, he had for the last seven years continually served in the imperial court as the Prime Minister. He was very good at handling relations between the Emperor and the officials. For more than thirty years Emperor Zhu Yijun did not meet with the officials, but the edicts issued by him were not contradicted by them. It was all to Fang's credit. The edicts were actually drafted by Fang Congzhe. He had managed to establish a very good relationship with Emperor Zhu Yijun's most favorite concubine, Zheng. After Emperor Zhu Yijun had passed away, Fang Congzhe helped Crown prince Zhu Changluo succeed to the throne. He thought that the new emperor, being just in the prime of his life, could definitely exert himself to make the country prosperous. At least, he could make comment on official documents in person, which would save Fang a lot of trouble. However, who could have imagined that the new emperor would be even worse than Emperor Wanli. Though Emperor Wanli had not

113

handled state affairs in person, he had been able and willing to make comment on the drafted edicts. But now the new emperor was not even able to hold the ink brush. Without edicts, state affairs could not be properly dealt with. The memorials presented by the ministers and other ranking officials needing urgent response occupied the desk every day. The most dangerous thing was that the officials in the cabinet had recently started to complain, saying it was all Fang's fault. Fang Congzhe was tortured by anxiety.

This morning, right after Fang Congzhe arrived at the Chaofang (antechambers to the throne room), an urgent official letter was sent to him from the imperial palace. The cause was the Emperor had lost trust in the imperial physicians and become impatient about his illness. So he drove the physicians away and asked the eunuch Cui Wensheng to make a diagnosis and give treatment. So Cui Wensheng wrote a prescription. But not long after the Emperor took the medicine, he started to have diarrhea which could not be stopped. In one night, he went to toilet more than forty times. Then he had lost consciousness. Therefore the cabinet members were expected to make a decision. Fang Congzhe was astonished and angered after he read the letter, because on the one hand, the Emperor was dying, and the state would be in panic, while on the other hand, he hated the incompetence of the inner court officials and attendants. There had not been even one person to persuade the Emperor not to take the dangerous cathartics given by an attendant who did not have any knowledge of medicine. So he informed the imperial physicians to go to the palace immediately to give emergency treatment. And at the same time, he notified the cabinet members to go to the Taihe Gate to await summons. He reckoned that if the Emperor was dying, he would definitely summon the officials to make arrangements for the future of the empire.

When Fang Congzhe arrived at the Taihe Gate with the cabinet members, the palace was in great confusion. The Emperor remained unconscious. The physicians had no idea what to do. No information could be obtained from the palace. Therefore no one knew how the treatment was going. But the sounds of chaotic running about from inside the Taihe Gate implied the situation was very bad. Fang Congzhe was very nervous while he waited for the diagnosis with his heart in his mouth.

It was not until noon that the physicians came out. Since the Prime Minister had given the word that the condition of the Emperor should be promptly reported, the chief physician came to the Chaofang to look for Fang Congzhe in particular. The physician was more than seventy years old. He had close association with Fang, therefore, he did not hide anything from him.

He said to Fang in a low voice, "His Majesty's illness is too far gone."

Fang seemed a bit puzzled. "Just past age forty, how can this be?"

The old physician shook his head and said, "It takes more than one cold day for the river to freeze three feet deep—the trouble has been brewing for quite some time. His vital essence has lost too much. As we usually say, 'The essence of life is vital essence, the more accumulated, the stronger life is.' Which is why the physicians always gave him medicine for controlling nocturnal emissions to help recover the shortage of Yin. This kind of medicine takes time. But what kind of disease can be cured with a single medicine? The Emperor complained that the medicine did not work, but would rather carelessly try cathartics instead. Now the recuperative medical treatment of several months has been completely destroyed in a flash."

From the old physician's words, Fang Congzhe realized that the situation was quite serious. He said without thinking, "Is it out of control?"

The physician replied with a sigh, "If no more quacks are trusted and he is strengthened with vigor-producing medicine, it is still hopeful, but if…"

Fang Congzhe cut in brashly, "I'll go persuade the Emperor to do as you say." The old physician bid farewell with his hands clasped in front, "Thank you for your trust, Sir."

Having seen off the physician, Fang realized that it was already noon. He had a rushed lunch, and was prepared to write the Emperor a letter with the intention of persuading him to trust the imperial physicians, when he heard a succession of quick calls from the Taihe Gate: "The Emperor is calling the Prime Minister in." Fang believed that the Emperor was really terminally ill. He stood there for a few minutes until he gathered himself together and then he followed the eunuch messenger to the inner palace.

Crossing the Qianqing Gate, he was depressed by the miserable atmosphere in the inner palace. Emperor Wanli's funeral not yet finished, the long mourning streamers were still hanging before the gates of every yard. Though it was blazing summer, the gates and doors were all closed. Seldom could any people be seen or any voice be heard, except one or two eunuchs passing by hurriedly. The leaves of the rare flowers and trees in the palace were curled by the sun and dropped wearily. Zhu Changluo's bedroom was in the Yangxing Hall which was to the southwest of the Qianqing Palace. The door was closed tight and a big bamboo curtain covered the door completely. Fang felt gloomy. He looked around and did not see one maid or attendant. There was ambergris burning in an incense burner which was in the middle of a big dragon desk. The room was full of the fragrance of incense.

The eunuch walked into the west side-chamber of the hall quietly and silently drew aside the bamboo curtain. Fang heard the Emperor say to the eunuch in a faint voice, "Please show Fang in." Fang did not delay for a minute. He walked into the chamber quietly, his face solemn. He knelt before the bed and said respectfully, "Your Majesty!"

"Get up and be seated."

An attendant had already moved to him a round stool with dragon motifs and asked him to sit down. Fang peered at Zhu Changluo out of the corner of his eyes. He found his face pale and his beard and whiskers well-combed. Around his head was wrapped a wet yellow cloth, which was obviously used to lower down his temperature. He could see that the Emperor was seriously ill, but not so close to death. Zhu Changluo grabbed Fang's hand with his shaking hand and said, "I've been dizzy and frail for days, so I can't deal with the state affairs. Thank you for settling all the affairs for me."

Fang said with reverence and awe, "Your Majesty, your grace is so vast and mighty. How dare I not devote myself to working for the country!"

Zhu Changluo nodded and continued, "You can comment on the memorials of state affairs for me with the red brush. The Crown Prince is weak in character. Please help him and support him. The wives and concubines haven't…" He was too fragile to finish the sentence. He was choked by something in his throat and panted for a good while. Then, he continued, "…they haven't been conferred titles. You can do it following past practices."

Obviously the Emperor was leaving instructions on the matters that he had left unfinished. Fang listened with great respect. After the Emperor stopped speaking, he comforted him, "Your Majesty, you are at the best age of your life. You are just suffering an ailment. Don't worry. All will be fine. Don't believe the gossip and hurt yourself. Please look after your venerable body."

Zhu Changluo shook his head softly. "Has the funeral chamber been properly prepared?" he asked suddenly. Fang did not know how to answer the question because he did not know which funeral chamber Zhu Changluo was referring to, Emperor Wanli's or his own. He paused for a while and said, "Don't worry, your Majesty. Emperor Dahang has already been buried properly. They started to cover the funeral chamber at Tianshou Mountain the day before yesterday…"

He was interrupted impatiently by Zhu Changluo: "I'm asking about my own funeral chamber."

Fang fell down on his knees in panic and said in a shaking voice, "The physicians of the Imperial Academy of Medicine have reported to me that Your Majesty is only suffering a poor constitution. Why would Your Majesty say such an ominous thing of yourself?"

Zhu Changluo said with disgust, "A group of quacks in the Imperial Academy of Medicine. I don't believe them."

"If Your Majesty doesn't trust the imperial physicians, I can send an official call out to the world for good doctors."

Zhu Changluo seemed to have been reminded of something by the idea. He asked Fang, "It's said that an official from the Court of State Ceremonial came to present some medicine. Why haven't I seen it?"

"The assistant director of the Court of State Ceremonial Li Kezhuo did once present a memorial saying he had a divine elixir which can cure Your Majesty's disease. But after I discussed it with the cabinet members, we believe it is not reliable. So we persuaded Li Kezhuo to leave."

Zhu Changluo looked a bit displeased. He paused for a while, then said, "The imperial physicians are useless and the divine elixir is not reliable. What do your expect me to do, wait for death hopelessly?"

Fang was frightened. He kept on kowtowing, and said, "Forgive me, Your Majesty. How dare I? But we really can't believe Li Kezhuo's words. Please think it over, Your Majesty."

Zhu Changluo stopped him by waving his hand impatiently. "Even if it can't cure my disease, it won't take my life, either. Isn't that so? Send my edict, I'll try this medicine."

Fang was aware that from the time of Emperor Wanli's grandfather, Emperor Jiajin, the imperial family had started to believe in Taoism. They believed that so long as they were sincere enough they could one day make pills of immorality. In his later years, every day Emperor Wanli had sat besides the stove to make pills together with Taoist priests. The new Emperor seeming to also tend toward such superstitions, it would be impossible to stop him. Therefore, Fang decided to find an excuse to get out of it, "Please, Your Majesty, let me discuss it first with the ministers and other senior officials."

Zhu Changluo had talked too much. He was too tired to argue with Fang. He waved for Fang to stop. Fang asked the maids to help him lie down. He saw the Emperor close his eyes panting, slightly, so he backed out of the chamber quietly after a kowtow.

In the following three days, the attendant from the inner palace kept on coming and asking if the elixir of immortality had been presented. Fang managed to delay it again and again until the afternoon of the third day, when the Emperor sent his close eunuch to the Hall. The eunuch said that the Emperor had issued on edict requiring Li Kezhuo to see him with the elixir pills immediately. Fang could do nothing more. After discussing it with cabinet member Han Lu, they decided to escort Li Kezhuo to the Emperor, in case the pills had negative effects.

Li Kezhuo was in his fifties. He looked hale and hearty and had an elegant bearing. The elixirs that he was going to present were put in an antiquated silk-covered box. As Fang opened the box, a kind of very special fragrance gladdening the heart and refreshing the mind came out and made him feel very at ease and happy. He looked at the pills which were dazzlingly red and sparkling, like agate. They did not look like the medicine which ordinary people could make. Li Kezhuo explained that the formula of the pills had been presented as a gift by a celestial being when he was gathering medicinal herbs on many Mt. Emei many years ago. The medicinal herbs for the pills had been plucked from magical lands and the pills were very efficacious for against any disease. Even Fang himself was convinced by these words. He showed Li Kezhuo to the Yangxin Palace immediately.

Zhu Changluo appeared more fragile than a few days ago. He was so weak that he could hardly sit up. He laid quietly in the dragon bed, remaining fully conscious however. As soon as he saw Fang Congzhe and Han Lu come in, he asked them anxiously if they had brought the elixirs.

Fang knelt down and answered, "Yes, Your Majesty, we have brought Li Kezhuo here, with the elixirs. But we are still in doubt about the efficacy of the pills. So, Your Majesty, please give further thought to your decision."

At this time, Li Kezhuo came forward and knelt right behind Han Lu, his hands holding the box before his chest. Zhu Changluo gave the sign that he should be given the pills. Fang turned around, took the box from Li Kezhuo and then moved hesitantly on his knees to the Emperor. One personal maidservant came over, took the box from Fang and opened it. All at once, the room was filled with a subtle fragrance. Li Kezhuo noticed the suspicious faces of the officials, so he took one pill and swallowed it. Seeing there was nothing wrong with Li Kezhuo after taking the pill, the officials were a bit relieved. When Zhu Changluo saw the pills were so uniquely red, and the fragrance of the pills so comforting, he could not wait to have the maidservant bring some water so he could take one. Almost all the people in the west side chamber were watching the Emperor. They waited nervously, anxious to see what would happen to the Emperor—especially Fang and Han Lu. But there was one person who was the exception. That was Li Kezhuo. He looked so confident

and calm as if he knew the pill would work on the Emperor.

The Emperor closed his eyes and lay there quietly after taking the pill. For about a quarter of an hour he did not move. The officials standing by could hardly stay calm. Fang hinted with his eyes to the eunuchs to watch Li Kezhuo and keep him from escaping. Right at this moment, the Emperor opened his eyes and asked the maidservants to help him up. Fang intended to stop him, but before he could do that Zhu Changluo had sat up. He seemed much better. There was even a smile on his face. "It is an elixir pill, it really is." He kept on saying this and praising Li Kezhuo. "Li Kezhuo is really loyal to me."

Fang Congzhe and Han Lu could not but be convinced by the Emperor's response. They asked at the same time: "How do you feel at the moment, Your Majesty?"

Zhu Changluo answered,, "I feel easy and light of body. I don't even feel weak." After this, he turned to Li: "Li Kezhuo!"

"Yes, Your Majesty!" Li answered. He was still kneeling on the floor.

Zhu Changluo said, "The pill is really efficacious. Please present another one tomorrow. I guess I'll be completely recovered if I take another one."

Li Kezhuo replied, "Your Majesty, I do have another one at home, but the celestial being told me that the second pill should be taken two days after the first one. So please allow me to present the pill two days later."

"I'll promote you in rank and position after I recover," Zhu Changluo said.

Li kowtowed and replied, "Your Majesty, I'm not

doing this for official promotion. So long as your venerable body is restored to health, I'm satisfied."

Zhu Changluo kept on nodding and praising him, "Loyal, really loyal."

Fang said to the Emperor, "Your Majesty, you have just recovered your health. Please calm down and take good care of yourself."

Zhu Changluo nodded and replied, "Yes, I know. You may leave now." Fang stood up respectfully and backed out with the others.

Late lunar August is called golden season in Beijing. In the yard of the Yangxing Hall, several luxuriant, sweetly scented osmanthuses were in flower. The faint breeze carried the heady fragrance to every corner of the vast yard. The gate of the hall which had been closed for more than half a month was open to allow the fragrant breeze to flow in freely. Zhu Changluo was seated full of happiness at the dragon desk. He had not felt like this for quite some time. He was still perplexed by the miraculous effect of the pills. It was just two days ago he had taken it, but now he felt his illness was almost totally gone. In these two days, he could not only read and contemplate by the dragon desk, but also walk to the osmanthuses to enjoy the flowers and fragrance. He regretted that he had missed enjoying the mid-autumn moon due to his illness. But when it crossed his mind that Li Kezhuo was going to present the second elixir pill this second day, he could not hold back his joy and expectations.

Zhu Changluo, just like his father, Emperor Wanli, had blind faith in so-called miraculous cures. And this experience made him respect further Taoism and its celestial pills. He clearly remembered the time once when his father Emperor Wanli had a severe stroke eighteen years ago. It was believed that there would be no way for him to recover. So he had made his will, entrusting Prime minister Shen Yiguan, with the Crown Prince and consorts. But after that one night, he recuperated his health completely. It was said that full credit was given to an elixir pill. When he recollected all this, he became even more anxious to get the second pill. Therefore, he sent eunuchs six times in the morning to urge Fang Congzhe to invite Li Kezhuo to the palace. Now it was almost three o'clock in the afternoon but Li Kezhuo had not yet arrived. Zhu Changluo got more and more impatient. He was murmuring to himself, "The Prime Minister bungles matters." It was not until four o'clock that he was told that Fang and Han Lu accompanied by Li Kezhuo were awaiting his decree outside. Zhu Changluo ordered that they be let in without delay.

Fang was really in a dilemma today. Three days ago he had shown Li Kezhuo into the palace to present the medicine under the Emperor's urging and force. Though the immediate effect was obvious to all, he believed that it might be caused by the Emperor's psychological reaction rather than the effects of the pill. After he returned to his place, several close aides and staff came for news. They held the same opinion as Fang and tried to persuade Fang not to lead Li to the palace again. The physicians from the Imperial Academy of Medicine unanimously agreed that it was not the effect of the pill. They all expressed the intention that if Fang guided anyone to the Emperor to present something like an elixir pill again, they would all resign. The next day, supervising censors jointly wrote to the Emperor to impeach Fang for failing to stop the palace attendant from presenting cathartics to the Emperor, and recommending absurd and unscientific medicine. Fang did not know how to explain it to the Emperor, but he thought the best thing to do was to stop Li Kezhuo from presenting the pill. But when the news from the palace said that the Emperor had been able to walk, a small hope for the elixir of grew in him. He had consulted the President of the Imperial Academy of Medicine and he was told that there were two possibilities which might have enabled the Emperor to get better. One was that the medicines given by the imperial physicians had started to work, the other was that it might be the momentary recovery of consciousness just before death. But anyhow, it had nothing to do with the elixir. Fang was at a loss. He could not tell right from wrong.

Very early in the morning of today, the Emperor had sent men several times to ask for the pills. Fang tried every possible excuse to delay it. But in the afternoon, the Emperor sent an imperial decree, saying that if anyone in the cabinet hindered the presenting of the medicine, he would be charged with blocking an imperial decree and deceiving the Emperor. Therefore, he could do nothing but bring Li into the palace. Before that, he called Li to appear in front of the cabinet and asked him in detail about the effects of the pill. Li Kezhuo guaranteed the celestial effects of the pill.

The Emperor met them in the same bedroom. He sat at the dragon desk and looked much better than two days ago. Fang was somewhat relieved. In fact, he had almost been convinced by the effects of the elixir. This pill presented by Li was slightly bigger and looked more sparkling. Zhu Changluo took it from a maid servant and gazed at it for quite a few minutes. His face shone with a kind of sentimental joy. Another maid servant held a bowl of light ginseng broth to him and he swallowed the red pill quickly with the soup. Seeing that the Emperor had taken the pill, Li knelt down on the floor and asked him to rest in bed.

But Zhu Changluo waved his hands, and said happily to him, "No, no. I feel great today. You have great achievement to your credit. I'll award you later, greatly."

After this, he stood up and paced with a few measured steps. He stopped before Fang and asked him with a smile, "Prime Minister Fang, what do you think? Can I go to the court tomorrow?"

Fang answered tactfully, "It's better for you to rest for a few days, Your Majesty. It will not be too late when you recover completely."

Zhu nodded, smiling. To prevent to Emperor from becoming too tired, a senior eunuch considerately halted the conversation and sent the three officials out.

The first of the ninth lunar month was the date to commemorate the new Emperor taking the throne one month ago. The officials in the inner palace saw that the Emperor had recovered his health very quickly, so they decided to take off the mourning streamers for Emperor Wanli that night and decorate the palaces with lanterns and colorful streamers to celebrate the new Emperor taking the reins of government. Therefore, the night before was a sleepless night. The Twenty-four Offices (collective reference of the units of palace eunuchs) organized decorating activities throughout that night. The Directorate for Imperial Accouterments and the Directorate for Imperial Regalia were even busier, because they had to send all the palace and red silk to every palace. The eunuchs were everywhere. Some were putting up lanterns and others were on their way to deliver embroidered clothes. None of them wanted to be criticized by the supervising eunuch of the Twenty-four Offices as he came to examine the five o'clock morning inspection.

But it seemed that something was wrong in front of the Qianqing Palace during the latter half of the night. Four young strong eunuchs ran through the palaces to pass on an imperial decree that the decorating be stopped immediately. And then, the Seal-holding eunuch of the Directorate of Ceremonial called the President of the Imperial Academy of Medicine to quickly send the physicians to the palace. After a while, verbal imperial edict was announced to call the Crown Prince and the ladies of the imperial harem to the Qianqing Palace for an edict. The cabinet members and other senior officials were called in at the same time. The calls hinted that the Emperor was approaching his last breath. When Fang led the group to the gate of the Qianqing Palace, the physicians were walking out from inside, their heads hanging in dismay. The women of the imperial family could not speak for weeping. The Emperor had passed away at two o'clock in the morning of the first day of the ninth lunar month.

The Emperor had almost recovered his health before taking the second red pill, but then he died shortly after taking it. And the pill had not been given by the physicians. The situation became very serious all of a sudden. Fang was very perturbed after the bad news had reached him, because he knew very well that there would be thousands of memorials calling for his impeachment right after daybreak. He might be made the scapegoat for the death of the Emperor. Though he kept cool outwardly, he was anxious inside, trying to figure out a way out. According to the practice of the Ming Dynasty, if the will was not properly drafted before the emperor passed away, it should be written by the Prime Minister on behalf of the Emperor. Fang thought it over and over, and came to the conclusion that the best strategy at the moment was to explain things in the will and make it clear that it had been the Emperor's own decision to take the red pill. He planned to remove himself from all the responsibility and blame. He had calmed down quite a bit after he figured it out. Then he started to carefully prepare for the funeral. The whole process of the funeral was properly arranged that very night.

As expected, the sudden death of the Emperor completely absorbed all the attention of the government. In two days, several hundred memorials were presented calling for through examination of the cause of the Emperor's death. Some memorials were very open in their blame. It said that Cui Wensheng, who had persuaded the Emperor to take cathartics, was once an official under the imperial concubine Lady Zheng who later recommended him to Zhu Changluo. He had used cathartics to torture the Emperor under somebody's instigation. Fang was shocked by the reproach because he himself had a very close relationship with Lady Zheng. If someone said that the red pill was introduced by him and connected him with Cui Wensheng, it would sound more like a well-planned conspiracy to murder. So long as rumors were blazing, it would be difficult to pour oil on the waters. And the more dangerous thing was that he would be the target. Even if he could have predicted all this, he was not ready for how quickly the situation worsened. He thought he was wise to have figured out countermeasures. He was still pretty confident that so long as the will of the Emperor was issued, all the chaos would vanish.

Therefore, Fang brooked no delay in obtaining consent from the cabinet and publishing the will. The will sang high praise for Li Kezhuo in the tone of the Emperor and awarded him with a lot of silver. Fang thought that this would surely shut the officials' babbling mouths. But he did not realize that he had in fact done a very stupid thing. The censors were enraged after the will was published. Everyone knew that the will was drafted by the Prime Minister. Naturally, the linked Fang and the introduction of the red pills tightly together. The will sounded more like a guilty person giving himself away by blatantly protesting his innocence. Some censors just unquestionably listed Fang in the group of murderers and asked for Cui Wensheng and Li Kezhuo to be severely punished and an investigation to find the backstage manipulator. The turmoil grew tenser and tenser. The Fang realized that the situation was out of his control.

Among the cabinet of the first year of the Tianqi reign period (1621), Han Lu was one of the ministers with the highest reputation. While all the officials wrote memorials for an inquiry after the incident happened, he remained silent, which drove Fang crazy. On the fourth day of the tenth lunar month, when they met alone in the cabinet hall, Fang asked him, "You were well aware of the whole process, right from when Li presented the pill. Why didn't you say something?"

Han Lu did not bother to answer him in words, just giving a slight smile. Fang could not discern what was

130

hidden behind his smile. In fact, Han Lu had been watching the development of the situation the whole time. He was sympathetic with Fang for the injustice, but he was more farsighted. As he saw it, when the officials demanded the case be thoroughly examined and the backstage manipulator be punished, Fang should have ignored then and let things go their way. Then after some time, the chaos would have died out little by little. However, Fang had jumped up, busied himself with drafting the will and making explanations, and so on and so forth. It was no different than hitching his own neck with chains. At the moment, Fang was targeted. Though Han Lu had been one of the two officials accompanying Li Kezhuo to present the pill, he had not been involved in the impeachment. If he stood up at this moment and spoke in defense of Fang, he would definitely land himself in a trap. Then it would be difficult to clear the case. But how could Fang realize all this?

In the middle of the tenth month, the turmoil reached a climax. The Minister of Rites, Sun Shenxing and Censor Zou Yuanbiao handed over two famous memorials, in which Sun Shenxing pointed out: "Even though Fang Congzhe did not mean to murder the Emperor, the result was that the Emperor was murdered and he may be exempt from the label of murderer, but he can never shrink from his responsibilities;" while Zou Yuanbiao criticized Fang Congzhe sternly: "As a Prime Minister, Fang Congzhe did not severely punish the criminal, but awarded him instead, which means he doesn't intend to deal with him. I don't know how he is going to explain this to the public." Sun Shenxing and Zou Yuanbiao were both reputed to be loyal, honest and upright. They never fell short of people's expectations.

Zou Yuanbiao especially was renowned as one of the "Five Upright Officials," because he had once suffered the cruel punishment of flogging due to his being against the previous Prime Minister, Zhang Juzheng, who had supreme power and influence at that time. Their memorials provided strong support for the proposal for a criminal investigation of the case. In this situation, Fang could in no way object to the investigation proceeding.

Fang could not stop his hands from shaking while holding the two memorials. He recalled the measures that he took to pour oil on the troubled waters and he believed that he had done nothing wrong. He thought of the moment that he had faced the officials, when he pointed out solemnly that it had been the Emperor who invited Cui Wensheng and Li Kezhuo to present the medicine. If there was an accusation of a conspiracy, the Emperor would be framed as a sovereign who did not pass away peacefully. How could the subjects stand such an image of their sovereign. He thought his words had been a powerful return attack. He thought it would force the truculent officials to retreat. But he had been disappointed. The return attack did not produce the expected effects, instead, it was like pouring oil on a fire. The voices calling to indict the criminal became louder and louder. I had only been some censors trying to impeach him before. But at this very moment, many senior officials were standing up and complaining of his mistakes. The previous memorials had just blamed him only vaguely. But now, all the reproaches and complaints were pouring out with the direct mention of his name. And moreover, some memorials even went right back through his past exposing his embarrassing history of relying on Lady Zheng. All these were the kinds of incidents which touched off the presentation of Sun Shenxing and Zou Yuanbiao's memorials.

The autumn wind blew the leaves off the trees and scattered them all around on the ground. To Fang the wind felt extremely cold. He felt as if his heart was frozen. He was too exhausted to bear the sharp criticism. He had never expected that he would be accused of murdering the sovereign after working conscientiously for the Emperor and the country for so long. For the time being, the best way to save his family was to ask for retirement. He had considered the situation over and over again, and this was the final resort. After he made the decision, he started to write the memorial, in which he carefully explained himself and sincerely applied for retirement.

In less than ten days, Fang Congzhe received the approval of Emperor Tianqi. At the beginning of the eleventh lunar month, the elderly official who had been the Prime Minister for eight years left the capital in bewilderment. At the rest pavilion near Lugou Bridge, the aides gave Fang the prescribed farewell and drank the parting goblet with him. What a bleak scene! The reeds were whistling in the wind, making a sound like weeping. The light of the setting sun was cold and gray. From high in the sky, drifted down one or two miserable sounds from some wild geese. Fang held a cup of liquor before his chest. All sorts of feelings welled up in his heart. He wanted to say something to the aides, but the words were choked back. His graying beard and mustache were blown wildly by the wind. The aides were all ever come with emotion and could not hold back their tears either. Fang finished the liquor in one gulp, and stepped out of the pavilion and on to the overgrown path. He was all alone, in the sighing autumn wind. But the tragedy had not yet come to an end.

Not long after Fang Congzhe left the capital, some other memorials were presented to Emperor Tianqi demanding that the inside story of the red pill be uncovered.

The young Emperor of only sixteen years of age had already journeyed the rough and ragged paths of life. His mother had died of illness after being beaten by others when he was still young. His grandfather Emperor Wanli for a long time had not trusted his father Zhu Changluo—once his title of crown prince had almost been taken away by Emperor Wanli. His father had eventually succeeded to the throne, but suddenly died of no reason, which aroused revengeful emotions in the heart of Emperor Tianqi. Unfortunately, Fang Congzhe happened to be the target for his suppressed hatred. Therefore, he did not hesitate in approving Fang's application for retirement. However, the officials did not stop reproaching Fang after he was dismissed, which made Emperor Tianqi more convinced that Fang was involved in the murder. It was difficult for Emperor Tianqi to apply severe punishment against Fang because he had served as Prime Minister for three emperors. Therefore, he kept all the impeachment memorials and waited.

One morning, Emperor Tianqi was looking through the presented memorials with the intention of looking for those demanding the impeachment of Fang Congzhe. He noticed one with very familiar handwriting. As he read down, he discovered it had been sent by Fang

Congzhe himself from his hometown. Fang wrote in an earnest tone: "I have never stopped caring about the court since I left the capital. I know the officials are still squabbling endlessly over the death of the former emperor. I was too old and foolish to stop the person from presenting the medicine. I admit my guilt. To be deprived of my official title and be exiled to a remote frontier region. I hope in this way the complaints of the officials could be cleared." Emperor Tianqi felt sorry for the previous senior minister. So he sent the memorial to the cabinet and asked them to discuss it. He did not know that this was actually what Fang had expected him to do.

In the whole course of the incident, Fang had made one mistake after another, except for this last move. Fang had two purposes in submitting the memorial. One was to clear up the public hatred with sincere words and stern self-blame. The other was to win over the officials who had sympathy for him to speak up for him. He succeeded. When the officials discussed the memorial, some started to complain on his behalf. Before long, the Minister of Punishments Huang Kezan, the supervising censor Wang Qingbai and the censor Wang Zhidao all wrote letters to the Emperor, in which they asked him to stop trying to unravel the mystery of the death of the previous Emperor. The reasons given in the letters were that, if the inquiry went on and on, the court would never calm down, and it would be also no good for the imperial family if the Emperor was found to have died of regular causes. If the reasons had been put forth by Fang, this would definitely have promoted public anger, but since they were presented by other officials, they sounded plausible. Emperor Tianqi was hesitant about what measures should be taken because he thought the case had not been cleared yet.

At this moment, the quiet cabinet member, Han Lu, came to see the Emperor. He told the Emperor that he had viewed the whole course of events in person. He gave the every detail of what had happened. Especially the moments when Fang was caught in a dilemma, he described very vividly. At last, Han Lu said that the case had been in limbo for more than a year, but Cui Wensheng and Li Kezhuo, who had given the Emperor the Cathartic and the red pills before his death, had not yet been dealt with. Though the two persons had administered inappropriate medicine to the Emperor, they had done so on the Emperor's demand. Therefore, Han Lu proposed that they should be punished appropriately, and the case should not be investigated any further.

Han Lu was an experienced and steady official famous during the Wanli reign period. Though he had been in the government for over a decade, he was straight forward about matters and never fawned upon rich and powerful persons. Therefore, he was sincerely respected by the officials. He had joined the cabinet only several days before the incident and assisted Fang Congzhe in dealing with the presentation of the red pills from then. But he was not involved in the conflicts between the factions in the cabinet. Therefore, what he said was believable. Days after he presented the memorial, the disturbances gradually calmed down. Before long, Emperor Tianqi issued an edict: "Li Kezhuo is to be dismissed from his post and exiled to the frontier. Cui Wengui is to be expelled from Beijing and relocated at Nanjing to serve a prison term." In this way, a great controversy finally died down.

But it was still a mystery why Zhu Changluo died suddenly that one night and what on earth those red pills actually were. For over three hundred years, though historians assumed various answers, none of them were convincing. Therefore, the case of the red pills will remain forever a mystery. However the political fighting related to the sudden death of an emperor brought out into the open the fierce fractional fighting among the imperial harem, nobility, eunuchs, maternal relatives of the ruling house, cabinet members, ministers, censors and provincial officials during the final years of the Ming Dynasty. From it, the accumulated social evils and misruled affairs of a feudal society on the decline were clearly exposed. Even now, "The Case of the Red Pills" and the "Attempt Assassination of the Crown Prince" are considered the key to understanding the course of political infighting in the Ming Dynasty.

A Murdered Wife Resurrected

Macheng was a small prosperous county in northeast Hubei in central China, with abundant crops of rice and other grains. With the Dabie Mountains to the north and the Ju River to the west, Macheng sat wedged between where Henan and Anhui provinces intersected. During the reign of Emperor Yongzheng (1723-35) of the Qing Dynasty, there lived a wealthy family in the county town, whose master was Tu Rusong. The Tu family's ancestors had all been merchants, and the family was rather rich in the county, so it came as a surprise when Tu Rusong decided to give up on business and concentrate on his studies.

Rusong was said to have been born very clever yet was rather headstrong. At sixteen, he married Yang, a daughter of a merchant, who was a year older than himself. She was pretty and lively, though frivolous at times. She even flirted with Rusong's studymates sometimes, embarrassing him. Rusong warned her over and over again to conduct herself with some dignity, but this had no effect on Yang at all. The rift gradually widened between husband and wife, and when Rusong lost his temper sometimes, he even beat Yang. Yang, however, never put up with this. She would run back to her mother's, and Rusong's mother would have to go there each time to apologize for Rusong and cajole his wife back. And so life went on like this for years with no sign of any rapprochement.

The winter turned especially cold one year, and it began to snow as early as the end of the tenth lunar month. Hubei people were not used to such cold weather and Rusong's mother caught a bad cold and couldn't rise from her bed. Rusong, ever the dutiful and obedient son, devoted himself to caring for his mother, administering her medicines and meals all day long, rarely leaving her bedside. Yang's mother entreated her daughter to help, but Yang, spoiled and pampered from childhood, was sick of taking care of her mother-in-law. When Rusong was not around, she would chastise his mother loudly. When he heard this at first, Rusong tried to hold his temper, but when he couldn't stand it anymore, he began to beat on his wife again.

One day, Yang reprimanded her mother-in-law again for spilling some tea on her bed. Rusong got so furious that he grabbed a stick to beat Yang. Yang, just as angry that her husband could be so cruel, packed a small bag and left the house. Rusong thought his wife had run back to her mother's as she usually did, so he took no notice. It also turned much quieter at home after Yang left, which was not a bad thing. Rusong now focused on looking after his sick mother, and after a month of tender care, the old lady finally recovered.

There's a saying: "There's no family without a wife, "and the first thing Rusong's mother wanted to do after she got well was to bring her daughter-in-law back home. Also, Rusong was still childless after ten years of marriage, and the old lady was eager to have a grandchild. She prevailed on Rusong to be more tender and considerate to his wife, and when Rusong realized his mistake, the mother prepared a trunk of presents for the Yang family. She let Rusong ride the horse which also carried the trunk, and she sat in a small sedan chair, and so together they went to bring the wife back. But when they arrived at the Yang's, they were informed that the wife was not there. At first, Rusong's mother thought Yang's family said this because they didn't want Yang to go back with them. She then apologized again and again. Suddenly Rusong's mother-in-law burst into a wail. She said if her daughter had left a month before and not made it to the Yang house, something terrible must have occurred. Rusong and his mother had remained calm until they heard this. Then they immediately put out posters, promising a handsome, hefty reward. They also called on their neighbors to find out where Yang might have headed toward, but more than a month soon passed, and no clue was found.

When there was no information forthcoming about their daughter, the Yang family began to suspect that Tu Rusong had murdered his wife. After his sister went missing, Yang's younger brother Yang Wurong—a lazy good-for-nothing who'd never done a decent day's work in his life and had grown into a rather rascal character—kept inciting his parents to charge Tu Rusong with murdering his wife. Under Wurong's constant harangue, Yang's family finally filed a suit at the county yamen.

The County Magistrate of Macheng was Tang Yingqiu, a righteous official who'd been a successful candidate in the highest imperial examinations. After he received the complaint, he looked into Tu Rusong's movements and decided there was little opportunity for Tu to murder his wife. Firstly, Tu's mother had been very sick when Yang went missing, and Tu had never left his mother's side during that time. Tu's neighbors could testify to this. Secondly, Tu's mother had prepared gifts and visited Yang's family with her son as soon as she was well. If Tu had committed the murder, they would not have acted like this to cover up. Thirdly, if Tu had killed Yang, how could he hide Yang's body? It was extremely cold that winter. The earth was frozen. Clear traces would be left on the ground if he had dug into the soil and buried the body. But when Tang Yingqiu examined Tu's property, he didn't find any suspicious evidence. Furthermore, the Tu family had gone from being merchants to becoming scholars. A scholarly family, he felt, would not have the courage to kill, although Tu Rusong did sometimes beat his wife. Based on these facts, Tang Yingqiu quickly cast aside the conjecture that Tu Rusong had killed his wife.

However, the key point of the case remained: Where was Yang? The search went on for a long time and unearthed no clues whatsoever. Tang could do nothing but postpone the outcome of the case.

When Yang Wurong found no progress on the case, he showed up at the yamen every day, crying out for justice. Magistrate Tang soon got irritated and told him the case couldn't be concluded if they didn't locate Yang's whereabouts. Tang told Wurong: "You'd better try to help the yamen find your sister instead of coming here complaining every day. As long as you can provide verifiable evidence, I will certainly give you justice." On hearing this, Yang Wurong said nothing. He kowtowed and left angrily.

Ten kilometers northwest of Macheng was the village of Nine Pools. Just thirty families inhabited the village, which was very famous for its scenic beauty. The village was set against the lush Dabie Mountains around which a small crystal-clear river meandered. Pear trees were planted thickly on the banks of the river, and when spring arrived, all the pear trees would blossom. Clusters of white flowers decorated the mountain and the river, making them even more beautiful. When the wind wafted through, the petals of pear flowers would scatter and drop lightly into the green water like a fragrant cascade of flowers. This unusual sight was most enchanting and the small river gained for itself a pretty name: Flower Rain River. Scholars of literature and calligraphy as well as wealthy people from Macheng came here each spring to enjoy the scenery. For this reason, most of the villagers didn't work in fields. Instead, they made a living running the pubs and trading pear trees.

Tu Rusong, the richest man in Macheng, often visited Nine Pools, and since he had a villa there, Yang Wurong suspected that his sister had been murdered there. As he hurried from the county yamen in anger, the villa at Nine Pools began to obsess him even more. He sneaked into Nine Pools quietly all by himself, and so as not to attract attention, he lived in a small inn, going out early and returning late. But after several days of close scrutiny, he found nothing suspicious on Tu Rusong.

One particular morning, a light rain had washed the mountains even greener. Yang Wurong headed for Tu's villa through the footpaths in the fields, hoping to find something around there. Along the way, Yang Wurong's attention was diverted by a village girl in a pub. About eighteen years old, she had shining big eyes on her round face, and long eyelashes and curved eyebrows which made her very pretty. Yang Wurong was a warm-blooded man, and his eyes at once latched on to the girl.

But the village girl, totally unaware of his staring, continued her friendly banter with her customers, a sweet smile adorning her face.

Wurong was locked in a trance. He stood there, frozen to the spot, until someone patted him on his back. Caught by surprise, he turned around and found a man in his twenties looking at him with sharp eyes, and an vacant smile on his lips. Wurong was taken aback.

The young man whispered: "So, the little beauty has stolen your heart, huh?"

Wurong blushed, greeted him with clasped hands and was about to leave. But the man pulled his sleeve to stop him: "I can read your mind very well, and that girl is a rose—pretty but prickly. Let's go inside and see if I can't put in a word for you." Yang Wurong was thus ensnared by the man. Hoping there was a way to get closer to the beauty, he followed the stranger into the small pub without even thinking.

Inside this simple but clean pub, several tables were already taken by customers. Yang Wurong sat down at a table in the corner. Without waiting to be asked, the stranger sat down beside him. Wurong ordered some dishes, but was a little disappointed that the village lass didn't come pour wine for him. The stranger bent toward his ear and said: "There are even more beautiful women in the Flower Rain River, and they're ripe for the picking. I'm Zhao Dang'er from Nine Pools. If you want, I can find you ten such beauties, how about it?"

Hearing Zhao Dang'er was from Nine Pools, Wurong had a brain wave. His lust diminished, and he brought up Tu Rusong's villa instead. Zhao Dang'er, who was just as villainous as Wurong, was suspicious of the stranger's queries about the villa. By leading Wurong on, Zhao learned of his intentions. In order to defraud Wurong of some money, Zhao Dang'er affected an air of mystery: "I've never been to Master Tu's villa. But a beauty did arrive there three months ago, a so-called Madame Tu. But she never left the villa."

"—Why didn't she come out?" Wurong interjected impatiently.

Zhao paused deliberately, and Wurong pressed three taels of silver into his palm. He then spoke haltingly: "Tu didn't get along with his wife. This winter, he coaxed his wife here with intent to murder. He got his best friend to help kill his wife. The poor woman died at her husband's hands!"

Yang Wurong couldn't believe he'd got the information he'd wanted so easily. To verify Zhao's words, he asked one more question: "Who's the other man?"

Zhao Dang'er blinked, then said: "Heard his name's Chen Wen."

Yang Wurong suppressed his excitement and asked: "My good fellow, are you telling the truth?"

"Absolutely!" answered Zhao determinedly.

"Dare you testify at the yamen?"

"What am I afraid of?" said Zhao with a shrug.

Wurong decided Zhao was not kidding. He stood up and bowed deeply: "To tell you the truth, I'm Yang Wurong, Madame Tu's brother. My sister went missing two months ago. Since then, we've found no trace, but I figured she was murdered by Tu Rusong. Since we had no proof, I came to Nine Pools to investigate. Now I've met you and learned the truth. I think you are very honest and brave. As the saying goes: 'A man shall abhor evil as a deadly foe.' But if you know the truth, how can you let that criminal escape justice! Please come back with me to the Macheng County yamen and let's charge Tu Rusong. If I get my revenge, I will reward you with fifty taels of silver."

On hearing Yang Wurong's words, Zhao Dang'er was so astonished he was momentarily struck speechless. He had hatched the story just to relieve Yang Wurong of a little money. He never even suspected he was Madame Tu's brother. Now, it seemed impossible to take back what he had uttered. But going with Yang Wurong to the yamen was no simple matter. He might get himself thrown into prison if someone saw through the fraud. What to do? Zhao's small eyes flitted about as he racked his brains.

Yang Wurong took Zhao's hesitation to be dissatisfaction with the price offered. He then added: "If you think fifty taels is not enough, I can give you a little more. How about sixty?"

With so much money as payment, Zhao Dang'er forgot all restraint. He pounded his chest and said: "Deal! It's not because of the money but because Tu Rusong broke the law. I'll go with you to the Macheng yamen." Yang Wurong was so overwhelmed by the desire to take revenge that he didn't see the holes in Zhao's story. He paid the bill right away and left with Zhao for the Macheng County yamen.

Tang Yingqiu hadn't slept well for days. He took his job very seriously. After some ten days of investigation, there were still no clues on Madame Tu's whereabouts, and this worried him. As he was discussing the search with detectives, the drum outside was beaten loudly and rapidly. After some commotion, he heard someone crying out for justice. Tang Yingqiu quickly adjusted his hat and called the court to order.

Tang Yingqiu was a little irritated to find that it was Yang Wurong again. But this time, Yang Wurong looked emboldened and forthright. He poured out the tale he'd heard at Nine Pools and demanded Tu Rusong's arrest, in order to confront the accused at once. Tang Yingqiu interviewed Zhao Dang'er who knew he couldn't retract what he'd said. So he stated boldly that Tu Rusong killed his wife at the villa together with one Chen Wen. Now that there was a witness, Magistrate Tang had to order the arrest of Tu Rusong.

When Tu Rusong was brought to the yamen, he vehemently denied the murder of his wife. He also said he'd never ever had a friend called Chen Wen. Furthermore, his mother was ill at that time and he'd stayed in Macheng County at her side. How could he commit the murder if he'd never gone to the villa at Nine Pools?

Magistrate Tang did not respond to Tu's argument. He summoned the housekeeper and servants from the Tu family to the yamen and interviewed them separately. These people all maintained that Tu Rusong had never left the old lady's side during that time. The housekeeper also said that an old doctor called Li Dechen could be called as another witness.

Magistrate Tang sent for Doctor Li and got to know he'd gone to Tu's house every day when the old lady was ill. Rusong had accompanied him each time. From this, the charge that Rusong had murdered his wife at Nine Pools seemed patently untrue. But Yang Wurong insisted that the Tu family had colluded together and fabricated false testimony to mislead the yamen. Then the accuser clung to his claim so tenaciously, that, fearful that emotions could get out of hand, Tang had to put Tu

Rusong into prison, while hoping the truth would come out soon.

In Macheng County, Tu Rusong was not only the wealthiest man, but he also happened to be a most warmhearted person. He often helped others out of difficulty and was therefore highly respected in his neighborhood, so it caused quite a sensation when he was thrown into prison on flimsy evidence. Within two days ten upright county officials and *xiucai** came to the yamen, appealing that Rusong was not guilty. They all said Tu Rusong had never left the county since winter. Someone also pointed out: although Zhao Dang'er had lodged an accusation against Tu Rusong, Yang's body hadn't been found yet. Nobody could decide whether Yang was alive or dead. How could the yamen throw an innocent citizen into prison?

On the third day an old man sent a petition to Tang Yingqiu. The father of Zhao Dang'er wrote in his plaint: "My son Zhao Dang'er is a scoundrel, well known in Nine Pools. He often commits fraud. The evidence he offers to accuse Tu Rusong is sheer fabrication without any basis. Please do not believe what he has said. If the yamen makes a wrong judgment from my son's false witness, I hereby request that I not be punished as his father if the truth comes out later."

Magistrate Tang remained calm after receiving so many petitions in favor of Tu Rusong. On one hand, he felt Tu Rusong had been wronged. On the other hand, he wondered if Tu's family paid money to assemble all

---

* Unofficial reference to all men qualified to porticipate in provincial examinations in the civil service recruitment examination sequence.

this defense. He didn't therefore set Rusong free. He instead ordered a closer watch on him in case something unusual happened.

Since Yang Wurong had Tu Rusong thrown into prison on Zhao Dang'er's testimony, he felt his accusation must be right. He went to the yamen every day, urging the execution of Tu Rusong. Magistrate Tang always tried to calm him, but refused to call a trial for further interrogation. This made Yang Wurong so upset that he would shake his finger at the Magistrate's nose and call him names.

This particular morning, as Yang Wurong finished his breakfast and was about to go to the yamen again, when a woman in her fifties came to him. She was dressed like a peasant, and seemed as if in a great hurry. She stammered, and couldn't even complete a sentence. Wurong felt she had something important to say, and so he offered her some tea to calm her down. After a while, the woman began: "I'm Madame Feng Wang from the Feng Village to the south. My son Feng Da is a dishonest businessman and is very licentious. Your sister had started a relationship with Feng Da long ago, so three months ago, she ran to our home after a quarrel with Master Tu. She then hid in our house and now shares the same room with my son. She wants to go back to Tu, but you and Zhao Dang'er have claimed she was killed by Tu Rusong and then filed a lawsuit at the yamen. Magistrate Tang is constantly sending detectives to trace your sister's whereabouts, and recently somebody asked us. Looks like she will be discovered sooner or later. We are all in a panic. Your sister asked me to come to you for help. What shall we do?"

Yang Wurong was stunned by the unexpected news.

He couldn't believe he was so totally wrong, and he was rather upset to find his sister still alive. In fact, his entire purpose for going to the yamen was not to find justice for her, but to extort some good cash from the Tus. It had not been cheap to have Tu Rusong thrown into prison using Zhao. He had been expecting someone from the Tu family to negotiate a settlement with him. Now, all of a sudden, here was somebody complicating matters. Not only would he now lose the fortune he'd dreamed of, he had also committed the crime of framing the richest person in the county. He might get himself thrown into prison. What now?

All these thoughts made Yang Wurong falter. Hiding his nervousness, he told the woman to go home and wait for a resolution. Wurong's bewilderment made Feng's mother realize the complications, and she almost cried out, as she rushed out in a tizzy, her hands cupping her mouth.

Yang Wurong was inconsolable after Feng's mother had left. He couldn't conceive of an easy way out no matter how hard he thought. In his helplessness, a name rang a bell: Yang Tongfan, who'd attained the rank of *xiucai* a few years ago. He had quite a wealthy household and was considered a celebrity in Macheng. He also was an unscrupulous businessman, addicted to gambling. Many a time, Wurong had picked up some dirty money helping him to gamble, so he could possibly be regarded as a friend. Besides it was an emergency, and Wurong had no choice but to ask for Tongfan's help.

To the southwest of Macheng, there was a small manor with blossoming trees and picket fences. The place appeared quiet and tastefully laid out, and along rows of willows, a pink wall was enjoined by an exquisitely wrought gate. A small board saying "Yang Residence" hung on the brown door of Tongfan's house. Although Wurong had been a regular gambling partner, he still felt nervous before the doorway of this famous *xiucai*. He was afraid of a cold reception or even being driven away, so he walked back and forth at the doorway for a long time before he sneaked up to the gate and knocked on the door.

Tongfan answered the door. Twenty-eight years old, his wide eyes on a broad face reflected his proud bearing. When he found the person at the door to be Wurong, he regretted opening the door himself. He asked coldly, with not one shred of a smile on his face: "Wurong, what are you doing here?"

Wurong was disheartened by Tongfan's arrogance, so he spoke with a humble smile, not daring to lift up his head: "Brother, I have come here for your help. I've found my sister's whereabouts..."

When Wurong mentioned his sister, the image of a beauty with a willowy waist and pink cheeks appeared before Tongfan's mind. He had met Yang several times and greatly desired her. When Yang later married Tu Rusong, he had long envied Tu's luck at acquiring such a beauty and regretted his failure at seducing her. Now when he heard that Yang was found, his lust was stirred again, and unconsciously his cold face melted into a smile. With as much friendliness as he could muster, he held Wurong's arm and led him into the house.

Wurong had never expected Tongfan to be so kind to him. He was so flattered, that he had hardly sat down before he blurted out to Tongfan everything about Yang leaving her husband and cohabiting with Feng Da, and of his own lawsuit against Tu Rusong at the yamen.

150

Tongfan became exhilarated upon hearing the story. He felt wealth and beauty were his for the taking today. It was no mere coincidence that he had heard some good-luck birds chirping happily this morning!

Tongfan didn't stir from his fantasy until Wurong finished his tale and begged him to think of a way out. Tongfan exclaimed: "It's simple. Let your sister come hide in my house for a while until the whole thing blows over.

Wurong looked a little hesitant: "But your house is not far from the center of the county. What if the yamen finds out..."

Tongfan burst into laughter: "I am a scholar with rank. Who dares come search my house? Nobody would know for a hundred years."

Wurong then asked: "What of the case against Tu Rusong?"

"After your sister hides, you can continue to sue Tu Rusong for killing his wife. If the Tu family wants a monetary settlement, you can demand a huge amount. If they don't want to settle, you can keep pushing the Magistrate to execute Tu Rusong."

With Tongfan's words Wurong could already begin to see the money flowing in. He asked the *xiucai* where he could hide his sister Yang, and Tongfan replied: "There is a double-layered wall in the main house. Between these two layers there is a bed and a table. Your sister can live there for now. Even if the yamen runners came to search, they would find nothing. Of course, they dare not search here." Wurong was elated. He bowed deeply to Tongfan then left cheerfully for Feng Village to get his sister.

Tongfan's heart was now on fire. He couldn't sit still. With a few words, the beauty he had fantasized about for so many years would be his. He became rather restless and went out to the street several times to see if Wurong was on his way, but was disappointed each time. Unable to contain his excitement he walked in circles around his study. Half an hour passed, and Wurong and his sister had not shown up. Tongfan suddenly felt his blue gown with the veiled design didn't fit him very well. He quickly changed into a black satin gown with a dark green waistcoat which was also embroidered with a veiled design. He went to the mirror and examined himself very carefully.

He heard steps. Tongfan looked out of the window and saw a small sedan chair following Wurong into the courtyard. Tongfan's heart burst with joy and he hurried out of the door just as Wurong lifted up the curtain of the sedan chair. Yang was helped out by her brother, one hand holding the edge of her skirt. Her pink cheeks and smiling face radiated an attractive elegance. She wore a lake green skirt which fit her very well, and her embroidered pink blouse hugged her slim figure, making her appear so charming. Tongfan adjusted his clothes once more before striking a studied pose to bow to her. Yang also made a greeting with an infatuating smile.

She opened her red lips slightly and said: "We are so indebted to you, Sir." Tongfan was totally overwhelmed by Yang's beauty. He returned the greeting and gestured for Yang and her brother to enter the main house.

Yang walked in quietly with small steps and great elegance. There's a saying: "Beauty is in the eyes of the lover," and at this moment, Yang's every movement seemed very alluring to Tongfan's eyes. He deliberately kept a little distance from Yang as they walked into the house.

After Yang sat down, Tongfan briefly showed her around his house, and then pointed to a back wall: "This is a double-layer wall built by our ancestors for refuge during upheavals. It's not very big but Madame can live there for now. You can hide there much of the time. When you are bored, you can come out for a while. Remember, I am a *xiucai*, and nobody would dare break into my house."

Yang asked: "How is my husband now? Is he still looking everywhere for me?" Tongfan deliberately scared her by answering: "Tu Rusong has filed a lawsuit at the county yamen. He accuses you of stealing his money and fleeing with your lover. The county is offering a reward for your arrest, and once they find you, they will throw you into prison, keeping you there for the rest of your life."

Yang's pretty face clouded over with anger: "It's hard to imagine he could be so malicious. He not only beats me but also wants to put me in prison. I will hide here—see if he can find me."

Tongfan soothed her with some nice words, and then stood up: "It's almost noon. Please have lunch before taking a rest." He ordered the maids to bring food to the table, as Yang thanked the *xiucai* and sat down first.

Tongfan showered his generosity on her, adding food to her plate and pouring wine for her, making Yang beholden to him. After lunch, Wurong stood up to say goodbye, and Tongfan made no effort to make him stay. He just exhorted him to come visit his sister from time to time, and Wurong left happily, his mind at ease that

153

he found Tongfan so warmhearted.

Now it was just Yang and Tongfan left in the room. Tongfan sat there, his eyes riveted on Yang so that she became a little embarrassed. She lowered her head and said quietly: "Please rest, Master Yang, I am a little tired."

The liquor, however, had given Tongfan some courage, and he cast a sidelong glance at the beauty: "Don't think of yourself as an outsider, my lady. As the saying goes: 'When you enter a house, you are part of the family.' I've admired your beauty for a long time. Can't I stay with you a little longer?"

Yang was clever, and she understood quickly Tongfan's intentions. She blushed and not knowing how to respond, she remained in silence, her head bowed over her chest.

His heart thumping heavily, Tongfan stood up and walked behind her, finding her delicate fingers twisting an exquisite handkerchief. She was flushed and slightly drunk, which added to her charm. Tongfan abandoned caution to the winds and put Yang's arms around him.

Short of breath, Yang became more flushed, and glared at him and mumbled coyly: "Do you want to seduce me, Master Yang?" The *xiucai* suddenly knelt down: "I've been crazy about you for a long time now and have regretted not being able to get closer to you. You've now come to my house to avoid trouble. Hasn't fate brought us together? Please understand my yearning for you..."

At this point, Yang didn't hesitate any longer. First of all, the alcohol had somewhat turned her on. Secondly, she was awed by Tongfan's rank and wealth. Thirdly, she knew she had lost control over her life when she entered his house. And so, the man and woman lay down together though the day was only half over.

From then on, Tongfan stayed inside the room where Yang hid every night. The two stuck to each other like beached fish returned to water, almost as inseparable as body and shadow. Yang, however, was still ignorant about her husband's arrest. Even as her brother Yang Wurong, egged on by Tongfan, kept going to the yamen, crying for Rusong's head, Magistrate Tang still didn't call the case. People in Macheng soon began to nickname him "Crazy Yang."

Tang Yingqiu had not been idle. For an alleged murder to take place with no corpse in such a small county, with a defendant who was the richest celebrity here, made it a highly publicized case. The whole county was aroused by it, and consequently, higher authorities heard about it, too. Despite facing official inquiries from above all these months, Tang Yingqiu could provide no answers. More recently, county officials had submitted a joint petition asking for a clear decision—either convict Tu Rusong or set him free, do not keep him in prison for no reason. All this put tremendous pressure on Tang Yingqiu.

However, after thinking the matter over and over, and balancing every factor, Tang Yingqiu felt it inadvisable to conclude the case without enough evidence. On one hand, he urged detectives to redouble efforts to find Yang. On the other hand, he wrote a detailed report to his superiors, asking for more time to investigate the case thoroughly. A year passed quickly, but there was not one clue regarding Yang's whereabouts. Magistrate Tang was so worried that several times he chastised the detectives as incompetent.

Summer soon arrived again, and Macheng was filled with the fragrance of tea flowers. There had been a lot of rain in the spring and the weather this year was clement. The peasants had enjoyed the fine spring and prayed to the gods for an even better summer. It was now the season for the crops to reach their peak, and with rain almost every ten days, a rich harvest was clearly unfolding. Tang Yingqiu had been the County Magistrate in Macheng for three terms in a row, but this was the first time he'd experienced such a bountiful harvest. He felt elated.

On an especially fine morning, Tang Yingqiu got up very early, and finding no urgent matter at hand, he went to his study to pore over a history book. As Tang Yingqiu immersed himself in his reading, the door of the study was quietly pushed open. Li Xianzong, the yamen secretary, hurried in without being announced. Tang Yingqiu sensed he must have something important to report, so he gestured him to sit down.

Li looked somewhat excited and reported hastily: "A decayed body has been found at the Ju riverbank, 15 kilometers west of Macheng. Looks like the body has been there for months. It was buried by the riverbank, but not deep enough, so some stray dogs dug it out. The local constable found it in time and drove the dogs away. Now the body is under watch awaiting a postmortem."

Tang Yingqiu's heart shrank for he immediately connected the body with the Yang case. He asked: "Male or female?"

"Can't tell because it's rotted so badly."

"Has anyone identified the body?"

"Nobody for dozens of kilometers around."

"Good!" Tang Yingqiu rose from his chair, "Inform

the coroner Li Rong and the detective He Xiong to come with me for the postmortem. And you must come too!"

Li Xianzong quickly gathered the coroner, the detectives and some yamen runners. They were standing outside the yamen gate when Tang Yingqiu came out in his official dress. Tang stepped into his palanquin and the group set out.

The weather in South China changes frequently even on the same day. When they got out of the county town, it was rather fine but before they had hardly walked five kilometers away, a blanket of clouds appeared from the southeast and covered the sky. The moisture in the air turned cold, and lightning broke through the clouds in the distance, bringing on the growl of thunder. Tang Yingqiu sensed a heavy rainstorm coming, and hurriedly asked the lead runner how far they were away from the riverbank. The runner answered: "About nine kilometers." Tang Yingqiu ordered the group to move faster, but before they had made the next few meters, raindrops as big as soybeans were splashing down. The rain fell fast and violent. Without any shelter in the open field, the group was drenched to the skin in no time. The heavy rain filled the ditches beside the road then turned the road paved with soil into a small river. It quickly became so muddy that the group could not move forward any longer, and Tang Yingqiu decided to return temporarily. In order to make sure the body wouldn't be washed away by the rain, he sent two runners ahead in the rain to exhort the local constable to carefully protect the site.

Li Rong, the coroner of Macheng, was already in his fifties. He had encountered innumerable cases since he came to work in the county yamen in his twenties. He was an expert in autopsies and examinations of wounds. When major cases came up in the province, he was often invited to assist in examinations. As soon as he showed up, any lingering doubts were soon dispelled. His colleagues therefore nicknamed him, "Magic Hands Li." Because of his meticulous work, the provincial authorities showered him with distinctions, hoping to transfer him to a higher yamen. But Li Rong had no interest in fame and didn't want to leave his hometown, so he still remained at his original posting.

Li Rong's wife had died two years before, and they had no children. He was now living by himself in a small alley off Cross Street. That morning, he had accompanied the county magistrate for the autopsy but was stalled by the heavy rain. Being drenched by rain at his age had brought Li Rong down with a slight fever and made limbs feel weak. He knew it would get worse if he lay down at this point, so with some effort he poured himself some liquor and drank it.

At dusk, the dark clouds which had covered the sky disappeared. In their place, brilliant clouds were seen with the sinking sun which shone through the window setting the whole room aglow. Li Rong, enjoying his liquor wrapped in this gentle radiance, got a bit tipsy. Suddenly, he heard someone rapping lightly on his door. Alarmed, he asked sharply: "Who is it?" A voice whispered from outside: "Please open the door, Master Li." Who on earth would visit on tiptoe?

Apprehensive, Li Rong opened the door. A young student stood outside. His conspicuous dress told Li Rong he was not from a small household, though his face was not a familiar one in Macheng. The stranger stepped inside and closed the door behind him.

158

Li Rong had worked in government office for more than thirty years and met people from all walks of life. The expression on the stranger's face told him at once that he had come about a case. Li Rong directly queried him before the visitor could speak: "Which case are you here for?"

Briefly taken aback by Li Rong's words, the visitor smiled knowingly: "Master Li is such a frank person. I will not let you down." With these words, he quickly took out some silver and put it on the table, his eyes fixed on Li Rong's face.

Li Rong maintained his composure as if he had not seen the silver. He turned his back on the visitor and asked: "Who sent you here?"

The visitor answered calmly: "We don't know each other and you don't have to know my name. The silver is a down payment. If you just say a few words, there will be more silver after."

Li Rong asked: "What do you want me to say?"

The visitor answered: "I heard that you are going to the riverbank for an autopsy. We want you to state that the dead person is a woman, twenty-three years old, dead by strangulation.' That's all."

Li Rong said: "If it's a man, no matter how I try to cover up, I surely can't cheat the eyes of other detectives and Magistrate Tang."

The visitor laughed: "Take it easy. The body has rotted badly, no parts are discernible. In such a hot weather, it also stinks awfully. Nobody will go near it. Furthermore, you are so famous a coroner, who will doubt your word?"

Li Rong felt the anger rising in his chest. Honest and upright by nature, the old coroner always hated

159

malpractice and corruption. He couldn't believe that someone would try to bribe him after all these years. It seemed absolutely absurd.

Li Rong's silent meditation made the visitor think the money had worked. He got closer to Li Rong and asked: "What do you think?"

Li Rong waited until the visitor was just half a step in front of him and suddenly grabbed his collar. His hands then straightened out and gripped the visitor's neck. Lifting his left hand, he slapped the visitor in the face from left and right until he howled. Veins bulged up on Li Rong's forehead as he yelled angrily: "You reckless rascal! Want to buy me with money! Dare you break the law? I have never seen such blatant bribery in all my thirty years!" He swept the silver to the ground with his palm and roared: "Take your dirty money and get out of here!" His right hand lashed out, and the visitor stepped back and fell to the ground. Li Rong spat on the ground, and slamming the door shut, he threw himself into bed. He was sweating all over but the aching was gone.

Two days later, it was a fine day again and Tang Yingqiu brought his group to the riverbank. By order of the county magistrate, the local constable had the area encircled by grass ropes and guarded by several villagers. Outside the rope barrier, many people stood awaiting the occasion. When Tang Yingqiu's palanquin arrived, the crowd stepped aside and made way for them.

Tang Yingqiu looked around when he got off the palanquin and instantly found a familiar face in the crowd: "Yang Wurong," he recalled this name and found Yang Wurong pushing people aside in front of him, trying to enter the circle. With swollen eyes, he cried out loudly: "Sister! Sister! My poor sister!"

Beside Wurong stood a smartly dressed *xiucai*, holding Wurong back and consoling him. Tang Yingqiu recognized him as Yang Tongfan.

To keep order, the runners had taken out their weapons, as Coroner Li Rong untied a little bag he had brought and took out the instruments for the postmortem. Tang Yingqiu turned his eyes to the body at the center of the roped-off circle. The body had rotted badly, and on the hands and feet there were marks of a dog's bites and large gouges. The face had already rotted away, and it was hard to tell it was male or female. Swarms of flies gathered around the body and the stink was unbearable.

Magistrate Tang looked at Li Rong, and he nodded and put on a pair of leather gloves. He then took out a bottle of liquor and poured some on his gloves. Li Rong walked inside the rope circle with a grim face, but when Li Rong got closer to the body, Wurong suddenly dashed out from the crowd and ran to the body. He threw himself on it, crying hysterically for his sister.

Expressionless, Li Rong pushed Yang Wurong away coldly: "How do you know it's your sister?"

Wurong wept: "My sister was wearing the same clothes when she left home; that's what she always wore to serve her mother-in-law. It's the same cloth, isn't it? Even the weave is the same."

With these words, he took out a scrap of cloth cut from some clothes and handed it to Li Rong: "Please have a look at it. Isn't it the same?"

Li Rong took the cloth and compared it with the clothes on the body. The weave was the same. He then put it into his bag. Yang Wurong knelt down in front of

161

Li Rong and entreated him: "Your Honor, please help us punish this criminal severely."

Li Rong seemed to hear nothing. He used a brass ruler to measure some parts of the body. Next he took out a silver pin and pierced the body's neck. Yang Wurong wailed: "Mercy!" Li Rong's pin was already out, and it hadn't changed color. He also examined the other parts of the body before he stood up and walked back to Tang Yingqiu. He bowed respectfully: "Your Honor, the dead person was a boy. He died of some disease two months ago. It has nothing to do with the Yang case."

"What!" Yang Wurong who had curled himself up on the ground jumped up: "Nonsense! It's obvious the dead person is my sister. Why did you say it's a boy?"

Li Rong glanced sideways at him; ignoring Wurong, he said to Tang Yingqiu: "Your Honor, shall we depart?"

Before Tang Yingqiu could answer, Yang Tongfan emerged from the crowd and said to Li Rong aggressively: "How can you judge such a major case so quickly?" He then turned to Tang Yingqiu: "I am *Xiucai* Yang Tongfan. I learned long ago that Yang Wurong's sister was murdered. It has not been easy for him to find his sister. If Your Highness don't support him but believe this coroner's false report, how can you genuinely convince people?"

Yang Tongfan's words immediately gained resonance among six other people present. But Li Rong said firmly to the local constable: "You can bury the body at the site. Don't let wild dogs dig it out again." But Yang Wurong and Yang Tongfan stirred some people to vehemently oppose this. When Tang Yingqiu saw both sides sticking to their own versions, he had to order the body put away for later re-examination.

During Emperor Yongzheng's reign in the Qing Dynasty, the capital city of Hubei Province was Wuchang. The residence of Mai Zhu, the Viceroy of Hubei and Hunan provinces, was located next to the beautiful She Mountain. The majestic gate and splendor of the residence showed that the Viceroy enjoyed luxury. In the east reception room in his backyard, Mai Zhu was absorbed in an orchid he had recently received. The plant had grown very tall, sprouting wide, thick leaves with clear veins. From within dozens of flourishing leaves emerged an erect flower stem, on top of which a cluster of red buds were about to blossom. Beside Mai Zhu stood an old aide in his sixties pointing at the orchid and explaining in great detail how precious the plant was. Mai Zhu looked completely engrossed in listening, with his head nodding, a self-satisfied smile on his lips.

After long scrutiny, Mai Zhu left the flower and sat on a carved wooden chair inlaid with seashells. He said to his aide, "Was this also sent by Gao Renjie?"

"Yes," answered the aide with an ingratiating smile, his back bent.

Mai Zhu nodded sternly and murmured to himself: "A conscientious man indeed!"

The aide rejoined: "Gao Renjie holds Your Excellency in great esteem. He often says to me he will never ever forget how Your Excellency sponsored and groomed him. As long as Your Excellency has a request of him, he will shun no difficulty and danger, not hesitating to lay down his life. This orchid was actually a family heirloom handed down by his father. He sent it as a gift to show that his respect for Your Excellency equals that for his father."

Mai Zhu felt so flattered when he heard these words, that he said slowly, "It's quite generous of him to give away such a legacy."

Finding the Viceroy pliant, the aide sighed: " Gao Renjie has been a substitute official for three years, and hasn't been designated a permanent position so far."

Governor Mai opened his shut eyes slightly. "Wasn't he nominated to Guangji County?" The aide awkwardly opened his mouth to speak but held his words. Mai Zhu asked: "Isn't he satisfied?"

"How can he not be!" exclaimed the aide. "However, he is still a substitute in Guangji County. Once the former magistrate resumes his post, Renjie must return his seal of office..."

Mai Zhu waved his hand to interrupt his aide. After a short silence, he said: "There are too many substitute officials in Hubei. No sitting magistrates have made major mistakes. I can't dismiss them. He has to remain this way for a while."

The aide said: "Renjie will surely not complain. As for dismissing an official, however, here is a possibility." Saying this, the aide took out a pile of papers and handed it to the Viceroy. "A murder case in Macheng County. Tu Rusong, the richest person in the county, has killed his wife Yang. Yang's family provided evidence to the yamen, but the County Magistrate Tang Yingqiu treated it with complete indifference. More recently, Yang's body was dug up by stray dogs at a riverbank, and the family went to complain again, but Tang Yingqiu has received bribes from the Tu family. He ruled Yang's body to be a boy's and refused to punish the murderer. The county has been aroused up by the case. The accuser Yang Wurong and *Xiucai* Yang Tongfan have bypassed their immediate leadership and presented their complaint to the provincial yamen. They have spread the details of the case everywhere. It is the talk of the province now."

Mai Zhu shook his head: "The murder in Macheng was announced a year ago. I too made a written inquiry. The County Magistrate Tang Yingqiu submitted a written response. The situation is not as you describe."

The aide said with a hasty bow: "It is well known all over the province that Tang Yingqiu has taken bribes and deceived higher authorities with a false report. It is only the people around Your Excellency who dare not tell you the truth."

Hearing this, Mai Zhu abruptly rose from his chair and read the petition written by Yang Wurong and Yang Tongfan. As soon as the Viceroy read a few lines he got angry. At the end of the complaint, it was written clearly: "The Viceroy has been tricked and the Provincial Governor deceived. A murderer is at large and the law is ineffective!"

These words made Mai Zhu even more enraged. He ordered right away: "The murder case in Macheng has been delayed too long. Gao Renjie from Guangji County is designated to go re-examine the body. A decision should be submitted within three days!" The aide quickly wrote down the Viceroy order and issued it to both Guangji and Macheng counties.

Gao Renjie, the substitute Magistrate of Guangji County was the son of a local tyrant in Sichuan Province. Born with a malicious and cruel heart, he had committed many crimes, gaining notoriety in his hometown. When he grew into his twenties, he toyed with the idea of becoming an official. Using the family's wealth, he donated a large amount of money on three occasions. The local authorities then offered him rank and made him a substitute official as a reward for his donations. However, his notoriety prevented higher officials from appointing him. He then bribed the Governor and was transferred to Hubei Province. Over the last three years, he had used all his relations to curry favor with officials everywhere. But he was rather dissatisfied that the large investment he'd made had only got him a substitute County Magistrate's post. So he kept his eyes wide open, hoping he could get rid of an official and occupy his post. At this time, the murder in Macheng caught people's attention, and Gao Renjie got the chance to bribe an old aide to the Viceroy. He was consequently designated the task of re-examining the body.

When he received the order, Gao Renjie was elated. He decided to make good use of this opportunity to get rid of Tang Yingqiu so that he could accumulate fabulous wealth in this rich county later. He ordered Coroner Xue Wuji to prepare at once for the postmortem in Macheng.

Yang Tongfan was rather weary these days. When the person he sent failed to bribe Li Rong, he realized it wouldn't be easy framing Tu Rusong. Yang Wurong and he had had to perform a two-man show to thwart the real identification of the body at the riverbank. Unfortunately, Li Rong saw through their plan. Luckily, Tongfan's aggressive intervention had made Tang Yingqiu compromise and not submit the autopsy report to the provincial authorities. Next, Yang Tongfan prodded Yang Wurong to propagate the complaint all over the provincial capital city, and put up a great fuss. Now his efforts had borne results: The review official sent by the Provincial Governor had arrived in Macheng. Quite arrogantly, he had decided to re-examine the body on the morrow without informing Tang Yingqiu and Coroner Li Rong who had done the first autopsy.

Yang Tongfan felt the tide had turned in their favor but worried whether Coroner Xue, who had come with the official, would uphold the judgment that the body was male. He then sent a servant dressed like a student to bribe Xue Wuji. The servant left at noon but didn't come back for a long time. The servant returned, just as it was getting dark, and Yang Tongfan 's anxiety only vanished when he saw nothing in the servant's hands—the coroner from Guangji County must have accepted the silver.

The servant told Tongfan: "Xue Wuji is quite greedy and cunning. He questioned me for a long time before he took the silver. He told me to tell you that he will get his chance to act tomorrow. He promises to do a good job but asks for more silver afterwards. I had to agree for fear of ruining the whole plan. He then insisted I write an IOU to him." Tongfan cursed Xue Wuji's blackmail silently, but on the other hand he was happy his initial plan had succeeded. He praised the servant and went back to Yang's room.

The next day was cloudy, yet the riverbank was packed with people awaiting the second autopsy. The local constable had lifted the body out of the icebox underground. People craned their necks to look inside the roped-off circle, but all they could see was a mass of flesh. Nobody could easily tell if it was male or female, and the heat released the stink again. People all around covered their noses. Then the sound of gongs clearing the way were heard from the road. The review

167

official Gao Renjie arrived with a large group of yamen runners.

Gao Renjie's palanquin was set down on a mound. He got off the chair and deliberately adjusted his hat and belt. Then he went directly to the body without waiting for the local constable to explain the situation. But when he got near to the body, the stink was so strong that he couldn't move one step further. He took out a handkerchief to cover his nose and gestured to Xue Wuji, who immediately knew what to do. He caught up with Gao Renjie and stopped him from going on: "Your Excellency can't be profaned. Let me do the examination and report to Your Excellency."

Gao Renjie nodded, and Xue Wuji took out the silver pin and the brass ruler. He walked over to the body and began the second autopsy. At this moment, hundreds of eyes were focused on Xue Wuji's hands.

Coroner Xue Wuji was an old hand. He looked at the body and a cold smile appeared on his lips. He suddenly turned the body over and exposed the most rotten parts. Now only a mess of flesh could be seen, and with this shift, the stink became intense. Many people couldn't stand the smell and started to leave. Hundreds of eyes began to lose focus—which was exactly Xue Wuji's purpose, to distract people's attention. When he found people starting to mill about, he began to examine the body, pretending to be very careful.

After a long while, Xue Wuji took off his leather gloves and poured out half a bottle of liquor to wash his hands. He then stood up and reported: "I have examined the body three times. It was a female, about twenty-four years old. She had severe wounds to her right ribs. She was struck to death with heavy objects."

With these words, a sharp wail was heard. Yang Wurong pushed away the crowd and ran to Gao Renjie. He knelt down and yelled with tears covering his face: "Your Excellency! Please help me find justice!"

Gao Renjie had the body put into a wooden case and buried at the site. He told Yang Wurong to follow him back to the county yamen for a final verdict. People around left slowly while continuing to discuss the case, some surprised, some grateful, some sighing, some doubting....

As soon as Gao Renjie returned to Macheng, as the specially designated official, he sent for Tang Yingqiu. In the courtroom, the two confronted each other. Gao Renjie handed his autopsy report with his signature to Tang Yingqiu and spoke in compelling tones: "From our public autopsy, we found the body was that of a young woman. Does Your Excellency have any objections?"

Tang Yingqiu answered: "You said you did a public autopsy. Why didn't you ask us to join you? Furthermore, the coroner of my county determined the body to be male. Since the two results are so different, Your Excellency should have called Li Rong to the site for an inquiry. Why did you order the body buried in such a hurry?"

Gao Renjie got angry: "Before hundreds of eyewitnesses at the riverbank, the body of the woman was found to have serious trauma to the right ribs. It means the woman died from being struck hard in the ribs. However, in Your Excellency's report, the cause of death was disease. Aren't you afraid of being blamed for deceiving higher authorities?"

Tang Yingqiu laughed: "I've been an official for more than twenty years, yet I have never heard of anyone dying from being struck on the ribs."

Gao Renjie struck the table and yelled: "Tu Rusong murdered his wife. But you protected him because he is a rich man. You won't get away with the crime of taking bribes."

Tang Yingqiu retorted: "If Tu Rusong wanted to kill his wife, why didn't he strike her in the head instead of the ribs? Can damage to the ribs be fatal? Was he playing games?"

Gao Renjie couldn't answer, but he announced that as specially designated official: "I'm here to review the case under orders from the Viceroy. You deliberately harbored a criminal and should be charged, too. As of today, you are stripped of your official title and shall await judgment at home."

Tang Yingqiu at once took out a copy of the Viceroy's order and argued: "By order of the Viceroy, you are only designated to re-examine the body, and are not permitted to review the case. Don't think yourself so important because of your connections that you can push us around in Macheng!" After saying this, Magistrate Tang turned to the two county secretaries: "Call the detectives to court!"

Gao Renjie was stunned momentarily, having no idea what Tang Yingqiu was going to do. When the detectives came, Tang Yingqiu shouted: "Drive this corrupt official out of the courtroom!" In no time, Gao Renjie, Xue Wuji and their followers were driven out of the gate by the detectives and other yamen runners. Tang Yingqiu then ordered Tu Rusong to be brought out of the prison, spoke some conciliatory words to him and set him free. Next, Yang Tongfan was arrested and strongly reproached. A report to the higher authorities was written in the court to remove his rank. At last, Yang Wurong was called to the yamen, too, and accused of fraud on the identification of the body and contempt of the court. He received twenty strokes before he was driven out of the courtroom. After all this, Tang Yingqiu's anger still wasn't completely assuaged. He wrote a final report to both the prefectural and the provincial authorities responding to their queries.

Viceroy Mai Zhu received two reports on the same day. One was the final report on the murder case in Macheng from the County Magistrate Tang Yingqiu. The other was written by the substitute magistrate of Guangji County Gao Renjie, impeaching Tang Yingqiu for bribery and harboring a criminal. Mai Zhu scanned the two reports, with his biases clear. The autopsy report attached to Gao's document showed the dead person was a twenty-four-year-old woman who had died from the blows to her right ribs. But Tang Yingqiu said the body was male. Obviously he was harboring a criminal. What made Mai Zhu suspicious most was that Tang Yingqiu had delayed judgment on the case for more than one year, yet concluded it in such a great hurry after Gao Renjie re-examined the body. Mai Zhu thought Tang was risking everything in a major ploy to deceive higher authorities.

Mai Zhu had no trust in Tang Yingqiu. Comparatively, he considered Gao Renjie a real talent because he had submitted the result of autopsy within several days and also raised grave doubts about previous conduct. Mai Zhu concluded that if Gao Renjie was designated to try this case, he would quickly uncover the whole truth, at which point, it would be quite natural to promote him.

171

With these thoughts, Mai Zhu opened Gao Renjie's report again. He found Gao Renjie had also criticized the misdeeds of the yamen secretary Li Xianzong and the coroner Li Rong. He concluded that none of the officials in Macheng County could be trusted. Perturbed, Mai Zhu sent for Gao Renjie right away and invested him with the power to review the murder trial in Macheng. He also issued an order to strip Tang Yingqiu of his official rank. All affairs in Macheng would be under Gao Renjie's dictate as of now.

Gao Renjie could not believe he had achieved such a commendation, and swelled up with pride. He left all affairs in Guangji County to his brother-in-law and recruited some able aides to accompany him to Macheng, all of whom displayed the same extreme arrogance.

As soon as Gao Renjie entered the county yamen, he immediately summoned Yang Wurong and asked him to submit a detailed complaint about Tu Rusong's murder of his sister. Yang Wurong handed him the complaint written by Yang Tongfan, and when Gao Renjie found the name of Zhao Dang'er in the complaint he summoned Zhao to court. Zhao Dang'er, who had been bribed by Yang Tongfan, stated categorically that he had entered Tu Rusong's villa at night and seen Tu Rusong and Chen Wen beat Yang to death with clubs. They then secretly hauled Yang's body to the riverbank and buried her in haste. Gao Renjie also sent for Yang Tongfan and asked him to be a witness to the verdict. Yang Tongfan agreed at once and also pointed out that Tang Yingqiu and Tu Rusong had connections prior to the case. Soon after, Gao Renjie ordered the arrest of Tu Rusong, Li Xianzong and Li Rong, who were then interrogated separately and severely tortured.

Tu Rusong was tried first. Gao Renjie figured that since Rusong had been born to a rich family, he was spoiled, and would confess obediently as directed after a few threats. But Gao was totally wrong. Tu Rusong had read many books and become quite knowledgeable at a very young age. How could he be cowed by such threats? He had also endured imprisonment for more than one year, during which he had already learned the tricks of interrogation. This "internship" added to his ability to guard against being tricked into a confession. Therefore, Rusong made his statements clearly and flawlessly, and Gao Renjie was at a loss to find any loopholes in his arguments. Severe torture was then applied, and Rusong given two hundred strokes all together, his legs almost reduced to a mess of flesh. Still he would not give in. Gao Renjie was so outraged that he ordered the wooden clamps—another instrument of torture. The vicious yamen runners clamped Tu Rusong's feet so hard that his bones could be seen though the flesh. He fainted several times yet still uttered not a word of confession. Gao Renjie had no way but to close the court, feeling a growing uneasiness crawl into his heart.

Gao Renjie knew if Tu Rusong did not confess someone would soon report the injustice done to him to the capital city of Beijing, and the Ministry of Punishments would make inquiries. His prosperous future, calculated carefully by him, would disappear like dust. After a sleepless night, Gao Renjie sent for his private adviser early in the morning. This adviser, a wily old fox, was well versed in governmental malpractice, especially in fixing court trials.

Since Tu Rusong would not give in, Gao Renjie said he wanted to target Li Rong. If Li Rong confessed, the case would be settled, but the adviser objected to the idea strongly: "Tu Rusong is already a headache, let alone Li Rong. If Your Excellency tortures all these people, you may be charged with inducing confessions under torture. The consequences would be terrible. A better way would be to torture Tu Rusong and let Li Rong and Li Xianzong watch until they get frightened. Once Tu Rusong is overcome, the others will not be a problem. They will go along with us."

Gao Renjie said: "We used all kinds of torture yesterday, but Tu Rusong was as hard as a rock."

The adviser said: "Although official punishments are severe, one can bear it. If Your Excellency wants a confession, some 'secret' punishments are necessary."

As vicious as Gao Renjie was, he had no idea about "secret" punishments. The adviser explained: "There have been unbearable methods of torture used throughout history. These tortures have been used generation after generation and get more and more cruel. They are called 'secret' punishments. In Hubei, they make prisoners kneel on hot iron chains, and wear iron clogs, and so on. If we apply these methods on Tu Rusong tomorrow, it will definitely work." Gao Renjie was elated to hear this. He asked the adviser to prepare the instruments without fail for the morning after.

The next day, Tu Rusong was dragged to the courtroom. He had wounds all over his body and couldn't even stand up because of the serious cuts on his feet. He could only lie flat on the ground, gasping in pain. Li Rong and Li Xianzong were already in court, bound in chains, watching. From the lighted flame in the fire basin, Li Rong knew they were going to use secret punishments, and he was overcome by compassion and

174

outrage when he saw Tu Rusong's condition.

Gao Renjie sat behind the judge's table and struck the court board, shouting, "Tu Rusong, confess your crime of murdering your wife! Now!"

Tu Rusong said nothing. Gao Renjie shouted again: "Yes or no?" Tu Rusong still remained silent, and Gao Renjie became angry. He called out: "Bring out the chain!" Two yamen runners took a red-hot chain from the burning fire with iron prongs and threw it on the ground. Two runners grabbed Tu Rusong up from the floor and rolled up his bloodied trousers. They then took him to the chain and jerked him down, forcing Tu Rusong to kneel on the chain. He gave a heartrending scream, as black smoke streamed off his legs. His muscles around the knees charred, Tu Rusong fainted away.

Gao Renjie ordered the yamen runners to pour cold water on Tu Rusong to wake him up. Tu Rusong was pressed again on another newly branded chain. Poor Tu Rusong, who had always believed in law and order, could not bear the cruel torture any longer. He begged them: "Your Excellency, please stop. I confess." Gao Renjie smiled and urged him to talk on. Tu Rusong , gasping for breath, rambled: "Yang and I didn't get along... So I had the intent... to kill her... Last February, I coaxed her to Nine Pools... and beat her to death with a club."

"Where did you hide the body?"

"Buried by the banks of the Ju River."

"Where is the accomplice Chen Wen now?"

"I gave him two hundred taels of silver... and he fled north."

Here was the break through in the case they'd been waiting for. Gao Renjie ordered Tu Rusong escorted back to prison and turned to Li Rong and Li Xianzong: "The criminal has confessed. Do you have anything to say?"

Li Rong suddenly stood up and yelled at him: "Gao Renjie, you used torture to get the confessions you wanted. Do you not fear the wrath of the gods?"

Gao Renjie broke into a cold chuckle: "Wrath of the gods? You'll get it right now! Today, if you confess completely how you faked the autopsy and judged that body a male, everything will go all right for you. Otherwise, I'll have your skin peeled off!"

Li Rong did not blanch, and instead shot back, "The body was male. You have made a male a female, like calling black white. Now you even want me to join in your fraud. You're an absolute daydreamer! Today, I came to the courtroom knowing I wouldn't go back alive. Do your worst!"

Li Rong's words encouraged Li Xianzong, who shouted: "Your Excellency, secret punishments are illegal. You shouldn't do this!"

Gao Renjie was enraged to find the two not scared at all. He struck the table: "Beat the two scoundrels one hundred strokes each!" The yamen runners pushed them to the floor, and these two ethical officials were beaten until their flesh was torn to shreds. But Li Rong still didn't stop calling them names. Gao Renjie then ordered the heated chain, but when they were about to torture Li Rong, Li Xianzong shouted: "Stop, I confess!"

Li Xianzong merely feared that Li Rong was too old to withstand such torture. He wanted to protect Li Rong, but Li Rong stopped him. He cried aloud: "Secretary Li, don't you fake a confession in order to avoid torture. We are both honorable—can't we bear this suffering?"

176

Gao Renjie got even more angry when he found Li Rong so bold. He ordered the burning chain wrapped around Li Rong's body. The group of yamen runners picked by Gao from Guangji were all pretty vicious. They picked up the chain and wrapped Li Rong in it. Li Rong's body made sizzling sounds, and he rolled on the floor until he fainted. Gao Renjie ordered him woken up with cold water and continued the torture—and so Li Rong died under torture.

Gao Renjie was not deterred by Li Rong's death. He just ordered him buried and then continued with the interrogation of Li Xianzong. The yamen secretary was bleeding with wounds all over his body, but his mind was still very clear. He knew that if he didn't confess as Gao Renjie wished, he would also die the same way. Death would be the result whether he confessed or not—but it was better to confess to avoid the unbearable torture. And so Li Xianzong didn't resist anymore. He confessed as Gao Renjie wished: that Tang Yingqiu had accepted eight thousand taels of silver as a bribe; that he had got five hundred taels for helping Tang write a false report; and, that Li Rong had received three hundred taels of silver to judge the female's body as a male. Gao Renjie let him sign the confession in court. Thus, a miscarriage of justice exacerbated by torture, proceeded unabated.

After the trial was over, Gao Renjie retired to the reception room in his backyard to enjoy a pair of newly purchased Ming Dynasty brass incense burners. Feeling proud and smug, the thick, heavy burner body and the exquisitely carved animal designs exhilarated him further. He decided to ask the assistance of the old aide again to send the furnaces to Viceroy Mai. If the Viceroy accepted them, he would submit the case report. Tu Rusong would be sentenced to death and Tang Yingqiu as well as Li Xianzong hanged. He would become the County Magistrate of Macheng.

Gao Renjie couldn't suppress his excitement as he imagined his brilliant future. He ordered some liquor and wanted a hearty drink to celebrate. But his adviser hurried in. Gao Renjie was most grateful to the adviser, and stood up to meet him, inviting him to join the celebration. But the adviser shook his head: "The case may be over, but we have a long way to go. Your Excellency shouldn't be too complacent."

Gao Renjie was shocked: "What?" The adviser answered: "People in Macheng are not so compliant. Tang Yingqiu and Tu Rusong have lived here for a long time. They have considerable influence. Although we got a confession, there is not enough material evidence to support Your Excellency's judgment, especially that Tu Rusong murdered his wife and Tang Yingqiu took bribes. If someone appealed for justice to the higher authorities, it is inevitable that another official would be sent for yet another review. I am afraid three loopholes would be found in another review."

"What loopholes?"

"Well, the body at the riverbank was decidedly male—I noticed it had no hair. If somebody examined it again and asked us about this, we couldn't answer this properly." Gao Renjie was stunned.

"Secondly," continued the adviser, "although Tu Rusong confessed he'd murdered his wife, there are no bloodstained clothes. If higher authorities requested them when reviewing the case, we would be in a tight spot. Thirdly, Li Rong died in court from severe punishments, yet there was no confession from him. If the higher authorities delved into it, Your Excellency wouldn't get away from the charge of coercion using torture."

Before the adviser could finish, Gao Renjie's face had changed color. He asked hastily: "Is there a way out?"

"Yes. As long as we force Tu Rusong to locate the hair and the bloodied clothes, everything will go easy. But Tu Rusong just underwent severe punishments, and his mind may not be very clear. Your Excellency will need to be especially patient when interrogating him." Gao Renjie understood that "especially patient" meant inducing Tu Rusong to confess. He lowered his voice and discussed how the interrogation should proceed.

The next evening, Tu Rusong was escorted to court again. The flame in the fire basin and the bloodstains on the clamps made him dizzy. Before Gao Renjie could strike the table and shout, Tu Rusong had already fainted away. Gao ordered a cold-water-soaked cloth applied to his forehead. Tu Rusong resumed consciousness after a long time. Gao Renjie asked him sternly: "Tu Rusong, you killed your wife, and cut her hair off?" Rusong didn't get what he meant and said hastily: "I didn't cut anyone's hair off."

Gao Renjie struck the table: "Nonsense! The body you buried at the riverbank had no hair. Who else could cut the hair off except you?"

Tu Rusong had lost all hope of living after he admitted to murder the day before. All he wanted now was to suffer less before his execution. When he heard Gao Renjie's words, he understood what they wanted him to say. He thought for a while then answered: "After

179

I killed my wife, I wanted to chop her body into pieces. But I got frightened after I cut the hair off. I couldn't continue."

"Where did you hide the hair then?"

"Among tombs in the western suburbs."

"Did you bury the hair together with the bloodstained clothes?"

"Yes."

"Would you be able to pinpoint it?"

"I vaguely remember it."

"Well! Lead the way! Let's look for this evidence!"

Gao Renjie ordered Tu Rusong hauled into a prison van. With some ten yamen runners carrying excavation implements, the group headed for the suburbs.

Only poor people were buried in this wild and desolate graveyard in the western suburbs. When the yamen runners asked Tu Rusong to point out where he buried the blood clothes, he became confused and didn't know what to say. The vicious group leader grew impatient and swung his whip at Rusong's head. As bloody welts appeared on Rusong's face, he quickly pointed at a high mound: "Here."

Digging began right away, but what they found after digging deep were just some pieces of wood—a rotted coffin. The runners were so angry, all their whips began to lash at Rusong. He begged them to stop: "I buried them at night in a hurry. I can't remember the position clearly. Please give me some time to look."

The runners pulled him out of the van and pushed him ahead to walk among the tombs. Rusong dragged his feet as he stumbled forward, his wounds from the court torture tearing open, paining sharply. When he could go on no longer, he pointed to another smaller grave mound: "This one."

The runners dug it open, but they only found an old man with a long beard. Exasperated, they vented their anger out on Rusong who had to point again. This time it was an old woman with white hair. Like this, they dug up the graveyard for a whole day and destroyed ten mounds. No bloodied clothes and hair were found, though countless welts were obvious on Rusong's body.

For the next two days, digging continued. The yamen runners were so tired of it that they got about thirty laborers to do it. After nearly a hundred mounds were dug open, no material evidence was found. People in Macheng found it strange and absurd that the new Magistrate did nothing but dig up graves after he had been designated. Secretly they began to call him: "Gravedigger Gao!"

After three days had dragged on, Gao Renjie was only told: "Nothing found." He was so furious that he punished Tu Rusong with the hot chain again. Rusong was singed all over his body and tortured until he was half-dead. Such cruel punishments, however, made some of Gao Renjie's runners feel sorry for Rusong. One of them who still had a conscience secretly ran to Tu's family. Rusong's mother was torn apart with grief. She couldn't bear it that her son was undergoing so much cruel torture and could not even ask for death. She cut her own hair, and pleaded with Li Xianzong's wife to cut her arm for some blood. She stained some clothes with the blood and then let a servant go to the graveyard to bury the clothes and the hair at a place that would be easy to find. The next day, while visiting the prisoner, the mother told Rusong where the hair and bloodied clothes were buried. Poor Rusong, on getting the information that could provide evidence for his own conviction, got so excited he could not sleep the entire night.

The next day, without being even asked, Rusong told the prison guards: "I thought all night and remember now." The yamen runners took him to the graveyard again and easily found the hair and the bloodstained clothes.

Now all the evidence wanted was found. Gao Renjie wrote a final report, arrogantly feeling that he had gotten all he needed. Tu Rusong was sentenced to be beheaded. Tang Yingqiu and Li Xianzong were sentenced to be hanged. In order to confirm the verdict quickly, he ordered the report sent overnight to the prefecture of Huangzhou. He believed that within days he would get a written response, and his carefully crafted scheme would succeed completely.

The Magistrate of Huangzhou Prefecture, Jiang Jianian, was a fourth-rank official who had worked in the Ministry of Punishments in Beijing. During the last ten years, he had been assigned to work in Anhui and Fujian provinces and became famous in the political arena. Three years ago, he was transferred to Huangzhou Prefecture from Fujian Province, and after he arrived at the post, he achieved praise for building irrigation projects, publishing masterpieces of literature and formulating policies to encourage farming. When he got the report on Tu Rusong's case from Gao Renjie, he read it without delay because he knew the Viceroy's eyes were on the case. At first, he found the material evidence and testimony recorded satisfactory. He also read of the County Magistrate's corruption. According to procedure, he would transfer the report to the Governor.

However, when he was about to write his comments,

he found between some files, the autopsy report written by Coroner Xue Wuji of Guangji County. He picked it out and read it casually, and at once found serious loopholes. Xue Wuji wrote that the female had been struck to death on the ribs. Years of experience told Jiang Jianian that damage to the ribs could break them, but would never cause death. Suspicious, he read the report more carefully again. This time, he noted that Li Rong, the coroner of Macheng had died undergoing court torture, and that Li Rong's determination at the earlier autopsy had completely contradicted Xue Wuji's. Jiang Jianian knew Li Rong well, and remembered several complex cases in Huangzhou Prefecture that were cleared up after Li Rong had come on the case. Li Rong's meticulous character and outstanding skills had left a deep impression on Magistrate Jiang. It seemed incredible that Li Rong would have judged a female body as male. Also, Li Rong's autopsy report was not included in the files.

To be more cautious, Jiang Jianian summoned some officials in charge of case files in Huangzhou. All of them had worked in this field for many year and were well informed through different sources. After their description of the murder case in Macheng, Jiang Jianian believed there was something amiss.

As the prefecture's magistrate, how could he let a faulty judgment stand? Jiang Jianian decided to handle the case himself, and secretly summoned some leading coroners from four counties. Not allowing Gao Renjie any time to make any preparations, they suddenly arrived in Macheng. Jiang Jianian ordered a third autopsy to be performed. Gao Renjie couldn't believe things had taken this turning. He had to send for Xue Wuji and accompany Magistrate Jiang to the riverbank. The rotted body was dug out once again.

News spread quickly that the Prefectural Magistrate himself and coroners from four counties had come for a third autopsy. Macheng County was aroused again. The site of the autopsy was packed with people, some even coming from neighboring Henan and Anhui provinces. The riverbank was so crowded that Jiang Jianian sent for a hundred soldiers from a nearby garrison to keep order.

The most nervous person now was Gao Renjie. The most frightened was Xue Wuji. Once the body was exhumed, his autopsy report would be reversed. However, Yang Tongfan assured Xue Wuji that gifts had been sent to the four coroners. This gave Xue some comfort, for if the gifts had some effect, the former decision would stand. The final conclusion simply depended on a few words by the coroners.

The body was carried out and created a disturbance among the crowd. Some craned their necks to look, yet others tried to jostle their way to the front, and some even climbed up trees. Hand in hand, the soldiers created a human wall, stopping people from pushing forward. The four coroners walked together to the body. They lifted the covering cloth and started a careful examination of the body. They measured it with brass rulers and pricked it with pins. They also took out two sharp knives to cut the body open to examine the ribs. After an hour, the four coroners put down their tools and called for Xue Wuji.

Full of dread, Xue Wuji walked toward the body slowly. The oldest coroner stared at him and asked, "Coroner Xue, did you say the body was male or female?"

184

Xue Wuji tried read his eyes, but the old man's eyes were expressionless. Xue Wuji murmured, "I think it's female."

The old man nodded and asked, "Cause of death?"

"Struck to death on the right ribs."

The old man nodded again, a slight smile on his lips: "Coroner Xue is well skilled."

Xue Wuji didn't know if he really meant it. He feigned humility: "I am quite flattered."

But the smile on the old man's face suddenly disappeared. "What if it isn't the case?" retorted the old man.

Xue Wuji was startled, but he recovered quickly and asked, "What do you think?"

Before the old man could answer, a quick-tempered coroner beside him spoke up: "It is obviously a male body. Not a rib is broken and no wounds were found on the body. How could you draw such a ridiculous conclusion?" Xue Wuji immediately flushed, and he opened his mouth but nothing came out.

Jiang Jianian silenced the agitated crowd and said to Gao Renjie: "Your Excellency Gao, what is all this about?"

Gao Renjie stood up: "The body must have been switched."

Jiang Jianian sneered: "You have already concluded the case. Why switch the body? This place is by the open road. It's not easy at all to dig open a grave and switch the body! Your Excellency is too distrustful."

Gao Renjie insisted that the body had been switched. He shouted at the top of his voice that he would not rest until he caught the person who did it. As Gao Renjie was the official sent by the Viceroy, Jiang Jianian could not chastise him in front of a crowd. He simply said: "Let's discuss after we get back."

An unexpected heavy rain poured down with a terrifying force not long after Jiang Jianian got back to the county yamen. The Ju River rocked with raging rapids, and the body by the riverbank was washed away by the water. Gao Renjie was ecstatic to hear the news, and he clung to his conclusion that the body was female. He sent a detailed report directly to the Viceroy, bypassing the authority of the Prefectural Magistrate and the Grand Provincial Governor.

Viceroy Mai Zhu had been presented with a pair of exquisite Ming Dynasty brass incense burners which he kept on his desk. A keen collector of antiques, he kept walking around and around his desk admiring the incense burners. When he heard they were sent by Gao Renjie again, he was even more impressed by him. He considered himself highly astute for promoting an official so capable and respectful of him. Then he remembered Gao Renjie's handling of the murder case in Macheng which was now the talk of the whole province. He wanted to learn what had eventually transpired, so when a pile of reports arrived Mai Zhu look through them one by one. When he found Gao Renjie's report, he pushed aside all the other documents and began to read.

According to the official procedures of the Qing Dynasty, a major case involving several lives should seek the approval of the county, prefectural and provincial authorities before being submitted to the Viceroy. The Viceroy would then transfer it to the Ministry of Punishments with his seal on the report. Gao Renjie's report had bypassed the authorities in the prefecture and the province, and should have been rejected—but Mai Zhu was so eager to promote Gao Renjie that he neglected proper process. He sealed the report and submitted it as an urgent document to the Ministry of Punishments. The death of Tang Yingqiu, Tu Rusong and Li Xianzong seemed but a matter of time.

After sending the report, Mai Zhu wrote a letter to Jiang Jianian, telling him to arrest Tang Yingqiu for trial. He also asked Jiang Jianian to choose a capable official from the substitute list as the County Magistrate of Macheng, to maintain law and order in the county. Mai Zhu's intent was quite obvious: he wanted to promote Gao Renjie using Jiang so that he himself would be above reproach. However, Mai Zhu hadn't counted on Magistrate Jiang not playing along. Jiang instead designated an official called Chen Ding to fill the vacancy, while Gao Renjie was sent back to Guangji County, still as a substitute Magistrate.

The news of the Viceroy's affirmation of Gao Renjie's report spread across the county in one day. Many people believed Tu Rusong had been wronged. They felt especially indignant about the principled Magistrate Tang Yingqiu. Some squires and scholars signed a joint petition and sent it directly to the capital city of Beijing. Many common people went to the prefecture of Huangzhou in groups, asking the Prefectural Magistrate to stand up and speak out about the injustice. Others went to Wuchang City to complain to the Provincial Governor Wu Yingfen. Many people sent food and clothing to the prison, expressing their sympathy for Tang Yingqiu and Tu Rusong. However, despite public opinion, since nobody could produce sound evidence to reverse the former judgment, the law would take its course.

Chen Ding, the new Magistrate of Macheng County promoted by Jiang Jianian, was twenty-eight years old. His courage, his determination and honest character had been well noted by Jiang Jianian. Within ten days of Chen Ding's arrival in Macheng, he had received dozens of complaints about the injustice done to Tang Yingqiu and Tu Rusong. In fact, even without these complaints, Chen Ding knew all about the situation. But the judgment of the case had been approved by the Viceroy. The body by the riverbank, the only material evidence which could directly reverse the former judgment, had disappeared. If Yang was not found, nobody could reverse the judgment. Chen Ding was in a real dilemma, for he knew that Magistrate Jiang had pinned his hopes on him. When Magistrate Jiang had promoted him from among so many substitute officials, he had hoped he would act impartially and free the wronged and punish the real criminals. Chen Ding also knew how dangerous Gao Renjie was, since he had the backing of the Viceroy. Chen Ding had to somehow get enough solid evidence to reverse the former judgment. He therefore maintained a studied silence despite raging public opinion. Secretly, he garnered as many personnel as he could to find Yang.

One day, after dealing with legal documents all morning, Chen Ding grew a little tired and took a break in his study. He was soon awoke by a yamen secretary. Chen Ding opened his eyes and asked: "What's the matter?"

The old secretary bent by his ear and spoke in a low voice: "Yang's been found!"

"What!" Chen Ding felt elation in his heart: "Where?"

The secretary gestured at him to lower his voice and

188

said: "In *Xiucai* Yang Tongfan's home."

"Where's the evidence?"

"Someone provided a clue."

"Where's the person?"

"Waiting outside."

"Bring him in."

"Right away!"

The secretary bowed and withdrew.

After a while, the secretary led a young peasant into the study. The young man tried to kneel down as a sign of respect when he saw the Magistrate, but Chen Ding stopped him, telling him to sit down and describe the story in detail.

The young man began, "My surname is Zhang and my given name is Xueli. I live in Xiaozhuang in the southwest. My mother Guo is a midwife, and our home is next to Yang Tongfan's residence. Earlier this morning, Yang Tongfan's lady was about to give birth, and my mother was called there to deliver the child. It was a difficult labor, and Ma tried to help the lady for four hours, but the child still wouldn't come out. The lady was in great pain, but Ma is old and didn't have enough strength. She then asked the lady to find a woman to help massage her abdomen. No other women were in the room, but when the lady was in great pain she cried out: 'Help me, Sister!' Ma didn't know who 'Sister' could be. But she also cried with the lady: 'Sister, please come help!' An attractive woman suddenly showed up from an inner room, but when she found a stranger, Ma, there, she tried to step back. Ma begged her to help save a life, and together they finally delivered the child. Afterwards, my mother asked the attractive woman who she was. The woman suddenly knelt down and whispered: 'I am

189

Tu Rusong's wife Yang. I am here at Tongfan's to avoid trouble. Please don't tell a soul about this.'

"Just at this moment Tongfan entered, and taking out fifty taels of silver, he put the money into Ma's sleeve, insisting that she accept it. He asked Ma to keep the whole thing quiet. My mother took the silver and went back home. But the more she thought, the more awkward she felt. If Yang was hiding at Tongfan's, how could Gao Renjie sentence Tu for murdering his wife? If Tu Rusong was innocent, why would Magistrate Tang take bribes to shield him? My mother therefore wanted me to report this to Your Honor. It has something to do with lives and conscience. We don't want innocent people killed and good people wronged."

After he finished the story, Zhang Xueli took out a small parcel and unwrapped it. The fifty taels of silver were there. Zhang Xueli put the silver on the table and said: "I know the silver is evidence. I have never seen so much money in my life. Please check it, Your Honor."

Looking at the forthright young man, Chen Ding felt so grateful he didn't know what to say. Zhang Xueli felt the Magistrate had understood all he said, so he made a deep bow to him and stood up to hurry out.

Chen Ding walked over and took his hands: "I thank you on behalf of Magistrate Tang and Tu Rusong. After you go back, don't let others know in case Yang Tongfan takes some countermeasures. I will immediately report this and make a judgment." Zhang Xueli nodded and stepped out quickly.

Yang was not dead! The truth would now be revealed, and Chen Ding got very excited. He secretly sent two experienced detectives to keep Yang Tongfan under strict surveillance. At the same time, he went to

190

Wuchang himself, and reported the case to the Provincial Governor Wu Yingfen. Wu Yingfen had been highly dissatisfied with Mai Zhu's neglect of proper process when he was dealing with this case. He had received numerous complaints in the last few days from squires in Macheng, demanding justice for Tang Yingqiu and Tu Rusong, and had been worried about what to do. After reading Chen Ding's report, he was overjoyed, but Wu Yingfen was a very cautious man. Since the Viceroy had interfered with the case, he realized that it was better to let the Viceroy himself rectify it. He asked Chen Ding to report the whole thing to the Viceroy.

Chen Ding felt a bit uncomfortable: "What if the Viceroy clings to his opinion, won't this remain an injustice forever?"

Wu Yingfen said: "It is a 'face-saving' device to let him end this fiasco. I am guessing he won't ignore it. If he really won't reverse his former judgment, I will not let it stand. It would be easier at that point to expose the case." The Governor's words made some sense to Chen Ding, and he left Wuchang and headed for Viceroy Mai Zhu's residence.

Mai Zhu was not in a good mood. He had just quarreled with his wife. When he was told that the County Magistrate of Macheng was there to visit him, his first reaction was to refuse him an audience. On second thoughts, he remembered it was Chen Ding who had taken the post he had set up for Gao Renjie. He was curious to find out what measures had been taken and what kind of person he was. If he didn't like him, he could pick out some mistakes in Chen Ding's report and have him dismissed. He immediately summoned Chen Ding, which was against his regular habit of keeping subordinate officials waiting for a while when they wanted to see him.

When Chen Ding entered the room, Mai Zhu was playing with a pair of jade vases. He didn't even spare a glance at Chen Ding when Chen Ding bowed to him. When Mai Zhu did not even turn to speak to him, Chen Ding got really embarrassed. After a long while Mai Zhu put down the vases and spoke, but his eyes still did not meet Chen Ding's.

"So you became the new Magistrate of Macheng? What tricks have you been up to, huh?"

Chen Ding understood what he was getting at, but he also realized the Viceroy was deliberately going to make things difficult for him. Chen Ding was very clever. He decided to make like he was hard of hearing, and did not respond to the Viceroy.

Keeping his back to Chen Ding, Mai Zhu said: "Aren't you the hard-working appointee of Magistrate Jiang? How come you have time to visit me?" Chen Ding still remained silent. Mai Zhu became surprised that there had been no response to his two questions. He finally turned around and looked at Chen Ding: "Why are you here? To act dumb?"

Chen Ding began to speak slowly: "I dare not act because I have come on an urgent matter."

"Oh, an urgent matter. What is it?"

Chen Ding responded firmly: "The murder case in Macheng."

Mai Zhu was a little startled but he remained calm and drawled back, "When are Tang Yingqiu and Tu Rusong due to be escorted to the provincial yamen?"

Chen Ding answered, "They are innocent. I dare not escort them."

"What!" All of a sudden Mai Zhu began to look carefully at Chen Ding and found he was just in his twenties. His studied manner exuded great confidence. "Looks like a capable young man. I should be careful," thought Mai Zhu to himself. Not waiting for another question from the Viceroy, Chen Ding narrated the situation about Yang calmly.

"What a ridiculous fabrication!" Mai Zhu exclaimed haughtily, "Yang's body underwent an autopsy. Bloodstained clothes and hair have been found. Is this all fake?"

Chen Ding countered: "Yang is alive, and the body, the clothes and the hair were meant to mislead us. Gao Renjie induced the confession through torture..."

"I appointed Gao Renjie to review the case," Mai Zhu interrupted. "The severe punishment followed oral testimony and hard evidence. How can you say it was obtained illegally?"

Chen Ding didn't shrink before the high official: "The wounds all over Tu Rusong's body are obviously from extreme torture. The coroner Li Rong died under torture without any confession. There is no precedent for such cruel interrogation. How can Gao Renjie avoid the charge of forcing a confession? Furthermore, the squires in the county have signed a joint petition exposing this injustice. Public discontent is at a peak. How can we report to the Imperial Court if we don't clear this up? I've found a witness who can prove Yang is hiding in Yang Tongfan's house. As long as we find Yang, the whole truth will be revealed. If I have permission from Your Excellency, I can definitely conclude this case in ten days."

Chen Ding's words irritated Mai Zhu, but there were

no loopholes in his compelling argument, just reasonable facts. Mai Zhu had to agree: "Since you believe Yang isn't dead, I give you ten days to arrest Yang and clear up the case. But if the case is not as you describe it, I won't let you off so easily. You're dismissed!" After saying this, Mai Zhu impatiently waved Chen Ding away. Chen Ding bowed respectfully and withdrew.

Chen Ding returned to Macheng quietly. He first summoned the two detectives to ask about the situation at Yang Tongfan's. When he learned that everything was as before, he ordered court held at once. Twenty competent runners were gathered, and together with the, headed at once for Yang Tongfan's residence.

They broke into the courtyard before Yang Tongfan rushed out in a frenzy, shouting: "How dare you break into a scholar's house?"

Chen Ding walked over and answered: "Someone has sued you for hiding a woman. I have come here on the Viceroy's order to track down and arrest the criminals. Search the house!"

The yamen runners pushed Yang Tongfan aside and ran into the house. These detectives and runners were all very experienced, and a false wall could never escape their scrutiny. An hour later, the wall was broken down and a gorgeously dressed Yang was smoked out. Chen Ding was happy to see it all go smoothly, and he ordered the detention of Yang Tongfan and the arrest of Yang Wurong.

It was only after Yang was found by using a lightning raid, did people in Macheng realize that Magistrate Chen had done a lot of legwork to make this sudden breakthrough in the case. The whole county was at a boiling point. Over thousands of people came out to see

Magistrate Chen, and a carnival atmosphere took over the small quiet county; even firecrackers were heard. Chen Ding did not rest after he arrived at the county yamen. He ordered a trial held at once, and the courtroom soon overflowed with people awaiting Magistrate Chen's judgment.

To Yang, who was kneeling in the middle of the courtroom, Chen Ding said: "You hid away and ruined your husband's family."

Yang seemed totally bewildered at his words. She had no idea yet of what had transpired—she only wept and said, "My husband beat me and sued me, saying I had taken his money and fled with a lover. I was afraid of being caught by the yamen and undergoing torture, so I hid in Yang Tongfan's house. I haven't hurt anyone."

Chen Ding replied, "I want you to see someone," as runners carried Tu Rusong into the courtroom. After so much suffering, Tu Rusong was in a terrible way, the wounds all over his body still bleeding, tangled hair hanging disheveled over his chest. He was so haggard and weak he could only lie on the floor, and had strength enough only to gasp. Yang became too afraid to look, seeing a half-dead man brought before her. Her heart was thumping as she unconsciously stepped back.

Chen Ding stopped her and asked: "Look carefully. Do you recognize him?"

Yang looked long and hard, finally realizing it was her husband. It also hit her that it was her desertion that had brought on so much suffering on her husband. Full of compassion mixed with guilt she dashed up to him. Holding him, not caring how dirty he was, she burst into tears: "It's my fault, it's all my fault..." Many eyes welled with tears as well.

Chen Ding in great indignation turned to Yang Tongfan and Yang Wurong, and roared: "Do you have anything to say?" The two scoundrels hung their heads in shame.

Chen Ding made the final judgment in court: Tu Rusong was to be set free at once. Compensation was to be offered for his recovery from torture. Tang Yingqiu was pronounced honest and incorruptible, and his earlier judgment in the case upheld. He was also set free from prison, to await further designation from higher authorities. Li Xianzong had been wronged, too, and would be sent home for recuperation and return as the county yamen secretary. Yang Tongfan and Yang Wurong were charged with fabricating false accusations against officials and framing innocent people. They were to be kept in prison, to await a final verdict when the case was concluded. Yang was to be charged with hiding in the villain's house and behaving against the moral code of conduct for a woman. She was also to be kept in prison, awaiting a verdict. When the judgment was announced, cheers rang out in the courtroom. Chen Ding sealed the trial report before the applauding audience and had it sent to the prefecture of Huangzhou.

Three days later, Governor Wu Yingfen received a detailed trial report from the prefecture of Huangzhou. Reading the report carefully, and finding no loopholes, he wrote a memorial to Emperor Yongzheng. At the same time, a copy of the memorial was sent to the Viceroy.

It seemed the case was over. However, because of Mai Zhu's attempts to cover up his role, and Yang Tongfan's cunning, another storm was whipped up.

The storm started in the provincial Viceroy's

residence. Mai Zhu had not expected Chen Ding to find Yang within two days and completely reverse a judgment affirmed by him. He also had not expected the normally cautious Wu Yingfen to directly write a memorial to the Emperor without discussing it with him. He had lost face in front of both the Emperor and common people. Furthermore, the official response from the Ministry of Punishments had arrived, approving Gao Renjie's judgment. According to this, Tang Yingqiu, Tu Rusong and Li Xianzong were ordered to be executed. But with the recent revelations, Mai Zhu could not uphold the former verdict. He had to eat bitter crow and not convey his sufferings to anybody. In the end he had no way out but to write a memorial saying new evidence had appeared in the case, asking for a postponement of the execution. After sending the memorial to the Emperor, Mai Zhu thought the matter over and over, considering it harmful to his fame to withdraw his former judgment. Without any choices, Mai Zhu felt trapped, so he sent for the old aide who had accepted gifts for him from Gao Renjie. The aide had also thought it over and seemed quite confident about a way to exonerate themselves. He offered an astonishing idea, which sounded quite feasible to Mai Zhu, who nodded his agreement as he listened, letting the aide lay out further plans.

The prison in Macheng was not watched closely, especially the women's prison cells. Several women prison guards worked the shifts. The keys to the prison cells were hung on the wall of the guardroom, and could be easily stolen as long as someone first made it through the gates of the prison. When Yang was imprisoned, two extra male guards were deployed to watch her—this was supposed to make things more secure. In fact, these male guards could no longer accompany visitors to the women's prison cells, and this provided an opportunity now for visitors and prisoners to conspire and concoct false testimony.

It was in the middle of the seventh month of the lunar calendar, and the weather was very hot. The prison gate was closed so securely not a breath of air could enter. The guard on duty could not stand the heat, so he picked up a bamboo chair and parked himself outside the gate. Just then, two overdressed young women arrived and said they were maids from the Tu family. They had come on behalf of Tu's mother to visit Yang, and the guard checked their belongings—just silk clothes and some food. He detained the food in case there was poison and let the visitors through.

Yang had not expected any visitors, and she had never seen these two women before. She was about to ask a question, but they stopped her. Yang was puzzled. One of the strangers began: "We have come to save you. Do you want to live or die?"

Yang was a little taken aback but said, "Of course I want to live. I want to leave this place."

The woman said, "You have admitted in court you are Tu Rusong's wife. By law, you are guilty of framing your husband. You will be hacked to death by autumn."

Yang was shocked, and quickly begged for help. The woman said, "You have only one way out. Retract your confession. Do not admit you are Tu Rusong's wife, instead say you are a prostitute. Yang Tongfan took you back home to live with him. This way, you will be released on bail and can marry according to the authority's wishes. If you want to return to the Tu family, we can make an effort at reconciling you with Tu Rusong. It will all go perfectly. What do you think?"

Yang hesitated: "Will the yamen believe me?"

"As long as you insist, Tongfan will find a way out."

Yang was frightened when she heard she might receive a sentence calling for her to be hacked to death. Since she was now assured that Tongfan would save her, she believed what they said and nodded her agreement. The two visitors then helped Yang concoct a series of lies for the trial. They left quietly after Yang could memorize her false testimony.

Governor Wu Yingfen had been very concerned about the trial in Macheng. He wondered why there had been no response from the Viceroy after he had sent him the copy of his memorial to the Emperor. Hoping to unravel the case as soon as possible, he had written a letter to Mai Zhu. In the letter, he had begged Viceroy Mai to stand up and rescind the former judgment, upholding justice. But Mai Zhu had not answered and Wu Yingfen was becoming impatient. He drafted a document to Chen Ding, asking him not to wait for the Viceroy's approval. After all the evidence was pieced together, the report could be submitted to the Ministry of Punishments through the Governor's yamen.

Before Wu Yingfen's document was sent out, an urgent message from Macheng arrived. Yang Tongfan had announced in prison that Yang was not Tu Rusong's wife but a prostitute. He admitted to the crime of harboring a prostitute in his house, for which he was ready to face punishment. Meanwhile Yang retracted her previous confession and denied she was Tu Rusong's wife. She said she was a prostitute. Yang Wurong had also claimed in court that Yang was not his sister. Now

Chen Ding's judgment had no basis in fact.

Wu Yingfen was very angry. He knew someone up high had interfered in the case and secretly instigated the three criminals to cook up their latest scheme. Now just as he was about to inform the Viceroy of his request for a joint investigation and trial, a document arrived from the Viceroy's yamen. It was a copy of the Viceroy's memorial to Emperor Yongzheng describing the current situation in detail and calling for the former judgment to stand.

Only when matters took this course did Wu Yingfen figure out that the man who had been interfering in the case all along was the Viceroy himself. It really enraged him to see Mai Zhu, an esteemed official with high rank and property, cover up such a gross injustice. Outraged and infuriated, Wu Yingfen forgot about maintaining cordial relations between Viceroy and Governor. He right away wrote a contradictory point-by-point refutation to the throne, impeaching Mai Zhu for promoting a repressive official and concocting false testimony to destroy innocent people.

Yuanmingyuan (the old Summer Palace) in the northwest of Beijing was where Emperor Yongzheng lived and dealt with state affairs in his later years. Emperor Yongzheng sat behind his dragon desk by the window, trying to wrap his brain around the two contradictory memorials. They had been submitted one after another by a Viceroy and then a Governor. He vaguely remembered signing an execution list submitted by the Ministry of Punishments about a month before. In that list, there was trial involving a County Magistrate, and today, the memorial from the Mai Zhu brought this matter up again. Yongzheng couldn't understand at first why he was bringing up a case that had already been affirmed. He quickly figured out why by the time he had finished reading the memorial from the Provincial Governor Wu Yingfen. Yongzheng assumed that the two officials were on bad terms and were trying to destroy the other's reputation. They had come to two totally opposite conclusions about a case that had created quite an uproar in Hubei. The Viceroy had named a man a murderer while the Provincial Governor did not believe that same man had killed anybody. Who was right? Both could not be! Emperor Yongzheng looked more closely, comparing both memorials carefully, noting the solid evidence presented in both. It was impossible to distinguish right from wrong based on their reports alone. The case concerned a prefectural Magistrate, two County Magistrates and quite a few other officials. If the case was not cleared up, it would certainly cause greater commotion in Hubei. The Emperor, therefore, did not leave his desk through the entire morning. He seemed so lost in contemplation, that the eunuchs were afraid to interrupt him for lunch.

It was already afternoon, and the sun shone on the flamboyant trees in front of a hall in the Imperial Palace. The sunshine filtered through the windows shaping dappled dots on the dragon desk. Yong Zheng felt a little tired, so he stood up and paced up and down, his hands behind him. He wanted to get to the bottom of the case. He wanted to distinguish the right from the wrong. He also wanted to win people's hearts by resolving this controversial case that had attracted so much attention. The Emperor thought hard for a while before writing down the imperial edict: "Mai Zhu and Wu Yingfen are removed from their present posts and transferred to the Capital for other assignments. Shi Yizhi, the Minister of Personnel Viceroy, is designated Viceroy of Hubei and Hunan provinces. He should gather officials together to jointly investigate the murder trial in Macheng. Within two months, the results of this investigation should be reported directly to the Palace." After finishing the edict, Emperor Yongzheng sighed as if he had discharged a heavy burden and walked out of the hall.

On receiving the imperial edict, Shi Yizhi took just four days to get to Wuchang City. Years of experience working in public office told him: In such circumstances, he would only get biased points of view if he went to either side for their opinions. He should start by unearthing detailed facts from all angles. He therefore did not summon officials from the different jurisdictions as former viceroys had done when they were newly designated. He chose to study the case files carefully in a quiet house for three days, and his wealth of experience quickly led him to the key areas of disagreement.

First, among the hair produced as one of the key exhibits in the case, he found some white hairs. The Yang was said to be an attractive twenty-four-year-old woman. Could such a young person have white hair? He doubted if the hair truly belonged to Yang. Next he looked carefully at the bloodstained clothes and got suspicious again. The texture of the cloth was clean and complete. It did not look like it had been buried in soil for a long time. According to Mai Zhu's case file, it had been buried for more than one year. There had been much rain in Macheng and the clothes had not been buried very deep. Wasn't it strange that the clothes had not at all rotted after a whole year?

With these doubts, Minister Shi began to meet the parties concerned. First, he quietly sent for Tu Rusong's mother. He found a lady well into her sixties with her hair wrapped in silk cloth, despite the hot summer. She obviously wanted to hide some defects in her hair by wrapping it up. Deliberately, Minister Shi brought up the topic of hair, and after some hesitation, the grieving mother removed the wrap and exposed her shorn hair. Minister Shi was very understanding and consoled the old lady with kind words. She then told Minister Shi about asking Secretary Li Xianzong's wife to cut her arm in order to stain the clothes.

After he saw Tu's mother, Minister Shi still did not summon officials for the investigation. Instead, he sent several expert investigators borrowed from the Ministry of Punishments to go to the site by the riverbank. Their secret task was to look for a boy who had died about two years before. Three days later, a report came back: A rich merchant, Huang Degong, had had a clever young servant who died of acute disease two years ago, and Huang Degong had buried him by the riverbank. He hadn't buried the body deep enough so stray dogs had dug it out. When the local constable found the body and issued a call for its identification, Huang Degong had been on a business trip to Wuchang. When he got back, his servant's body had been judged to be a woman's body by Gao Renjie. Huang Degong then remained silent for fear of offending the new County Magistrate. Secretly he had found it all quite preposterous. This time, the investigators sent by Minister Shi found Huang Degong and asked him for details on where he had buried his servant. Only then did Huang Degong speak out about the actual situation.

Only after Shi Yizhi had gathered all this solid evidence, did he think he had an airtight case. He began to summon officials from all levels, and interviewed everyone related to the case, particularly Jiang Jianian, Chen Ding, Gao Renjie and Tang Yingqiu. After comparing each party's statement, it was very easy to tell truth from falsehood. In accordance with the Emperor's edict, Shi Daizhi decided to hold a joint trial on a case which had been postponed now for more than one year. Officials from three levels would join in the court session at the beginning of the eighth month of the lunar calendar.

This type of a combined trial was big news in Hubei. On the day of the trial, Wuchang City was packed with people, some of whom had come from dozens of miles away, even from Henan and Anhui. Heavy security was arranged outside the Viceroy's yamen, as soldiers patrolled up and down to keep order. All the prisoners and witnesses were summoned into the courtroom one by one. The striking of the court board and the exclamations of the judge were frequently heard. The court session lasted an entire day.

At dusk, when an evening glow lit up the western sky, the gate of the Viceroy's yamen was opened. A silver-bearded old aide walked out, holding up a trial announcement. People who had gathered in front of the gate pushed forward to get a look through the surging crowd.

Quickly stuck on to the wall, the trial announcement written on white paper gave the final verdict of the trial: "Tu Rusong is an innocent citizen. He had been framed and is now to be set free at once. Tang Yingqiu was fair and honest in judging the case. He is restored to his seventh rank and remains the County Magistrate of Macheng. Li Xianzong obeyed the laws and regulations and acted as an honorable official. He will gain a promotion in the county. The righteous and honest Li Rong refused bribes and died for upholding the truth. He is to be given a posthumous commendation throughout the province and will be buried with honor befitting a deceased County Magistrate. The newly designated Magistrate Chen Ding was fair-minded and virtuous in judging the case. He is promoted to new posting in the prefecture of Huangzhou. Gao Renjie, out of greed, fabricated false evidence and extracted confessions through extreme torture, and even caused a person's death. He is stripped of his rank and will be imprisoned, awaiting further trial. Yang Tongfan and Yang Wurong conspired together in cheating and bribing officials and fabricating false evidence. They also committed the crimes of framing innocent people and hiding a woman sought by the law. Their grave crimes deserve grave punishment, and they are now sentenced to death and will be executed in the autumn. Yang deserted her husband and committed adultery, in acts against social morality. She will be banished to the frontier for a lifetime of labor. Xue Wuji took bribes to cheat on an autopsy, and caused a person's death. He will be executed together with Yang Tongfan and Yang Wurong. The scoundrel Zhao Dang'er was greedy for money and concocted a false story to frame an innocent citizen. He is to be beaten forty strokes and will be sent to Heilongjiang Province to join the army."

This evenhanded judgment surprised and pleased both officials and common people. The squires of Macheng bought red silk from the silk shops of

Wuchang City and put up a red banner in front of the Viceroy's yamen. Fireworks and cheers resounded while the people discussed the happy outcome of a case that had lasted almost two years. Meanwhile, Minister Shi's impartiality and expertise deeply impressed the people of Hubei.

Spring arrived and the trees and the grass turned green throughout Macheng. A young man in a plain gown slowly walked toward Li Rong's grave. He placed a box of offerings in front of the grave and knelt down respectfully, tears streaming down his face. The young man, Tu Rusong, then whispered: "Respected Benefactor Li, you died for me and for the truth. Rusong will never ever forget your kindness and sacrifice." As he spoke these words, Rusong could not keep himself from sobbing uncontrollably.

The mountains silently stood still as streams rippled and white clouds came floating by across the sky. The flourishing pine trees and willows spilled their green shadows around Li Rong's grave. Gazing at the lush trees and grass, Rusong felt somewhat comforted—the people of Macheng would never forget this conscientious coroner.

Murder in Seven-Ravine Bridge

The winding Jialing River was rising in the Jialing Valley in Shanxi Province. It surged forward to merge with the Fu and Qu rivers as it passed Hezhou County in Sichuan Province. This provided more water and made a magnificent broad stretch of river. When the rivers crossed the nearby Huaying Mountains, the famous Little Three-Gorges of Sichuan Province were created. From ancient times, men of letters had been attracted by the beautiful scenery. The county which was located at the delta of the three rivers was called Hezhou Subprefecture (later renamed Hechuan). It was a vital communications hub in the center of the Sichuan Basin. The fertile land and abundant rain in this area provided perfect growing conditions for tangerines and rapeseeds.

In the years of Emperor Xianfeng's reign (1851-61) in the Qing Dynasty, a murder case in Hezhou Sub prefecture occurred which became much talked about throughout southwest China. Because of the muddleheaded ness of the corrupt officials and avaricious subordinates, a woman of virtue was almost put to death on a charge of adultery. She was lucky to encounter a wise Viceroy who appointed a clever County Magistrate as the judge to clear the case and bring the real murderer to justice after going through a lot of difficulties. The county grew famous because of the case. Since the end of the Qing Dynasty, Hezhou Prefecture has been a well-known tourist attraction. And those who came to Hezhou are always curious and eager to hear the whole story.

During Xianfeng's reign, a family named Ju lived at Seven-Ravine Bridge, a village in the east of Hezhou Prefecture. There were four people in the family: Ju Hai, his wife Xiang, and one son named Ju An, about twenty years old, who had just married a girl from the Zhou family living next door. The newly wedded couple did not have any children yet. Both the mother and the daughter-in-law were quite good-looking. The mother-in-law Xiang was just over forty. But her fine features and fair complexion made her look much younger than her real age. The daughter-in-law Zhou had always been considered beautiful in the village. Her radiant youth added to her beauty, so she was prettier than her mother-in-law. Villagers all said each generation of Ju family had beautiful wives of because their ancestors must have accumulated plenty of virtue and merit.

Ju Hai and Ju An made a living by curing snake bites. This unique skill was inherited from their ancestors. No matter what kind of poisonous snake bit the victim, so long as he was sent to the Ju family before he breathed his last, he could be saved. Therefore the family was very well known as snake physicians around the area. Ju Hai had a kind character. He never forced sick people to pay and only charged a small amount of money. In case patient was too poor to pay, he often offered treatment and medicines for free. So, the family was not at all wealthy, in stead barely supported themselves. Ju An resembled his father in nature. Besides practicing medicine, he also farmed in the fields. They worked very hard but were not after fame and money. The family atmosphere was quite harmonious.

In this particular autumn, there was a big harvest of tangerines in Seven-Ravine. Tangerines hung in the trees all over the mountains. The Ju family also had two *mu*,* of tangerine orchard. Their tangerine trees were growing much better than others' and they harvested much more fruit because Ju An had worked harder and spent more time in the orchard. The mother was very happy. She was busy collecting tangerines with her daughter-in-law. She couldn't even have a relaxed meal during this time. Only after they finished collecting all the tangerines did she breathe a sigh of relief. One evening, Xiang cooked some of her special dishes and took out a pot of liquor which had been kept for a long time. The families had a thoroughly delightful dinner to celebrate their harvest. It was quite late when they finished eating. Ju Hai was a little drunk. He could not help being overcome by dizziness from the liquor and went to bed first. It took Xiang and Zhou quite some time to clean the kitchen. When everything was done, it was already midnight. Then they said good night and went to their respective bedrooms.

The temperature varied by quite a large range in late autumn. It was hot in the day but cold at night when the mountain breeze blew its coolness over. Xiang was very considerate. She took out two thin quilts from a wardrobe, giving one to her son and daughter-in-law and covering her husband with the other. Then she gradually dozed.

_____

* 1 mu=1/15 hectare.

A tiring day brought a sound sleep. When Xiang woke, it was already dawn. Day had not yet fully broken. The quarter moon shone its white and cool light on the floor of the bedroom, adding a cold ambiance to the room. Xiang turned around to find the bed felt empty. She stretched out her arm for her husband, but she discovered he was not in bed. She waited for a while, but there was still no sign of him. Xiang became a bit worried. She got up quickly and went to the lavatory in the courtyard to look for him. He was not there, either. "Where has he gone?" An ominous feeling rose in her heart. She hurried to the door of her son's room and called for him. But only her daughter-in-law replied from inside. She said Ju An was not in, either. Xiang was really thrown into a panic this time. She asked her daughter-in-law to get up quickly. Holding a lamp in shaking hands, they went out together to look for their husbands.

As they came to the gate, trembling with fear, they found it was open. Xiang remembered clearly that she had slid the bolt in before going to bed. Obviously, someone had walked out from here. As they came out on to the street, they found a person lying on the ground about a dozen steps away. Xiang forgot all the fear as she ran over. Then she recognized it was her husband. His body was all covered with sticky blood. With a shaking hand, she tested for his breath before his nostrils. There was no breath. It seemed he had been dead for a long time. She looked up in panic and found another person lying a dozen meters ahead. Zhou rushed to the person and found Ju An was in a pool of blood too. His body was already rigid. Catastrophe had befallen the family overnight. How would they bear it? The mother and daughter-in-law burst into wailing. Neighbors were

211

waken by the crying and came out. The bloody scene sent chills up their spines, too. The two women cried themselves hoarse. Many people could not hold back their own tears at the miserable scene.

The family was very popular in the village. Upon seeing this family met with such a sudden tragedy, their neighbors could not just stand by. Some tried to calm down the mother and daughter-in-law. Some helped them away from the dead bodies. Some ran to get the local constable. Some senior people already had the site guarded by some young men.

After a short while, the local constable arrived. The situation was simple and clear. Ju Hai and his son had been murdered. No lethal weapon was found. It was the first time that the local constable had encountered such a horritic murder case in the village. But he was quite capable at his job. He arranged people to accompany Xiang and Zhou back home. At the same time, he had the corpses covered by bamboo mats and sent a young man to report it to the sub prefectural yamen. When all these things were done, the sun was way up in the sky already.

Rong Yutian, the Magistrate of Hezhou Prefecture, was a dissipated man, lacking in both learning and practical abilities. On the basis of his family's wealth, he had bought a seventh official rank. He had lubricated his ascent fill such a good post at this richly endowed Hezhou Prefecture. But he did not embezzle or take bribes after he took up the official post. What he cared most about was to keep the rank which he had paid ten thousand taels of silver for. Therefore he devoted himself to ingratiating himself with higher officials but was lazy in dealing with the county affairs. He never concerned about the condition of the people and the local economy. Though he had been the Magistrate for two years, he even had no idea how large the subprefecture was. All the county affairs were handled by his secretaries. What he did every day was just to absentmindedly sign the documents drafted by the secretaries. The secretaries were happy to have such a Magistrate. In his way, all the subprefectural affairs were actually under their control and all the people's lives were in their hands. So they tried their best to satisfy the Magistrate and fool him. It was really lucky for Rong Yutian that Hezhou Prefecture was fertile and people here were honest and innocent. Since he had come, nothing serious had happened. Rong had become quite settled at his official post. But the good times didn't last long. Who would have expected that a murder case could happen at the village of Seven-Ravine Bridge. However, when the report was presented to him by the local official, he thought it was just another run-of-the-mill document. He stamped it with his seal and had it sent to the Prefectural Magistrate with the other documents.

When Du Guangyuan, the Magistrate of Chongqing Prefecture received the report, he found it preposterous and infuriating. He thought to himself, "Look at this Rong Yutian. I heard he's muddleheaded. But how can he be as silly as this! He has directly sent me the same report submitted to him by the local official!" In great anger, he picked up his brush and wrote at the bottom of the document: "Human lives are of greater value than anything else. But the murderer is still at large. You are given one month to catch the criminal." After this, he still did not feel relieved from his anger. He decided to ask Rong Yutian to visit him and talk to him in person.

213

When Rong Yutian received the notice, he was wondering why the Prefectural Magistrate wanted to see him. "There are more than ten subprefectural and county magistrates in Chongqing Prefecture. Why does the Prefectural Magistrate want to see me alone? Maybe he's fond of me. Maybe he'll promote me or give me an award or something." When he thought of this, he felt full of happiness. He ordered his sedan chair quickly prepared and hurried to the mansion of the Prefectural Magistrate, his brain full of magnificent illusions.

When Rong Yutian saw the Prefectural Magistrate, he kowtowed to him respectfully then stood aside, waiting. Magistrate Du was irritated to see Rong Yutian stand there as if nothing were amiss. He said to him coldly, "Master Rong, do you know why I invited you here?"

"I don't know, Sir." answered Rong Yutian.

"You don't know, huh? Do you know a murder happened in Hezhou?"

Rong Yutian was flurried a little by the inquiry. He thought for a few minutes but could not recollect any murder that had happened recently in his subprefecture. So he had to reply cautiously, "I don't know, Sir."

Hearing this, Du Guangyuan became more angry. He asked sternly, "Then what do you mean by sending me this report of a murder case?" Rong was completely confused. He turned the question over in his mind for a while then answered in a low voice, "What, what report? I, I really don't know."

It made Du Guangyuan further exasperated to find Rong Yutian did not know a thing about the document he himself had submitted. He took the document and threw it at Rong Yutian, shouting: "What's this? Read it carefully!" The Prefectural Magistrate's great anger made Rong realize the situation was very serious. He took the paper with trembling hands and unfolded it to read. He began to sweat after reading only a few paragraphs. He peeked at the Magistrate and quickly moved his eyes back to the paper again. He faltered but did not know what to say.

Du Guangyuan had no interest in further talk. He ordered in a strict tone: "As the magistrate of a subprefecture, you don't even know your people were murdered. How preposterous! Go back now and conduct an investigation immediately. The case must be cleared in a month. Its progress has to be reported to me on each reporting day. If the criminal is not caught before the time has expired, I'll definitely not let you off so easily!"

Rong didn't dare to say anything for himself. He had to consent obediently and then backed off.

The Prefectural Magistrate was quite serious about the case. On every reporting day, he would send people to urge Rong Yutian to hurry up with the investigation. Rong found himself at his wits' end. He had sent people to research and investigate. But after ten days had passed, nothing had been obtained. Meanwhile, Xiang, the wife of the victim Ju Hai, came to subprefectural yamen quite often to make entreaties. She begged the Subprefectural Magistrate to find the murderer and avenge her husband and son. Furthermore, the letters of urging from the Prefectural Magistrate drove Rong mad. He could not rest his brain for a single moment.

After twenty days had passed, Rong was called to the prefectural yamen and was scolded for his ineffectiveness in the investigation. He was told that if he could not break the case in the next ten days, he would be dismissed from his post. Fortunately Rong was smarter this time. He took two capable secretaries with him to see the Prefectural Magistrate. The secretaries appealed piteously to the Prefectural Magistrate for more time. Then the Prefecture Magistrate agreed to give him two more months.

Walking out of the gate of the prefectural yamen, Rong felt his legs too heavy to move, like they were filled with lead. He quite well understood that if there were no leads soon a case like this would only become more and more difficult. Although two additional months had been given, he had no idea how to clear up the case yet.

After returning to his yamen, Rong was not even willing to go back to the inner court. Wearing a long face with knitted brows, he went to his office to deal with daily affairs. He hunched over the desk and thought hard about how he could get rid of this trouble. He thought over and over again and the only result he could come up with was to ask the legal Aide for suggestions. The legal Aide of Hezhou was already in his fifties. He had a good knowledge of yamen matters. And because of his years of investigative experience, he had some clever ways of catching thieves. In consideration of the future of his own official career, Rong Yutian was very sincere and respectful to the legal Aide. This completely won over his sympathy. The old Aide narrowed his eyes and contemplated seriously for Rong Yutian.

After thinking for quite some time, he suggested, "This really is a hard case. It won't be easy to track down the criminal in three months. But now the time is strictly limited. The only way to remove ill fortune is to ask for the help of Chen Laolun, the legal Secretary of the

Office of Justice."

Rong asked with doubt, "Chen Laolun is usually so quiet, and he is only a little over thirty. Do you think he can really solve such an important case for me?"

The Aide retracted the smile on his face and said sternly, "Don't look down upon the young man. Though he is young, he knows the ways of the world very well. He's smart and has seen much of life. He is the most capable man in the yamen of Hezhou. If he can't handle it, there's nothing we can do."

Seeing that the old Aide recommended Chen Laolun so energetically and seriously a ray of hope flickered in Rong Yutian's heart. He sent for Chen Laolun right away. The Aide knew how to behave in this delicate situation. He immediately saluted a farewell to Rong. It was the first time that Rong broke custom to see an aide to the door.

The curtain of night in late autumn fell early and quickly. Rong lit a big candle and waited for Chen Laolun patiently in the light of the jumping flames. He had already put everything, his future and fate, on to Chen.

Rong did not know how much time had passed before he heard quiet footsteps approaching the door. Rong stood up to greet him. But before his hand reached the handle of the door, the door was pushed open and Chen came in. Chen was around thirty years old, thin and tall. His complexion was fair and clean. His eyes were big and deep, sparkling with a kind of cunning light, which made it difficult for others to pin him down.

Rong invited him to sit down and directly poured out his troubles, then asked Chen if he had a way to break the case in two months. It seemed that Chen had already acknowledged the purpose of inviting him here.

217

He let out a slight smile and said, "The murder case has been well known throughout the province. The detectives in our subprefecture haven't cleared the ins and outs of the matter, however. There exist only three possible causes leading to any murder: revenge, money or adultery. Before a thorough investigation can be carried out, the cause of the case has to be ascertained. Then we can trace down the clues and eventually break the case."

Rong agreed with him, and could not help nodding his consent. "You're absolutely right. I'm going to entrust you with the case. Do you have the courage to take it and solve the problem for me?" he asked eagerly.

Chen thought for a few minutes and replied, "I'm afraid I can't." His face showed signs of reluctance. Rong stood up and walked close to Chen, speaking in a low voice, "I know what you're thinking inside. The saying goes: 'Nobody gets up at five o'clock unless it's profitable.' You won't do it for nothing. You'll be awarded with five hundred taels of silver when the case is closed. And of course, I'll make great effort to get you promoted, too. What do you think?"

Chen's brow loosened. He replied respectfully, "I'm not asking for a promotion or rewards or anything. I'm just afraid the case is too difficult to handle properly. I don't want to make any mistakes and bring Your Excellency more trouble. Now that you'll bestow special favor, I can't insist on refusing any longer."

"Then in how long do you reckon the case can be cracked?" asked Rong anxiously.

"Since the situation of the case is not clear yet, I can't guarantee you an exact date. But don't worry, Sir, the case will be closed within two months, anyway."

218

Rong was pleased beyond his expectations. He was ready even to enshrine and worship this young man. He repeated his promises again and again before he saw Chen out of the gate of the yamen. Then he strode toward the inner court, brimming with happiness.

Seven-Ravine Bridge was a scenic spot in eastern Hezhou. The famous Fishing Castle was not far from it. In late autumn, the leaves of the tangerine trees turned reddish. They mingled with the green bamboo leaves all over the mountains and presented a magnificent view. A path wound out of the layers of valleys and led to Seven-ravine Bridge, in which the houses were all covered by trees. From outside, it was hard to notice the village's existence. The Jus' house was located at the edge of the village, beside a small bridge. The bridge, the flowing water, the bamboo and the village houses were blended together harmoniously and created a sweet, tranquil picture.

Chen Laolun arrived at the village at length after climbing over mountain after mountain. On his back he carried a sack of documents. It did not take him much trouble to find the Jus' house. Several bungalows built of straw and grass, a small courtyard surrounded by a low wattle wall and an unpainted gate of the yard all told him that this was an average villager family. Chen paused at the gate for a while before he knocked on it. But there was no answer until he knocked several times. Then a woman's voice came from inside: "Who is it?"

Chen answered in a calm and kindly voice, "I'm a secretary of the Hezhou yamen. I came for the investigation into your case."

Very soon, the gate was quietly opened. Ju Hai's wife

Xiang appeared inside the gate. Though deep grief and suffering were expressed in her eyes, she had not lost her refined and elegant manner. Chen couldn't help think privately, "Such a good-looking woman in such an isolated village!" Seeing that Chen was not dressed like an ordinary person, Xiang hurriedly curtsied to him respectfully and invited him into the sitting room. After being seated, Chen looked casually around the room and found baskets of tangerines were everywhere inside and outside the room. Some had started to rot. Obviously the mother and the daughter-in-law did not have the ability, or maybe the interest to deal with such things anymore after the terrible tragedy which had befallen them.

Xiang could not hold back her tears as she recollected the scene when her husband and son were found murdered. She was sobbing too much to speak. But Chen was very relaxed and calm. He waited quietly until Xiang had gathered herself together, then asked carefully about the details of the day. When the topic touched the most painful part in Xiang's heart, she was so grieved that she could no longer continue talking. She had to ask her daughter-in-law to come out from the inner room to answer Chen's questions. So Zhou came out to greet Chen. The moment Chen Laolun laid eyes on Zhou, he was completely enchanted by her beauty. He forgot himself entirely and fixed his eyes on Zhou's gorgeous face and figure. Zhou became flushed and embarrassed by Chen's staring. She lowed her head and hid behind her mother-in-law, rubbing the sash of her clothes nervously. Chen came to himself again and realized he had lost his manners. So he composed himself and gave some comforting words before he continued the inquiry.

His questions were very detailed and complete. He asked many questions, from everything that happened that very night to the daily behavior of the father and son, from their economic situation to possible family feuds. Zhou answered honestly and thoroughly. When the question led her to the horror of the past, she also broke down sobbing tearfully. Chen found her even more beautiful in her sorrow. At last, Chen could not keep himself calm any longer. He could hear his heart pounding heavily and rapidly. Secretly, he would rather stay longer with the two beautiful women. But when he finished asking all the questions, he had to leave. He really felt a reluctance to leave.

Chen Laolun's heart was changed forever after he returned to Hezhou. Zhou's pretty and charming face kept flashing before his eyes. His wits told him to drive the image away. But the more he tried to forget, the more deeply he missed her. Chen was thirty-one years old. He was not yet married. In this restless and excitable mood, an idea hit him—marry Zhou. After this thought emerged, he could not get rid of it again. For the whole sleepless night, he tossed and turned in bed, until finally he figured out a wicked idea, which would get two birds for him with one stone.

Very early the next morning, Chen went to the yamen and asked to see Rong Yutian alone. Rong had been anxiously expecting good news from him. So he asked the yamen runners to invite Chen in immediately. When Chen saw Rong, he bowed deeply to him and said happily, "Congratulations, Sir, congratulations."

Rong asked joyfully when he heard this: "Have you found a clue in the case?"

"It's true, though it'll take some time to catch the criminal."

"Did you find the suspect, then?" asked Rong Yutian. Chen replied, "I went to see the Ju family yesterday. In the light of the family's circumstances and the behavior of the father and son, murder for revenge or money seems unreasonable."

"Why do you say that?" asked Rong. Chen looked at the Magistrate with smiling eyes, and answered, "The father and son made a living on farming, and also treating snake bites on the side. Although they have a great reputation, they don't have much money. Financially, the family could barely be counted as an average family in Hezhou. They have neither rare treasures, nor accumulated silver, which means the family had nothing attractive to burglars. Of course, nobody would commit murder for one or two baskets of tangerines. Therefore, there is little possibility of murdering for money."

Rong was convinced. He kept on nodding his head, "That's right, that's right."

"The other thing is," continued Chen, "the father and son were law abiding and behaved themselves. They were very kind to their neighbors and had harmonious relations with everybody. Especially Ju Hai, who was warm hearted in nature. He never counted on payment for curing snake bites. For many miles around Hezhou, there are hundreds of people who were cured by him. How could a person like him have an enemy? Murdering for revenge is absolutely impossible."

Rong was completely impressed by Chen's reasoning. He eagerly asked further, "Then was it a crime of adultery?"

222

Chen nodded his head slightly and said, "Ju Hai's wife is a little over forty. But she's a very good-looking woman and looks just about thirty. Her daughter-in-law Zhou is very young and very pretty, too. Both the mother and the daughter-in-law are well known for their beauty around the area. Beautiful faces always attract attention. And the Jus live in poverty. It's inevitable some men would seduce women with their wealth and power. Women have long hair, but short wits. Who can guarantee they won't be lured? I noticed that Xiang is a woman of loose morals. Her eyes are constantly exuding tenderness and love. Therefore, I reason that it probably was she who enticed an intrigant and had Ju Hai and her son killed by him."

Rong Yutian said, "If that is so, let me issue an emergency order and arrest Xiang for trial. Then everything will become clear."

Chen shook his head and replied, "It's not as easy that. At present, everything is only assumption. We don't have any material evidence at hand. Who is the intrigant? Who did he gang up with? How did they commit the murder? We know nothing about these things. If we arrested Xiang and she would rather die than admit it, what could we do then? Besides, the intrigant would be alerted."

"Then what shall we do?"

A cunning smile appeared on Chen's face. He said, "I have arranged a marvelous plan, Sir. I came to ask for your permission. So long as I'm allowed to carry it out, I can ensure you the case will be cleared in two months. However, Your Excellency, please don't ask me how I'm going to do it."

Rong was not quite sure what Chen was talking

about. He completely lost his wits again. He kept his eyes on Chen through his dizziness. It was clear to Chen that Rong was unsure about his plan, so he said in an emphatic tone, "So long as my actions are authorized, I will offer an apology with death if I can't catch the criminal in two months."

Seeing that Chen was guaranteeing with his life the cracking of the case, Rong heaved a sigh of relief. "All right, all right. I'll not interfere with your actions. As long as you can get the murderer in two months, you can do anything you want."

Chen said, "To make it convenient for clearing up the case, please notify the prison that I'm authorized to take out any prisoner for interrogation and no other person is allowed in sight."

"That's easy," said Rong. "You're the secretary of the Office of Justice and you are authorized to go in and out of the prison freely. I'll have Chief Huang notified to provide you with every convenience."

Chen stood up from his chair and thanked Rong for his trust and support. But when he was going to salute goodbye, Rong stopped him. "Please wait, I've promised you a five hundred taels of silver in reward after the case is cleared. Now that the case is settling into shape, I can't go back on my words. I'll give you the reward now so that you can cover your expenses during the investigation." Not expecting this, Chen was pleasantly surprised. He hurriedly thanked Rong. Rong asked the servant to bring in ten packages of silver and, with his own hands, handed them to Chen.

On the morning of the third day, while Xiang and her daughter-in-law were busy doing housework, they heard someone knocking at the gate. To avoid meeting a stranger, Zhou hurried to the inner room. Xiang laid down the work she was doing and went to the gate, asking: "Who's it?"

"Sister, it's me. Can't you recognize my voice?" A voice answered. Xiang felt she was very familiar with the voice, but she could not right away tell who it was. She opened the gate and saw a middle-aged woman standing outside, her face shining with an intimate smile. Xiang recognized her at once. She was Madame Sun who sold fresh flowers in the town of Hezhou.

Xiang had been very fond of make-up since she was young. She also used flowers to do face applications. Madame Sun came to the village very often to sell flowers and make-up and Xiang was her regular customer. Every time Madame Sun passed by the village, she would stop at Xiang's place for some time. Besides the flowers and make-up, she would bring some beautiful thread and needles for Xiang. They often spent time together for more than ten years, therefore were acquainted with each other. Madame Sun was a smooth talker. She lived in the town and had seen a great deal. When Xiang was at a loss for ideas to solve her problems, she would ask Sun for suggestions. The suggestions were always reasonable. However, for some unknown reasons, they had not seen each other over the last three years, which was why Xiang could not recognize her voice.

As soon as Madame Sun saw Xiang, she quickly caught her hands. "Sister, it's been years since we've seen each other. How are you doing? Why are you so weary? How is Brother and my nephew? I moved away three years ago which is why I haven't come to see you. Nobody else has sent you any rouge since then, right?"

Xiang was deeply touched by the warm and intimate

greeting. She felt her nose twitch and said with a sobbing voice, "Sister Sun. Please, come in."

Madams Sun appeared to only just notice something wrong with Xiang. Her smile froze on her face when she saw Xiang was dressed in full mourning dress. Since the tragedy had befallen the family, Xiang had not met a friend as close as Sun. Seeing Sun had been shocked into silence, she could not hold back her emotion anymore. She threw herself on Sun's shoulder and burst into tears. Sun tried to console her while she supported her to the sitting room.

It took Xiang quite some time to control her emotions. Then she slowly told Sun the whole story. Sun was shedding tears with Xiang while listening. When Xiang finished the story, Sun asked about the details of how they reported the case and the current progress in pursuing the criminal. At last, she said, "It looks that the Hezhou yamen isn't working very hard on tracing the killer. I'll go to town tomorrow and ask some influential acquaintances to push the thing—I have some good friends in the yamen. Some of them are in important posts."

Xiang stood up hurriedly and expressed her gratitude with a curtesy. Sun quickly returned the courtesy. After a while, she said, "It has been three years, and your son had gotten married. But who could have expected that the poor daughter-in-law would suffer such a terrible tragedy? Where is she now? Still here or has she gone back to her mother's?" Only now was Xiang reminded that she had forgotten to let Zhou greet Sun. " My girl, come to see your Aunt Sun."

Zhou had been hiding inside and listening to their conversation. She didn't know who the person was, so she did not come out. Hearing the mother's call, she slowly walked out and shyly greeted Sun. Sun walked up to Zhou, holding her hands and praising her: "What a beautiful girl! It's the Ju family's fortune to have such a gorgeous daughter-in-law. But what misfortune..." With these words, tears fell down her cheeks.

When they had all calmed down, Xiang asked about Sun's present situation. Sun answered that everything was fine with her. After they had chatted for some time, Sun found the house was in a mess. She then started to tidy up the room. When lunchtime came, Xiang invited Sun to stay for lunch. Sun accepted without hesitation and began to help with the preparations.

It did not take long for the three of them to get food ready. They ate while continuing their chat. Sun did not show any dissatisfacion, though the dishes were only some simple preserved vegetables. After a while, Sun let out a deep sigh and said, "There is something I want to say. But I don't know if it's appropriate."

Xiang answered, "Sister, you are not an outsider, so go ahead."

"Your family had undergone so much suffering. Both Brother Ju and my nephew have passed away. How are you going to spend the rest of your life? Today I still can have a simple meal here. But what will it be like when I come next time? Now the killer is still on the run. It seems even if the yamen devotes itself to the investigation, it won't be clear in a short time. The ways and morals of the world are so bad. Pressing charges or suing somebody. Is there anything for which we don't need money? The more the case is prolonged, the more expenses it will need. How are you going to manage? I know you don't have any savings. On the other hand, the girl is still so young. Is she going to live in widowhood for the rest of her life? My words may sound rude. But why not choose a good family for her and let her remarry? In this way, one person's living expenses are reduced and you can also get some money from the betrothal gifts so that you can lubricate the palms of people working on the case. Then these'd be hope for avenging the murdered. We've been together for ages and that's why I'm bold enough to put it to you straight. What do you think, Sister?"

Sun's words made Zhou blush. She dropped her head and did not say anything. Xiang considered what Sun said to be very reasonable. She agreed with Sun that she could not let Zhou live with her as a widow for the rest of her life. That would be too cruel to her. Actually, if it were not because it had been too short a time after her son had died, she herself would have brought up the topic. In addition, there was no reliable person to approach to recommend a man. She was afraid that it would not be easy to find a dependable man for Zhou. That was why she had thought of the matter, but had never talked to Zhou. Now that Sun put all this out on the table, Xiang showed her agreement.

She turned to Zhou and asked her in a concered tone, "Daughter, did you hear Aunt Sun's words?"

Zhou was so embarrassed that tears were streaming from her eyes. Seeing this, Sun interceded to ease the situation: "Zhou, we both are your dear ones. We wouldn't let you down. You still have a long life. Remarry or not, it's all up to you."

Zhou paused for a few minutes and, with her hands rubbing the corner of her clothes answered: "I'd rather live with Mother and never marry again."

These words made Xiang's heart ache. She said to Zhou affectionately, "Life is not a matter of one or two days. You're still so young yet your husband has passede away. Besides, you don't have a child, so why should you live alone for the rest of your life? Even if you chastely remained here, the officials in the yamen won't be moved. Your mother-in-law can't afford to bribe the fellows who are working on the case. The killer is still freely enjoying the sunshine. Your husband won't be lying easy under the earth." Hearing this, Zhou could not control her emotions any longer. Tears fell into the bowl in front of her. Suddenly, she pushed the bowl away, stood up and ran into her room.

Xiang exchanged glances with Sun and said, "You're surely right, Sister. We village people don't beat about the bush. About the marriage of my daughter-in-law, would you please look for a good family for her? So long as they can live happily together, I'll be satisfied."

"There are several good families. But I don't know if they would agree with the marriage. Let me talk to them first. You just wait for my news with your heart at ease. As long as one family agrees, I assure you that your daughter-in-law won't need to worry anymore about a living." Xiang thanked her profusely.

It was getting late and Sun took her leave. Before they parted, Sun took out one tael of silver from her waist pocket and handed it to Xiang. "Sorry, Sister, I am not wealthy. We don't have much savings, either. This is just an expression of my good will to Brother Ju."

Xiang would not accept it. Sun was a bit upset: "We've been sisters for ages. Aren't we close enough for you to accept a small gift like this? If you refuse it, I'll never come back again." Xiang could not refuse any longer. She took the silver reluctantly. Then they parted and Xiang stood there until Sun's back disappeared down the winding path into the mountains.

In fact, Madame Sun's trip had been arranged by Chen Laolun. Since the day Chen had met Zhou, he had become completely obsessed by her beauty. He wanted to have her right away. After he got the reward from Rong Yutian, he became more confident of his plan. Of course, the first step was to find a reliable matchmaker to persuade the mother and the daughter-in-law. He had been worried that Xiang would refuse. He had not expected it that would go so smoothly. After hearing from Sun about the positive response, Chen took out ten taels of silver and gave it to her in gratitude. Then he urged Madame Sun to bring up the proposal as soon as possible.

Sun answered with a smile, "A watched pot never boils. You'd better wait here on a firm footing. In two or three days, I'll bring you the good news." Chen took out fifty taels of silver as the bride-price. Sun took the silver while repeatedly warning Chen not to divulge the secret. Then she hurriedly took her leave.

Four days later, Madame Sun arrived at the Ju's with the bride-price. Xiang was so excited to see the shining silver that she asked Sun eagerly who the groom was. Madame Sun, full of joy and pride, congratulated Xiang: "It's really your daughter-in-law's luck. He is Chen Laolun, the secretary of the Office of Justice. He doesn't mind that Zhou was married before and is willing to hold a formal wedding. Chen is the most capable man in Hezhou. The Magistrate thinks highly of him and just rewarded him with five hundred taels of silver. He is really fortunate in life and money. Having

Zhou marry into his house, on one hand, can give her guaranteed glory, splendor, wealth and rank; on the other hand, it can encourage Chen to capture the killer. In this way you can even save on your legal costs! Wouldn't it be good on all sides?" Xiang was glad to hear this. She immediately found Zhou and explained to her what was going on.

Zhou had not thought to marry again. But her mother-in-law's description of the marriage sounded perfect. Besides, she had seen Chen before and knew he was not ugly in appearance. In fact, compared with her former husband, Chen excelled much more in various aspects. So she did not refuse anymore but shyly and mournfully nodded her consent. When Xiang realized her last surviving relative would soon leave her in the near future and she herself would be left in the empty house alone, she became very sad and could not hold back her tears. Madame Sun tried to console her until Xiang finally stopped weeping. Then she left the Ju's.

Chen was very pleased when he received the message that the Ju family had agreed to the marriage. He hired some people to clean the house and paint it all over again. Then he prepared clothes and furniture for the bride. It took him four to five days to have everything ready. In mid-October, he hired a squad of trumpeters and buglers and invited shifts of yamen honor guards to liven things up. In this festive atmosphere he moved Zhou into his household. After the wedding day, Chen Laolun gave Zhou whatever she wanted and let her do as she liked. She got the best food at meals. She did not wear the same dress every passing day in half a month. And Chen gave every care to Zhou and made her so happy that she did not know how to express her gratitude. Compared with her life in the Ju family, though Xiang had treated her as her own daughter, those living conditions could never match the Chen family. Zhou felt like rejoicing, that she married a good husband and the rest of her life would be stable. For the first few days after the marriage, Zhou had missed her mother-in-law. But bit by bit, she gave all her heart to her husband. There were no secrets between husband and wife. Chen Laolun quickly got to know every detail about the Ju family.

Time really passed very fast. Before one noticed, one month had passed. Now it was already mid-winter. One day, Chen had still not come back after dusk. Zhou had dinner prepared and was anxiously waiting for her husband. But there was still no sign of him when the moon hung high in the sky. Zhou became more and more worried. She had lost a husband and would never want to see any accident be fall her new husband. She felt like she was on hot coals. It was already very late when Chen Laolun returned. He looked so tired, his face full of worries. Zhou's fond greeting did not even get a smile in return. He slumped numbly down in the chair and let out a big sigh. It seemed that he wanted to say something, but at length he swallowed it.

"Why did you come back so late today? What are you sighing for? Is there some trouble?" asked Zhou, full of care and worry.

Chen Laolun waved his hand to stop her and did not answer for quite a long while. "I'm not sighing intentionally. But the case of the Jus really troubles me."

Zhou was frightened, "How are you related to the Ju case?"

Chen answered, "I always urge the Magistrate to

pursue the murderer for your mother-in-law. When I talked to him again yesterday, an urgent notice from the Prefectural Magistrate happened to arrive, in which the Subprefectural Magistrate was ordered to crack the case in half a month. So he asked me to clear up the case and find the murderer. But so far, there is not a single clue and it is impossible to stop your mother from applying pressure. Just now I discussed it with the investigators for more than two hours, but we still have no idea where to start. Now the time is severely limited. If the case can't be cleared in the end, not only will I not keep my rank, but I myself might be accused and put into prison. How can I remain calm at this?"

Zhou was torn with anxiety as she heard this, but she also could not figure out any solution. She paced up and down in the room and did not know what to do. When she thought of the terrible things that might happen to her husband, she buried her face in Chen's arms and burst into tears.

Chen Laolun fretfully pushed Zhou away. He contemplated for a few minutes before he sent out feelers: "Can you go back to Seven-ravine Bridge to persuade your mother-in-law not to press the yamen anymore?"

Zhou shook her head in disagreement: "She won't listen to me. Her husband and son were both killed and a happy family was destroyed. With such a deep hatred, how can she let it go so easily?"

"I know she won't easily give it up." Chen Laolun let out a frustrated sigh. "But can you go and persuade her not to press too hard? She has to give me some time. I believe she won't give you a rebuff if you go to ask her. I think she's a sensible lady."

"I'm afraid I can't do this, either." Zhou still shook her head. "It has been more than one month since my father-in-law and Ju An were killed. But the killer is still at large. Everybody knows the longer the case is delayed, the harder it will be to clear. My mother-in-law can't wait to catch the killer and get revenge. To ask her not to press is to kill her. I dare not be rebuffed."

Seeing that Zhou was not going to help, Chen's face clouded over with coldness and unhappiness. He went to bed without having dinner. Zhou was so worried and sorry. She tried to calm down and comfort Chen in a soft voice. But Chen did not say anything after that and only went to sleep.

The next morning, Chen Laolun got up before daybreak. After a hasty wash, he left home without speaking a word to Zhou. He did not come back for the whole day until it was totally dark. He simply had a little food and then went to bed. Zhou was driven to greater anxiety. She tried to find out what was going on, but Chen never gave her a clear response and only prevaricated ambiguously. All the tenderness and kindness had gone and Chen looked worn out.

For a whole week, Chen kept leaving early and coming back very late. He also talked very little. One day he did not come back until midnight. Zhou often cried privately when she saw her husband so distressed. She missed the good days so much. She had never imagined that the foundation of a loving family could be so shaken by such a situation. She had expected that their peaceful life would go on. She had expected that they would be affectionate like that forever. But now, everything seemed impossible. What could she count on if Chen was dismissed from his post or put into jail due to his failure in the case? She was so sad that she hated herself for not being able enough to share his burden. She had thought to go to Seven-ravine Bridge to persuade Xiang. But considering the pain and loss Xiang had endured and the affection Xiang had for her, she felt she could never speak out. These days, she seemed even more nervous and upset than Chen. She thought and thought all day long with the intention of finding a way to help her husband out of his dilemma. She was willing to suffer for Chen so long as he could tide over these difficulties.

It was already very late one day, but Chen Laolun still had not returned. There was a gale blowing outside. The old tree in the yard was shaken so violently that it made terrible noises. Zhou was so scared that she checked if all the doors and windows were closed properly time and again. But the windows could not stop the strange roar from squeezing into her ears. She waited and longed for her husband's familiar footsteps. Finally Chen came back, dragging his heavy feet. He said nothing, but threw himself into bed and didn't moved at all.

When Zhou eventually took off his clothes for him, she asked with much affection: "Dear, any more troubles?"

Chen opened his eyes with difficulty and said wearily, "Another official paper came from the Prefectural Magistrate, urging that the case be closed. Magistrate Rong scolded me and ordered me to get the killer in one month. Otherwise, he would cut off my head as punishment. Well, well..., looks like my life is doomed..."

"Oh, my..." Zhou was so shocked that she suddenly

lost consciousness and fell to the ground. Chen got up immediately and helped her up. He pinched her Renzhong acupressure point for a long time before she came around. Her tears fell wildly like pearls falling from broken strings. Chen carried her to bed and looked at her compassionately.

Zhou held him tightly and cried, "No, you can't die! I won't let you die! Tell me what to do. I'll do anything for you." Chen shook his head hesitantly. Obviously he was hiding something.

Zhou now realized he was hiding something from her. She held him more tightly and asked, "Is there anything you can't say even between you and me? What are you hiding from me?"

Slowly, Chen answered, quite hesitantly, "To be honest, all these days, I have been over the case with the investigators again and again. We also did a lot of investigating. Now the case is completely clear. But I was afraid you would not be able to accept the result, so I didn't tell you..."

Zhou let her hands go in surprise. "Why can't I accept it?" asked she earnestly, her eyes staring at Chen, wide opened.

My foolish girl, do "you know who on this earth murdered your father-in-law and your former husband?" asked Chen.

"No!" answered Zhou, completely at a loss.

"It was your mother-in-law, Xiang!" Chen answered with curt finality.

Zhou could not believe her ears. She was dumbfounded, her mouth opening unconsciously and her eyes staring in front blankly. Chen seemed to regret he had let out the secret. He looked at Zhou with his

236

eyes full of unease. They just stood there, looking at each other with all kinds of thoughts between them. Suddenly, Zhou seemed to realize something. She shook her head hard and murmured with a hoarse voice, "No, no, it can't be true. I know her, very well. How could she kill her own husband and son? I don't believe it! I can't believe it! No!" She burst into tears again.

At this moment, Chen regained his composure. He said to Zhou coldly, "You don't believe it, but the case has been cleared. Xiang had an affair with a man for more than two years. This time, it was she who had planned it out with the man who did it. They lured the father and son out at midnight and killed them separately."

"My mother-in-law is an honest woman," retorted Zhou in disbelief. "She is steady and virtuous. She, committed adultery? No way! It is a matter of her life. Please check it again and don't accuse her wrongly."

"It's also hard for me to believe that she had done such a thing to injure public morals. But now the man has been found and the whole course of the crime is clear. Xiang can't shift her guilt."

Zhou still insisted on her point, "I was in the family for more than a year. I never saw her conspiring with any man. Trust me, and please check it again."

Chen Laolun scoffed at her opinion: "Nobody will show off an adulterous affair. How could she let you know her secrets? Looks like she's pretty smart—she can even hide things so well from you."

Zhou turned her face toward Chen and looked straight at him. She was hoping to discover Chen had just been teasing her—but she failed. Chen looked serious, not showing any sign of joking. Zhou became uncertain. She didn't know whom she should trust, her husband or her former mother-in-law.

It seemed Chen understood her very well. "I should not have told you all this. But now with things already like this, how could I cheat you? If Xiang hadn't pretended to pursue things so avidly, we would have pretended to find nothing. But who could have expected this with Xiang always coming to the yamen, crying and making a fuss? Maybe she thought in this way we would be deceived and not suspect her. Magistrate Rong had no choice but to order me to clear the case. Now there isn't much time left. If I disclose the real situation, your mother-in-law will definitely be convicted and given the death penalty. I would have a feeling of guilt toward you all my life. Because of you, I had tried, when I first discovered the truth, to absolve her from guilt. But if I don't catch the criminal, I can hardly save my own life. Thinking about it over and over again, I'd made up my mind not to expose her affair. After a month, my death would end the case and everything... I feel so sorry to you. You have just remarried and will become a widow again." With these words, tears fell from Chen Laolun's eyes.

Zhou was completely torn at this moment. Of course she would not let her new husband sacrifice his life. Nor was she willing to let her mother-in-law die like this—their lives had depended upon each other. But what could she do? She couldn't come up with a single idea. She was so desperate that she buried her head in Chen's arms and burst into tears again.

Chen did not stop her. After quite a few minutes, he said slowly, "Don't be too sad. Let me think again to see if I can find a way that would satisfy both sides."

Zhou lifted her head and said hopefully, "If it will satisfy both sides, I'll do anything you want."

Chen supported her up gently, paused a long while and then said with hesitation, "There is a way, but your mother-in-law has to put up with it."

"What is it?" asked Zhou eagerly.

"I'll arrest Xiang for committing adultery. And you'll be needed to testify against her in court and..."

"What?!" Zhou was horrified again.

Chen quickly continued, "When the case is closed, I'll be exempt from charges. At that time, I'll try to bribe the officials in charge to save her life." Chen finished his idea in one breath before Zhou could interrupt again.

Still, Zhou shook her head in disbelief: "Is it possible a criminal who had committed both adultery and murder can be exempted from execution?"

"You don't know the yamen's tricks. So long as I can keep my rank in the yamen, I can manage to let somebody go freely even if he commits treason, let alone adultery and murder."

Zhou was not impressed. She dropped her head in silence. "As long as I can get away from a conviction, everything is possible," said Chen. "I'm your husband, can't you save me first and then we'll try to save your mother-in-law?"

Zhou balanced the different sides again for a few minutes and then gave a sigh,

"Do whatever you like." Chen was so excited to see that Zhou was persuaded, he gave Zhou a tight hug to show his appreciation.

Two days later, it was the eighth day of the eleventh lunar month. According to the Qing Dynasty relevant regulations, it was a day for common people to lodge their complaints. The morning wind was quite freezing. Just past 7 o'clock, the gate of Hezhou yamen was opened. Soon after that, Rong Yutian convened the court, attended by a huge crowd. The courtroom looked awe-inspiring. Rong issued his order to allow those who were wronged to submit their plaints. Just after the order was announced, a middle-aged woman started to cry out for justice. She was wearing a white mourning dress, and a of mourning scarf. Her face was completely bathed in tears. But the grief didn't keep her face from radiating her beauty. It was Xiang. To get to the yamen in time, she had got up at 2 o'clock in the morning. Neither darkness of night nor danger on the mountain paths could stop her from coming to beg the Magistrate to avenge—catch the murderer and avenge her husband and son. She remembered very well it was already the ninth time in just over two months that she came to complain in the yamen.

The Magistrate ordered the complainant be brought to court. The order was transmitted through the court by a series of runners. Their voices were so loud and the atmosphere was so threatening that a timid person might have been scared out of his wits. But Xiang was used to this. She followed the ushering runner obediently into the courtroom. Before she had finished the kowtow, Rong asked her impatiently, "Xiang, why are you here again?"

Xiang felt her heart quaking and answered in a voice full of misery, "My husband and son's deaths have not been avenged. How can I give up?"

Rong sneered, "You want me to catch the murderer?"

"Please, Your Honor!"

240

Rong paused for a while and then asked slowly and suspiciously, "You really don't know who killed your husband and son?"

Xiang realized that he was implying something. She thought for a while, but could not get Rong's meaning. She answered, "I really don't know, Your Honor."

"Nonsense!" Rong suddenly struck the table harshly with the wooden mallet and shouted at Xiang: "Why do you try to fool me? The Ju father and son were killed by you and your intrigant. You don't admit the sins you committed and come to confess your crime, but utter nonsense and make trouble. How can you play with the law like this? Today, you came freely, but will not be able to leave so easily."

Xiang felt like she had been struck by a lightening bolt. She saw shining stars flashing before her eyes, then her vision blurred. She fainted and fell down softly onto floor.

Rong gave a glance at Chen Laolun who was standing beside him, and stood up, "I exposed this woman's secrets. She fainted because of her panic. You can pour cold water to wake her." A runner took a basin of water and poured onto Xiang's face waking her.

Rong glared at her viciously: "I must know everything. You committed adultery for almost two years. In order to avoid being discovered by your family, you two planned to kill your husband and son. Is that so?" Xiang was over come with such fury that she forgot that her life was in Rong's hands. She protested loudly:

A murder takes place in Hezhou, and people were killed! You can't break the case but take me as the scapegoat. What a shocking action! Now if you say that I have committed adultery, where is the intrigant then?

You say that I planned to kill my husband and son with someone, so where is the evidence?"

Rong had thought that Xiang was timid and weak, but now she dared to oppose what he had said. He was furious: "You shrew! You have seduced men with your face. How can you get away from punishment? Now you dare to contradict me in court! Aren't you afraid of the law of the land?"

"The law won't kill the innocent. The injustice that happened to me hasn't been cleared, yet now I'm unjustly accused of adultery and murder. I'm too angry to keep myself calm. Please pardon my offense."

Rong's face became twisted when he saw Xiang refusing to give in. He said to her sternly, "You said you are unjustly accused. Do you mean I have wronged you? It looks like you won't confess until you face grim reality. You want a face-to-face challenge!" "I have done nothing wrong! I'm not afraid of a face-to-face challenge."

Rather than exchange more words with Xiang, Rong ordered the runners in a severe voice: "Bring out the intrigant!" Xiang was shocked again when she heard this order. She looked around and found all the people in the courtroom were staring at her, in a deadly silence.

The court fell quiet for a few minutes. Then the sound of chains could be heard drawing near from outside. When Xiang looked back, she saw a husky fellow walking slowly into the courtroom under the escort of two prison guards. The fellow's face was squarish. With a heavy beard and mustache, he looked really ugly and ferocious. Xiang disliked this man very much at the first sight. But the man did not lower his

242

head at all while he was kneeling on the floor. Instead, he looked at Xiang greedily, as if he wanted to swallow her in one bite.

"Do you know this woman, Jin the Sixth?" Rong asked the husky man.

"Yes. She is Xiang, living in Seven-ravine Bridge."

"Did you have an affair with her?"

The man gave a leer and said with an extremely lecherous tone, "She slept with me..."

"Nonsense!" Rong stopped him sternly and retorted: "Xiang is so pure—how dare you say she slept with you?"

For a few seconds, the man seemed to be confused a bit. Then he regained his calm. "Don't be angry, Your Honor. Not only did she sleep with me but we have been having an affair like this for more than two years!"

Xiang was so ashamed and enraged, she pointed at the man with her finger and scolded, "You shameless scoundrel! When did I ever see you before?! How dare you frame a woman from a good family in court? You, aren't you afraid of being punished by the god of heaven?"

The man did not flinch one bit. Instead, he became even more provocative and debauched. He murmured to Xiang as he bit by bit inched closer to her, "My beauty, I've confessed everything. I'm afraid you can't hide it anymore. It's better for both of us to tell the truth."

Rong cut in at this moment: "Xiang, do you have anything else to say?"

Xiang turned to Rong and retorted sternly, "Your Honor, don't listen to his nonsense. I don't know him at all!"

Rong did not answer Xiang, but said to Jin the Sixth,

"Jin the Sixth, confess the details of how you committed adultery with Xiang and how you hatched the plan to kill the Ju father and son."

"Yes, My Lord." Jin the Sixth answered obediently. Then he narrated a story of how they had become acquainted two years earlier and how they had started an affair. The description sounded more like reciting than recalling. When it came to the part about the killing, he said, "We often met when the Ju father and son went out to treat patients and we had illicit relations in her room. One month ago, the Ju father and son went to the Huaying Mountains on medical rounds. They had planned to be out for ten days. So I sneaked into Xiang's room. But unexpectedly, Ju Hai returned earlier than planned because he had broken his ankle. He saw me in Xiang's room. Lucky for me we were only talking at that moment. Then I found an excuse and got away. But Ju Hai grew suspicious. He had his son called back and wanted to investigate my background. Xiang was afraid of being exposed. So she came to me and discussed strategy. It was my fault. I shouldn't have concocted the idea of killing them. We made our plan: Xiang would befuddle them with drink first, and at night she would pretend to elope with me so as to trick the drunken Ju Hai outside of the house. I would hide somewhere in the darkness and come at him quietly and kill him. But unfortunately, when I killed Ju Hai, Ju An heard the noise and came out, too. He discovered what we were doing. But before he could react, Xiang held him from behind and I stabbed him in the chest and killed him, too."

"What did you do with the knife?"

"I wrapped it up and threw it into the river from the

Seven-ravine Bridge."

"Did Xiang say anything after this?"

"She said now that we had killed them, she had to pretend innocence and go to complain at the yamen, that probably we could mislead the officials."

"Where did you escape after that?"

"I had thought to escape along the Fujiang River. But I got lost in the mountains. I came across the investigators and got arrested. I think the Ju father and son's ghosts were chasing after me. I deserve punishment."

"Are you telling the whole truth in your confession?"

"Nothing but the truth, Your Honor."

"Press your finger print on your confession now."

"Yes, Your Honor."

Chen Laolun, who had written down the confession took the record to Jin the Sixth. Without looking at what was written, Jin immediately put his fingerprint on it. Rong tossed the confession toward Xiang and brought her to account: "Do you have anything to say?"

Now Xiang realized that today's trial had been deliberately arranged by the Magistrate. The blood debt had not been repaid, but she herself would be banished to the lowest depths of hell. She knew very well that she had no way to get out of the trap. Though she had always been kind to people, she was actually also very strong in nature. After she saw through all this, she calmed herself down. She had made up her mind privately to struggle to the end. She would rather die than satisfy Rong Yutian. Therefore, she straightened her back and answered Rong loudly, "I'm wronged."

Rong struck the warning mallet on the table and

shouted, "With the witness' testimony in court, you dare to deny your crime! Slap her in the face."

Right after the order was given, three yamen torturers ran to Xiang. Two of them held Xiang's shoulders to fix her at the kneeling pose. The other one slapped Xiang's face hard with a piece of wooden board, left and right in turns. How could Xiang's delicate skin stand such a beating? Only some ten slaps left Xiang's face torn and swollen. Blood was oozing out from her mouth. Her head dropped down weakly.

Rong stopped the runners and asked Xiang coldly, "Are you going to confess your crimes?"

Xiang took a deep breath, spat out blood from her mouth and closed her eyes without saying a word. Rong asked again, "Yes or no?"

Xiang couldn't speak anymore, but she gathered her strength to shake her head. Rong became more angry and shouted his order:

"Put the clamps on her!" No sooner the runners put the torture instrument on Xiang's fingers than he shouted impatiently, "Pull, pull, pull hard!" Xiang felt her ten fingers were tightly clamped up and then a fierce pain electrified her whole body. Immediately sweat poured out from her face and sparks flew before her eyes. She let out a heart-rending scream and fainted.

Rong asked the runners to wake her with cold water. After seeing Xiang let out a painful breath and her body twitch, Rong realized that the torture was too much for her. She could barely regain consciousness after it. So he signaled the runners to take the clamps off. He asked Xiang once again, "Are you going to confess or not?"

Xiang felt her cheeks hurt as if they had been burnt.

The pain in her fingers also pierced into her very heart. She didn't even dare to move her hands a little bit. She uttered vaguely and with difficulty, "I'm... wr...onged, wr...ronged..." Rong waved his hand and wanted to order further torture. Xiang was terrified. She said hastily, "I lived with my daughter-in-law. We supported each other to survive. If I had committed adultery, I couldn't have hidden it from her. Your Honor, please bring Zhou here and ask her. Then everything will be clear."

Rong let out a grin and said, "You think Zhou will help you out of this? Summon Zhou to court for testimony." Hearing this, hope sprang up in Xiang's heart. She had treated Zhou like her own daughter and they got along well with each other. She thought as soon as her daughter-in-law appeared in the courtroom, all the injustices against her would be cleared up.

After a while, several runners escorted Zhou into the court. When Zhou had been at the Ju's, she seldom went out of the house. Therefore she had no knowledge of the larger society. When she saw all the fierce-looking yamen runners around, she started shaking with fear. Then she saw Xiang curled on the floor, her hair disheveled and her face stained with blood, and she shuddered even more severely in terror. The only thing she did was to beg for mercy from the judge with her shaking voice.

Rong said sternly, "Zhou, don't be nervous. Answer my questions. Did your mother-in-law, Xiang, ever commit adultery?"

Zhou was almost scared to death. She could not wait to finish all this and get out of here. When she heard the inquiry from the judge, she did not spare a second to think before she answered as she had been told by Chen

Laolun: "Yes, she did…"

The words created a disturbance in the courtroom. Xiang heard the words clearly, too. But she could hardly believe her ears! She lifted up the hair in front of her eyes and fixed her eyes on Zhou steadily, her eyes full of shock and doubt. Zhou was terrified by her appearance and more by her eyes. She let out a scream and wanted to escape. But two yamen runners stopped her and pushed her on to the floor. Since Rong's goal was achieved, his voice became soft and slow. He said to Xiang in a haughty tone, "Now Zhou has testified against you. What then is your alibi to deny your guilt?"

Gradually, the situation dawned on Xiang. She understood very well that she would suffer all the punishments and probably die from them if she were to insist any longer. But if she confessed, the worst result was also death—but she could avoid more torture. At first, her heart burst with hatred for Zhou. She had never expected she would offer false thought against her. But then, she thought maybe she had been given no choice at all. After she thought through all this, she considered it better to be executed by guillotine than go through the punishments. Therefore, she decided to give up. She gave Zhou a hard and sad glance then said with great grief, "I confess…" She fainted before she finished her words.

The next day, an announcement of the results of the case, signed by Magistrate Rong Yutian, was put up at the city gate. It was written that the murder case of Seven-ravine Bridge had been cleared. The immoral woman Xiang had seduced Jin the Sixth and murdered her own husband and son. She had committed the serious crime of killing two people and was sentenced to be put to death by dismemberment. Jin the Sixth, the intrigant and the accessory offender, was sentenced to life imprisonment. When the spread, the whole region was stirred up. Some gave high praise for Rong's great speed in cracking the case; some were shocked by Xiang's atrocities; but others had doubts about the case because Jin the Sixth, the actual killer, was not sentenced to death.

When the news got to Seven-Ravine Bridge, all the villagers were filled with indignation. None of them believed that kind and tender Xiang could have murdered her own husband and son. Some brave and righteous ones even called upon the villagers to go to the yamen to reason with Rong. The villagers gathered at the Ju house and discussed how to defend Xiang. Someone suggested informing her maternal brother to protest the injustice. They all agreed with the idea. They quickly selected two venerable elders to go to the Xiang family to discuss the strategy.

Xiang's mother's home was a beautiful place not far from Seven-Ravine Bridge. Her little brother, Xiang Ji'an was an honest and unassuming man. He had been working on his land almost all his life. Sister and brother kept in regular contact. Almost every month, Ji'an would send his nineteen-year-old daughter to see his sister. Xiang also spent a few days at her mother's every year. Each time when they got together, they always had a lot to talk about. When tragedy had first befallen Xiang, Ji'an had gone to her home several times to persuade his sister to move back to her mother's, but Xiang had refused. On one hand, Xiang did not want to leave her daughter-in-law behind alone. On the other hand, she had made up her mind to press the officials to catch the killer. She did not want to have her brother involved in her trouble. Therefore, she had kept on living at Seven-ravine Bridge. When Xiang Ji'an learned Xiang had just been thrown into jail, he became extremely anxious and worried. But he was weak in character and tenderhearted by nature. He had never won an argument before, let alone debated in a court trial. He had no idea what he could do. Just as he was feeling at such loss, the two venerable old men arrived.

Xiang Ji'an expressed his appreciation and invited them into the sitting room. He could not hold back his grief and almost sobbed out lord. The two men tried to console him with kind words. Then they honestly described the feelings of the villagers at Seven-Ravine Bridge. At the end, they asked Ji'an tactfully what his plan was. But Xiang Ji'an only repeatedly be moaned the injustice done his sister and had no idea what to do. Seeing that Ji'an had no definite views of his own, they helped him analyze the case. They told him there was no material evidence. And the witnesses were not exactly dependable, either. They encouraged him to bring the lawsuit to the prefectural yamen.

Ji'an looked uncomfortable. "Certainly I will go to protest the injustice done my sister. But I haven't seen much of the world. And I've never gone through anything like this. I'm only afraid that, even with the justice on my side, I will not be able to make it clear to the prefectural yamen. Everything will then be messed up."

The old men knew very well that it was not an easy thing to reverse former verdict. The Prefectural Magistrate and the Surveillance Commissioner, maybe even the Provincial Governor and the Viceroy would have to be disturbed. Why let Xiang Ji'an lodge such a serious complaint when there was no hope of winning? But such a suit could only be pursued by a relative of Xiang's. They were all at a loss.

While they were sighing over the dilemma, a girl's voice spoke up from the inner room: "How can we stand such a great injustice? I'll go on my dad's behalf to complain over my aunt's injustice." Before the words were finished, the curtain was pushed aside and a beautiful girl walked out. She was tall and slender, and had a pretty face and a fine complexion, but most attractive were her eyes which were so clear, shining with an intelligent and courageous light. The two men were surprised. They exchanged glances and turned to Ji'an.

Xiang Ji'an hurried to make introductions: "This is my daughter—Xiang Juhua. She is nineteen years old. She was brought up in the village and is not familiar with many customs and rules. Please excuse her."

Before Ji'an had finished his words, Juhua continued: "The injustice suffered by my aunt was entirely caused by the Subprefectural Magistrate. There's only one way to clear it up—go to the higher court. People always say 'officials shelter each other.' We might be rejected by the Prefectural Magistrate. But we won't give up. We'll go to the provincial capital to the Provincial Administration Commissioners yamen and the Provincial Governor's yamen. If we are rejected again, we'll go to the capital city and bring the case to the Censorate. My aunt has treated me like her own daughter. I don't deserve the love she gave me all these years if I don't cry out justice for her. Trust me, Elder uncles, I'll never quit even until the case is brought to the Emperor."

"Great!" The elders could not help praising her.

They had no idea that Xiang Ji'an had such a bright, bold and strong daughter. Next, they instructed her on all the matters she should be aware of and to be careful on the journey. They also wrote a plaint for her. At last, before they went back home, they insisted on leaving thirty taels of silver which had been contributed by the villagers.

To the east of Hezhou was Fishing Mountain, atop of which was a Fishing, Castle built in the Southern Song Dynasty. It had won much fame in the Sichuan area. At this time spring had already come, and the trees on Fishing Mountain were bursting into green and flourishing.

One day, around 10 o'clock in the morning, a fleet of splendid ships cave sailing downstream, under the guidance of four tiger head warships. When they came to Fishing Mountain, they all slowed down and the most luxurious official ship was the first the moor dock at the pier. Then a canopy embroidered with a green dragon was opened immediately on the deck. Attended by a crowd of well-dressed officials, a middle-aged official strode on to the shore. He wore a mandarin jacket and on his head two sparking peacock feathers. As soon as he stepped ashore, the tidily lined-up soldiers of the famous Eight Banners greeted him with loud voices, "Salute to the Excellency Viceroy!" The official nodded modestly while waving his hand to them. He was Huang Zonghan, the Viceroy of Sichuan Province, who had taken over the post not long before.

Since the day he had arrived at his office in Sichuan, Huang Zonghan had been engaged in official affairs and seldom spent any time touring around. Even today, he did not come particularly for viewing historical sites. He had heard that Fishing Castle located at the junction of

Jialin and Fu jiang rivers was one of the most important fortifications in Sichuan. In the Southern Song Dynasty, General Wang Jian had fought against the Yuan troops here for thirty-six years. Huang was a thoughtful man. He had found that the current government was deteriorating quickly. Some powerful foreign countries had been for a long time greedily eyeing China's fertile lands. War was imminent. If war broke out, Sichuan itself could feed half of China's population. But how to protect Sichuan from war? He had been thinking of strategies for a long time. Today, the particular purpose for which he had traveled here from Chengdu was to have a geographical survey of Fishing Castle done.

When he made plans for the visit, he did not want the local officials to be disturbed. He only had informed the Chongqing Prefectural Magistrate. But he had not expected that the Chongqing Prefectural Magistrate would report his trip to the Provincial Governor of Sichuan. How could the Provincial Governor ignore his visit? He had the Provincial Administration and Provincial Surveillance Commissions informed. The whole of Sichuan Province was stirred up. The Provincial Surveillance Commissioner came to Fishing Castle in person to arrange security measures. The Provincial Governor and the Provincial Surveillance Commissioner hurried to Chongqing to greet the Viceroy. Huang Zonghan found it both amusing and annoying and did not know whether to laugh or to cry. He managed to persuade some of the officials to go back. But the Surveillance Commissioner ordered by the Governor to stay and accompany the Viceroy because he was the official in charge of security and criminal cases. Also the Magistrate of Chongqing Prefecture and the

Magistrate of Hezhou Subprefecture accompanied him to the destination. But on Huang Zonghan's side, he only had his aide, Li Yanggu with him.

It was only about half a kilometer from the pier of the Jialin River to Fishing Mountain. But it took them about two hours to get there because the path was very steep and dangerous. Huang watched the road carefully. He found it truly an ideal fortification. So long as the shabby gun emplacements were repaired, one man could hold ten thousand enemy soldiers at bay here.

While they were carefully walking, a woman's miserable cry of injustice reached Huang's ears. It was so mournful and so loud. They all stopped in astonishment. The most nervous and irritated one among the officials was Rong Yutian, the Magistrate of Hezhou. He thought to himself, "All the entrances at the foot of the mountain were safely guarded and there was one guard every five meters. How could the woman sneak over to the very path which the Viceroy would pass?"

Still surprised, the soldier who was leading the way started to whip the girl kneeling on the ground. No doubt the soldier had been prompted by someone. The girl let out a heart-rending cry. Rong reckoned that whoever the girl was, she would definitely run away. But what in fact happened was completely beyond his imagination—the girl would rather receive such a vicious whipping than move her body an inch. When Rong caught sight of the girl's face, he almost cried out. No one recognized the girl better than him. It was nobody but Juhua, the girl who had been running from Chongqing to Chengdu to prosecute him, and would never give up, not even if she were driven out of every yamen.

The memory was still so fresh in Rong's mind how highly Prefectural Surveillance Commissioner of Chongqing and the Provincial Surveillance Commissioner Sichuan praised him when he had sentenced Xiang last year. But suddenly at the Congqing yamen there was a girl complaining over the injustice done her aunt. To keep his rank, Rong had bribed the Prefectural Magistrate with one thousand taels of silver and then the girl from the Xiang family was beaten out of the yamen. Before long, an official notice was sent to him from the Surve Hance Commissioner of Sichuan, saying that Juhua had walked several hundred kilometers to Chengdu to hand her plaint to the Provincial Surveillance Commissioner yamen. Rong had no choice but to send the Provincial Surveillance Commissioner three thousand taels of silver to stop the girl from prosecuting. Juhua was detained for ten days and escorted back to Hezhou. Rong Yutian had ordered a close watch to be kept on the girl to prevent her from lodging her complaint again. But who would have expected that the girl would manage to run to the yamen to make the charge. Fortunately, Provincial Administration Commissioner and the Provincial Surveillance Commissioner were relatives by marriage. He had Juhua beaten with a bamboo stick and driven out. From that point on the troublesome girl had disappeared. He had sent people out looking for her for more than one month. But they just had not been able to find her. But today, she had evaded the guards and managed to run directly to the Viceroy to accuse him. If the inside story were to be discovered by the Viceroy, Rong would be dismissed from his official post forever.

When Rong thought of this, he became filled with

hatred and anger. Before any of the other officials could react, he had already given his order: "Pull the shrew down the mountain and punish her severely!"

When the guards answered "yes" and were about to seize her, they heard the Viceroy shout: "Hold on!" They all stopped right away and knelt on the ground, waiting for his further directions. Huang did not say anything to them but walked to the girl who had been beaten by the soldiers and looked at her carefully.

Juhua's appearance had changed a lot. Maybe an acquaintance would not have been able to recognize her at this moment. She had been traveling for several months to protest the injustice that had befallen her aunt. However, every time she had handed over the plaint to the yamen of different levels, she was whipped and beaten by the yamen runners and driven out. She had never heard any sympathetic words from any official. Whip scars were all over her face. The formerly lovely face had become so thin. The only thing left unchanged were her bright piercing eyes. She knelt beside the path. Her clothes had been torn by the whip. Layers of fresh and old scars could be seen on her arms. Huang had noticed that though she was being whipped by the soldiers, her arms were held tightly in front of her chest. Now he found she was holding several pieces of paper with curling edges. "It must be the plaint," Huang thought to himself.

He bent down to her and said kindly, "Don't be scared! What's the injustice? You can tell me now. I'll support you." Juhua looked up and realized this was a high-ranking official. His yellow mandarin jacket, the peacock feathers and his dignified manner all showed his extraordinary status. When she saw the canopy was

embroidered with green dragons and the officials beside him all holding their breath, she immediately knew this man was nobody else but the Viceroy of Sichuan Province. He was the person who could shake the whole of Sichuan by stamping his foot. After months of complaining, Juhua had gained more experience, courage and wisdom. She was not even a bit nervous before the Viceroy. She succinctly, confidently and unhurriedly, described the background of the case. Then she held the plaint high above her head with both hands. Huang took it, had a quick look at it and then handed it to Lu Dao'en, the Provincial Surveillance Commissioner, "Try the case and report the result to me in ten days!" After this, he told Li Yanggu to give the girl two strings of cash. "Now, you'd better go home and await the result. Don't run around any longer!"

Then he said to the Prefectural Magistrate of Chongqing and Rong Yutian, "Don't make things difficult for her. Wait until every thing is cleared up." Finishing these words, he waved to the guards to bypass the girl and proceeded on toward Fishing Castle.

Two months later, Huang Zonghan had forgotten everything about the plaint he had encountered on the road to Fishing Castle. It being the first time he was governing the border province of Sichuan, he had sensed the hidden difficulties in handling the province. The officials at different levels were all like fired ovens with high flames—you could feel the warmth from them, but you could never get too close to them. Some of them, such as the officials of prefectures and counties, were always obedient in appearance, but opposing in private. They always spoke highly of the decrees that he launched, but none of them put them into action. In such a big province, he could not find even one official he could trust. The only one he could open his heart to was his aide Li Yanggu who he always had with him. With all these thoughts on his mind, Huang Zonghan could find no way to relieve his mounting frustration. One day, some famous scholars held a party at the River Viewing Tower. They insisted on inviting Huang Zonghan to join them. Considering it was a good thing anyway and he could not let these celebrities down, Huang reluctantly went. Unexpectedly, he was greatly moved by the atmosphere when several young poets expressed their sentiments with their poems. His increased interest in the party made him drink heartily. Time passed quickly before he realized it. He did not leave for his mansion until it was already nightfall.

As long as the Viceroy's sedan chair was on the street, the guards who struck gongs would warn the people on the street and drive them into their yards so that the sedan chair would get to the Viceroy's mansion without hindrance. Huang sat in the sedan chair, eyes slightly closed. He was a little tipsy and almost fell asleep. Suddenly, he felt the sedan chair stopped with a shake. Before he could make an inquiry, a sad and touching woman's cry complaining of injustice reached his ears. The voice was so sad, so shrill and somewhat familiar to Huang. But he could not recall where and when he had heard the voice. At this moment, Huang heard the lead guards whipping the woman, as she let out moans of pain. Huang's heart shrank. He pushed aside the curtain and looked out. He saw a girl kneeling in the middle of the street, on her pretty face appeared several reddish scars of the whip. Even so, she was reluctant to give way.

"Isn't she the girl named who I encountered on the

way to Fishing Castle!" Huang recognized her all of a sudden. "Stop!" cried Huang. The guard was a bit frightened by his voice and looked at him nervously. Huang ordered the complainant brought to his sedan chair for an inquiry.

But Juhua refused to move her body one bit. She just kept murmuring, "Your Honor, please help me find justice!"

Huang asked her, "Xiang Juhua, last time you stopped me at Fishing Mountain and asked me to clear your case. I've transmitted it to the Provincial Surveillance Commissioner. Today, you stopped me again to complain of injustice. Do you intend to get another two strings of cash?"

Tears covered Juhua's face. She sobbed and answered miserably, "My aunt is suffering a great injustice. There isn't even one official in Sichuan willing to uphold righteousness and justice for the Imperial Court. I have no choice but to take the chance of stopping Your Highness, sedan again. How would I dare to disturb Your Highness for strings of cash?"

"You said there was not even one person upholding justice in the whole province? Did the Provincial Surveillance Commissioner's yamen play favoritism and commit irregularities?"

"I dare not criticize the government. But my aunt has been wronged and the Provincial Surveillance Commissioner and the prefectural and subprefectural magistrates together put pressure? Use force on me and forbade me to indict. The only result of Your Honor transmitting the case to the Provincial Surveillance Commissioner was to bring me another cruel beating," Juhua said, her voice full of hatred.

At this point, Huang Zonghan noticed whip scars all over the girl's face. Her clothes were in rags and stained with blood. He felt so sorry for the girl. He thought to himself that if there had not been a great injustice done to the girl's aunt, this teenaged girl would not have ignored all risks and stopped him twice to cry for justice. Privately he blamed himself for not asking the Provincial Surveillance Commissioner about the progress of the investigation. He felt the excuse that he had too many official affairs to deal with could not exonerate him from blame. He immediately called the *qi pai guan*(officer with a bannered warrant) to him and gave him a command arrow and said, "You take my command arrow and the girl to the Provincial Surveillance Commissioner's yamen. I order Lu Dao'en to crack the case in a limited period. If no clear conclusion is obtained this time again, I'll definitely write to the Emperor to dismiss the official!" The official accepted the order and went to the Provincial Surveillance Commissioner's yamen with Juhua.

A myriad of thoughts crowded into Huang Zonghan's mind. He was wondering how the legal system in Sichuan Province had deteriorated to such a terrible state. Suddenly an idea hit him: "Maybe the current tendencies in society can be corrected by clearing the injustice in Juhua's case. At least, I can get rid of the group of corrupt officials who were directly involved in the case. However, it's not an easy thing to clear the case. From the subprefecture to the prefecture, and from the prefecture to the province, the case has already involved officials of different levels. If the behind-the-scenes facts can't be discovered, there will be no hope to clear things up and reverse the former judgment..." Huang

Zonghan thought it over and over and made up his mind to clear the case no matter what was hidden behind it. "I'll take this case as an example for all officials and for the whole of Sichuan Province." When he thought further about the strategies for pursuing the case, he found that he had no one except his aide Li Yanggu to share his ideas with.

Therefore, he did not stop a minute to rest after he returned to the yamen. He asked for Li Yanggu to come see him immediately. When Li arrived, he told him that he had been stopped for the second time by Juhua with complaint about officials. He also told Li what was on his mind. Then he told Li sternly: "Clearing this case will be the foundation for rectifying the working style of the yamens in the whole of Sichuan Province. I'm going to entrust you with the matter. Please don't refuse."

Li Yanggu used to be a magistrate of a county. He was very familiar with the hardships of the common people as well as the inner workings of how the yamens dealt with cases. He had a lot of experience investigating strange cases. From the introduction given by the Viceroy and from his tone, he had sensed the difficulties in clearing up this case, But he did not refuse. He was born with an honest and upright character. He was always ready to uphold righteousness and justice. "Your Excellency is entrusting me with such an important task. I will devote myself to it so as to thank you for understanding and trusting me. However, it will not be easy to pursue the case. It might take quite some time. Please allow me to go out and do the investigation in civilian dress. It'll be easier and quicker to find the truth in this way." Huang Zonghan gave his consent right away. Then Li Yanggu approached to the Viceroy and whispered a few words in his ear. Huang nodded his agreement and appreciation. He then asked Li Yanggu to proceed with his plan.

That very evening, four sedan chairs came out from the Jiceroy's yamen in succession and headed separately in the four directions of east, west, south and north. In front of each sedan chair, there was a servant-boy holding a lantern to lead the way. On each of the lantern was written "LI." The sedan-chair carriers walked very fast. It seemed that they were all in a great hurry and had some important things to do. The strange thing was, each time after a sedan chair left the gate, about half a kilometer away, there was also a pedlar who had been doing business near the Viceroy's yamen following. The sedan chairs did not stop for a second after learing the yamen. They were carried around the streets of Chengdu for a long time and finally all came to an isolated, simple yard near Qingyang Palace. They stopped there and when the carriers pushed open the curtains of the sedan chairs, the pedlars following were all dumbfounded. All the sedan chairs were empty!

These pedlars were all yamen runners sent by the Provincial Surveillance Commissioner's yamen. They were ordered to watch Li Yanggu closely and report all his actions to the Provincial Surveillance Commissioner. Li was circumspect and insightful. He had foreseen that the Provincial Surveillance Commissioner would become uneasy because the Viceroy had twice accepted Juhua's plaint. The Viceroy's inviting of Li Yanggu to his place at this particular time was clearly telling people that he would be entrusted to investigate the case. If the Provincial Surveillance Commissioner really had hidden something during the trial, he would definitely take precautions against Li Yanggu. And he would probably send people to secretly keep a close eye on him. In order to avoid the spies, Li Yanggu had played this trick to decoy these people away. While the empty sedan chairs were turning about in the center of Chengdu, Li Yanggu had disguised himself as an old servant and come out of the back gate of the Viceroy's yamen and left the city unencumbered.

After Huang Zonghan had sent Li Yanggu away on his task, he felt more lonely. For the next several days, he could not even calm down enough deal with official affairs. Each time when he thought of the serious situations where officials in the province had acted in collusion and been involved in illegal transactions, he felt very disheartened.

One day, he was informed by the Imperial Court that He Shaoji, one of his former colleagues, had been designated the Director of the Education Commission in Sichuan and had just arrived at Chengdu. Huang Zonghan was very glad. He decided to visit his old colleague. Unfortunately, upon arriving at his place, he was told He Shaoji was not in. He had been invited by the Governor to visit Emei Mountain. Huang had come on an impulse only to be disappointed. It was then nine o'clock. Huang Zonghan dejectedly told the yamen runners to go back to his mansion. On the way back, they did not take the same route by which they had come. They took another route instead, which happened to pass by the Provincial Surveillance Commissioner's yamen. Huang Zonghan thought to himself, "The murder case in Hezhou has been in the hands of the Surveillance Commissioner's yamen for almost a week. How much progress have they made now? Why not drop in on the way and have a look?" So he told the runners to stop at the Chief Prosecutor's yamen.

The building of the Surveillance Commissioner's yamen was really grand. There was a large square in front of the outer gate, inside of which there was another square. The inner gate of the yamen was at the far end of the square. Looking into the yamen from the inner gate, some tiger-head saying "Avoidance" lined both sides of the courtroom, creating an awe-inspiring atmosphere. Today the yamen was open for court trials. In front of the outer gate there was a crowd of soldiers who guarded the yamen. They all looked angry and vicious. Passersby knew that the street in front of the Surveillance Commissioner's yamen was not an easy road to take. So they all took other roads to avoid passing by the yamen. Therefore, there was hardly a single person walking on such a broad street.

No sooner was Huang Zonghan's sedan chair placed on the ground than two malicious-looking bannered warrant officers came and shouted at them: "Where the hell are you from? How dare you stop at the Surveillance Commissioner's yamen?" Then Huang Zonghan realized that he had come out to visit his old friend in unofficial dress, without all his flags and ceremonial guards. There was no sign to indicate whose sedan chair it was. That was why the officers were so rude to them. Before he could lift the curtain and answer his question, one of the soldiers guarding the yamen, already impatient, gave the sedan chair a whip and threatened: "Get out of here quickly!"

He was only a guard of the Provincial Surveillance Commissioner's yamen! How dare he treat people like this? Huang was infuriated, and shouted loudly from the sedan chair: "How dare you take such liberties?"

The guard was a bit taken aback. Before he put forward his inquiry, two of the Viceroy's guards had already grasped his whip and roared at him: "How dare you! This is Viceroy here!"

The guards were all scared out of their wits. They immediately knelt down on the ground and did not dare to look up. Huang Zonghan walked out of the sedan chair, his face clouded dark with anger. He ordered his guards: "Put that soldier in custody and punish him severely!" Then he said to the guards kneeling on the ground, "You are overbearing and unbridled! It looks like you are used to doing this to common people. That is why you dared to treat me like this! Get away and wait for your punishment!" None of the guards was bold enough to utter a sound. They all backed off dejectedly.

Huang Zonghan tidied his attire and walked toward the gate with his hands folded behind, his eyebrows knotted. But unexpectedly, he was stopped by another guard before the gate. He gave the Viceroy a courteous salute and said, "Please wait a minute, Your Excellency!"

"Can't the Viceroy of the province enter a small yamen like this?" Huang retorted angrily.

The guard answered, "There is an important trial being held in the yamen at this moment. According to the law, officials of any level can be stopped here while a trial is proceeding. I'm just doing my duty! Please don't make things difficult for me, Your Excellency!"

Huang grew more incensed, and he raised his voice to ask further, "What important trial?"

"The murder case in Hezhou."

"Good! I came especially for this case! Get out of my way!" With these words, he impatiently pushed the guard aside and walked toward the inner gate of the yamen. The bannered warrant officers followed immediately and said to the guards around, "Get all unnecessary personnel out of the way. And no reporting of the Viceroy's arrival. The Viceroy only wants to listen to the trial." The guards dared not hinder them any further. They just watched as Huang Zonghan walk into the courtroom.

The courtroom was shrouded in an awe-inspiring atmosphere. The Provincial Surveillance Commissioner Lu Dao'en sat rigidly upright in the seat of honor. On both sides of the courtroom had been placed several official desks, at which were seated more than ten judicial officials. In the middle of the courtroom knelt an emaciated woman, her hair disheveled, bloodstains all over her face. She was nobody else but Juhua. From the wounds on her cheeks, it was not difficult to tell that she had been slapped more than once.

Lu Dao'en had heard the chaos outside the gate. But before he could send people to find out, Huang had walked into the courtroom with a stern face. He had not expected this. It made him very nervous. He stood up in a flurry to greet the Viceroy. Huang did not say a word, but gestured with his hand to go on with the trial. The gesture did not work as he had thought. All the officials in the room stood up and bowed down to greet him: "Salute the Viceroy!"

Huang answered coldly, "I told you to continue! Who asked you to stand up to greet me?" With this, he walked directly to the seat of honor. Lu Dao'en hastily offered his seat to him. But Huang held him back: "This is still your seat! Give me another chair!"

Lu Dao'en kept repeating that he did not dare to

take the seat. Huang became more impatient: "What the hell is all this mere courtesy about?" Then Lu Dao'en reluctantly sat down in his chair. Another chair had already been placed on the left side of Lu's seat by a close officer.

Huang seated himself in the chair and said, "Now you can continue with the trial!" All the judicial officials just looked at each other and did not know what to do. They all looked embarrassed. Huang Zonghan gave Lu Dao'en a nudge and urged, "Go ahead, Master. Lu!" Lu seemed to wake up and answered, "Yes, yes, continue..."

"Bang!" The sound of the warning mallet broke the uncomfortable atmosphere in the courtroom. A judge with a long beard and mustache pointed at Juhua and asked sternly, "Xiang Juhua, tell the court, is it not true that twice on the road you brought a false charge against the Magistrate of Hezhou?"

Juhua retorted in a strong voice with her head lifted high: "Every word of mine is true. Why do you say I have brought a false charge against him?"

Another judge immediately howled at Juhua: "The witness has solidly testified against Xiang for murdering her husband. And the case has been reviewed by the Chongqing yamen and then the Provincial Surveillance Commissioner's yamen. There were no suspicious points. But you, you complain on behalf of an immoral woman, and accuse all the yamens in the province. Isn't this a false accusation?"

Juhua wiped off the blood oozing out from the corner of her mouth and rebuked them: "The Hezhou yamen sentenced my aunt to death by dismemberment. But they don't have any material evidence. All the yamens made the judgment relying on the same witness' testimony. This is a case concerning a human life. How could the judgment be made in such a careless manner?"

Hardly had Juhua finished her words, than an ugly-looking judge with round eyes and thick brows shouted at her: "Nonsense! You are so young, but already so devious! I know there's someone behind you! Looks like you won't confess without undergoing severe torture. Pull her down and slap her with the stick twenty more times!" The yamen runners standing beside assented loudly and pulled Juhua some steps away and started to slap her on the face. Her cheeks, already torn by the slapping, took only one slap for the uncoagulated blood to be squeezed out and splatter from her face. The flesh of her cheeks became mangled and a portion of bloody gums was clearly visible. Juhua was moaning in pain, her whole body trembling hard. But she did not utter one word to call for mercy.

Huang was greatly impressed by her strength of character. He stretched out his hand to stop the runners who were about to carry out the torture. He glared at the judges sitting with great composure, and said with a gloomy countenance, "The girl walked hundreds of miles alone to protest an injustice. There might be something amiss. She's so weak and lonely! But you judges don't show any mercy for her or let her finish her words. Must you try all the severest tortures on this fragile girl to show your power and ability? Don't you ever think about what other people would say about you?"

The official who ordered Juhua punished answered self-confidently, "People in Sichuan are known to be unruly and crafty. The girl has been traveling between Chongqing and Chengdu several times to level

269

accusations against the Magistrate of Hezhou. Obviously, she is a shameless pettifogger. If we don't administer punishments, she will never admit her guilt!"

Huang Zonghan gave a cold smile and retorted scornfully, "If an unmarried girl of nineteen years old is already a pettifogger, isn't everyone in Sichuan a thief?"

Lu Dao'en immediately went along with Huang: "You're definitely correct, Your Excellency! We won't use any torture."

Huang said to Lu with no expression on his face, "Master. Lu, you're in charge of the criminal cases in the province. It's better for you to judge the case!"

Lu wiped the sweat off his forehead and replied, "Yes, Your Excellency!"

But he did not proceed with the trial, but looked at the officials on both sides of the room. It seemed that they already understood Lu, since no one had said anything since then. Some looked up at the ceiling, some were tidying their beards and mustaches while others had even closed their eyes to rest. The courtroom which had been very lively a few minutes ago, had now fallen into a dead silence. The trial atmosphere had cooled down extremely.

Huang did not say anything for quite a long time. He had figured out the essence of the case while quietly observing all the officials in the court. After about a quarter of an hour, nobody had still said anything. Huang Zonghan stood up and said slowly, "Looks like this is really a hard case! Why do you only interrogate the girl? Master. Lu, isn't Xiang's intrigant imprisoned here? Why not bring the witness to court to confront her? He will contradict all the false accusations of the girl, won't he?"

Lu Dao'en did not expect the Viceroy to make such a proposal. He blamed himself for lack of wisdom. He had to obey: "You're right, Your Excellency! Bring the intrigant to court!"

In no time at all, the intrigant was escorted to the courtroom by four strong yamen runners. Huang stared at him steadily from the time he walked into the courtroom. He found the so-called intrigant very strong. The husky man walked normally and his eyesight showed his avaricious, lecherous, frivolous and crude character. He looked in good health. It seemed he had been very well fed. The prison clothes that he was wearing were old but quite clean. Hardly any scars could be found on the visible parts of his body. If this was not in court and he was not escorted by guards, no one would believe that he was a prisoner who had been in jail for more than half a year!

Huang could not keep down his rising anger, he asked in a stern voice, "Are you the rogue who committed adultery with Xiang?"

The fellow answered with a nonchalant giggle, "Yes, I am!"

Huang Zonghan shouted, "You killed two people and still act so rude! Looks like nobody told you how to be serious before! Runners, pull him out and cane him eighty strokes and then we start the interrogation!"

The yamen runners carried out the order and pulled the man to the entrance of the court and began to cane him heavily. After just one stroke, the so-called intrigant could not stand it. He howled like a butchered pig. Huang grew more infuriated and ordered the runners to beat him more severely. The fellow shouted hoarsely, "You guys are cheating me! You told me that you'd never

271

torture me. Why are you beating me like this today?"

Hearing this, the Surveillance Commissioner Lu became extremely incensed, and howled at him: "Nonsense, beat him to death!"

But Huang Zonghan waved at them to stop the beating and asked solemnly, "Who told you that you wouldn't suffer any tortures? What deal did you make in the prison? Tell the truth, otherwise..." Now the intrigant sensed the changed atmosphere in the court today. He looked up at Lu Dao'en for help, but found Lu had dropped his head low. He would not get any help from him.

Huang saw the husky fellow looking around at random, and knew that he had lost his bearings. He shouted again at him severely: "Beat the rogue, severely!" The torture runners wanted to cater to the Governor, and lifted up the canes boards high and gave him two hard whacks with the edges. The fellow's head cracked open and blood oozed out and streamed down his face. Though the guy looked strong, he was not strong willed. The beatings had frightenened him out of his wits. He kept on asking for mercy: "I confess, I confess, I confess everything!"

Huang stopped the runners and continued his questioning: "How did you end up in the Hezhou jail?"

The intrigant panted heavily and answered docilely, "I'm fond of women and I was attracted by a girl in our village. So one day I climbed into her room at night and raped her. But who was to know that the girl would be so ashamed and stubborn that she hanged herself on the beam the following day. Then the yamen of Hezhou arrested me and was going to sentence me to death. But one day, a secretary with the surname Chen came to my

272

cell and asked me to confess to I committing adultery with Xiang of Seven-Ravine Bridge. He promised me that after I confronted the accused in court, my death penalty would be commuted and I could spend the rest of my life comfortably in the prison. He also promised that so long as I did as he told me to, I would never suffer tortures in court. I wanted nothing but to live, so I accepted. After the trial in Hezhou, I was really treated very well and I have never been beaten since then. But who knows why they changed their minds today. It hurts so much..."

All the people in court were struck dumb by his words! Huang Zonghan looked around the courtroom with a smile. Finally his sharp eyes rested on Lu Dao'en: "Master. Lu, do you have anything to say?" Lu was so embarrassed that he turned all red. Sweat streamed down his cheeks. He prevaricated, "Isn't it strange that the courts at all levels concluded the same foolish verdict on this case? It's funny...!" He let out a dry laugh in embarrassment.

But before his laughter had died away, an official from the jury stood up and said to the Viceroy after giving him a deep salute, "I really admire Your Honor's wisdom in judging the case. But the case is not yet finished! If Xiang is not the murderer, then who is? Please explain to us, Your Honor!"

Huang answered back sarcastically, "So, is it your meaning that so long as the real murderer is not captured, the wrong judgment against Xiang should not be overturned then? And Xiang Juhua's charge against the yamen is still a false accusation what's more, the so-called should intrigant be well treated in the jail and allowed to enjoy life?"

The official answered, "Since the murderer is still on the run, it's too early to correct her injustice. Investigations should be conducted. Only after the real situation is clarified, can we know if the accusations brought by Xiang Juhua are true and if the testimony given by Jin the Six is solid."

Huang found he had no sound reasons to dispute him. He had to order that Xiang, Juhua and Jin the Six all be put under close watch in prison. He would not reconvene the trial again until the murderer was caught. He repeatedly warned Lu to treat Juhua fairly: "She is alone and so fragile, but she had suffered so many tortures. You can't administer any more punishment. You shall also keep a careful eye on Chen Laolun and Rong Yutian in case they conspire to make a false confession."

Huang felt today's court trial was not to his heart's satisfaction. The murderer had not been caught and there was not enough evidence. He could do nothing more than this. He was anxious to know the progress of Li Yanggu's investigation. He thought to himself, "Li Yanggu, Li Yanggu, it all depends on you to clear the case, capture the criminal and clean up discipline in Sichuan!"

There were two routes that connected Chengdu and Chongqing. The land route was quite mountainous, and the water route contained many dangerous rapids. Therefore, most people preferred to go by land, though it was quite zigzagging and a little further than by water. But Li Yanggu chose the latter. On the one hand, it took less time; on the other hand, he could evade the spying of the local government so that his investigation would not disturbed. Now he was fully dressed like a merchant.

There were two attendants accompanying him. One was Li Yi, an old servant who had been with him for years; the other was a guard of the Viceroy, who was proficient in Chinese Kungfu. They were travelling with the wind and the boat sailed down the river very smoothly. Li Yanggu was a very careful man. When they berthed the boat at night, they always found a place with few boats. Seldom did they go ashore except to buy necessary food and spirits. So their simple boat did not catch many eyes.

The view along the river was always beautiful. But Li Yanggu never stood out on the deck for a minute to enjoy the scenery. In this way, the small boat sailed along the river quickly for half a month and finally reached the dock of Chongqing quietly.

Li Yanggu exhorted the two attendants to stay away from any trouble in Chongqing. He asked them to observe more and speak less. Everything had to abide by his plan. When he finished his talk, Li Yanggu walked out of the cabin and strode on to the dock.

The dock was really crowded and noisy. There were passengers, porters, sailors, as well as people who had come to meet friends and relatives or to see them off, and also pedlars who hawked bamboo mattresses, baskets, fresh fruits and Li Yanggu elbowed his way through the crowds and walked to the entrance of the dock. But suddenly, he heard the clamor of voices and found people shrinking back on the sides of the road. When he looked up, he saw some runners driving people back with sticks. Following them was a steward, who was holding an invitation card of a splendid red. They were heading toward the dock in a great hurry.

Li Yanggu thought to himself: "They must have come from the Chongqing yamen to meet someone. I'd better hide away." So he signaled his men with his eyes and they hid quietly in the crowd. However, it seemed that the steward was deliberately making things difficult for them. He walked straight to the place where they were hiding. Li Yanggu was very surprised when the man stood right before him and said to him with a smile, "Lord Li, our Prefectural Magistrate asked me to meet you here especially. Why are you so late, Lord Li?"

These words were totally beyond Li Yanggu's expectations. He was shocked and replied hastily, "My last name is Wu, Master. I'm a merchant passing by. I don't have much to do with the government. Why do you call me 'Lord Li'?"

The steward was still smiling at him: "Beard Li, Lord Li, is there anyone who doesn't know about your beard? Though it's the first time I've met you, I've heard so much about you. This time you have been ordered by the Viceroy to investigate the Hezhou murder case. And the Chongqing yamen has been expecting you. But it's not a matter you can finish up in a day. Why don't you stay at our yamen so that our Magistrate can express to you the hospitality of a host and offer all the help you need?"

Li Yanggu touched his thick beard subconsciously and secretly blamed himself for his carelessness. But he managed to calm. He gave him a smile and answered, "You really have a sharp eye, Steward! I am Li Yanggu. But this time I have come to Chongqing just to collect some personal debts. That's why I did't dare give you my real name. As for the case you mentioned about the murder in Hezhou, I don't know much about it and I'm not going to put my hand into it. Please thank the Magistrate for me and please tell him that I am not traveling as a county magistrate at this point and dare not disturb him. I'll go and visit him at some later time when I am free." With these words, he saluted the steward farewell, and said to his attendants, "Let's go!"

However, the steward just would not take no for an answer. He half bent his knees and begged him earnestly, "I was ordered by the Magistrate to invite you back to the yamen. If you passed here without stopping by for a while, the Magistrate would definitely scold me for my incompetence. How am I supposed to answer the Magistrate? Besides, our Magistrate has admired you for a long time. He has some dishes and spirits prepared for you. How could you let him down, Lord Li?"

Li Yanggu shook his head and answered, "I've said I'm not going! You just give him the reply and thank him for me."

The steward knelt down on the ground and would not get up. He turned to the accompanying soldiers and pursed his lips as a signal. The soldiers got the hint and out of nowhere quickly led three horses to them. The steward took reins over and said to them courteously, "Your horses are ready, please do me the honor!" Then he stood up modestly and prepared to support them to get on the horses.

Li Yanggu was taken by surprise. "How strange!" he thought to himself. "We managed to leave Chengdu so quietly. But how could they know even about the exact number of people in our group? It looks like we've been making every move right before their eyes all these days! Now a private investigation seems impossible! Since the situation has changed, why don't I meet the Magistrate in the Chongqing yamen? I'll see what kind of person he is and what kind of tricks he is up to!" Thinking of this, he did not refuse any longer. He folded his hands in the front to thank the steward, "It's really our pleasure to be invited by the Magistrate. It's impolite to refuse such kindness. We'll go with you!" The steward was very happy. He supported Li Yanggu to climb on the horse and their group headed for the yamen of the Chongqing Prefecture.

Du Guangyuan, the Magistrate of Chongqing Prefecture was already waiting at the gate of the yamen. It seemed that he had known Li Yanggu would come for sure. When Li's horse drew near, he quickly approached him in a modest manner and gave him a deep bow, "It's my pleasure to have Your Excellency visit our prefecture! And it's my honor to meet you, Your Excellency."

Li Yanggu got off the horse and was going to salute him in a manner of a junior greeting a senior, but he was stopped by Du Guangyuan. Du stretched his hands out to help him up. Then he made use of the opportunity to hold Li's hand and walked him into the sitting room.

At the night, it was arranged for Li Yanggu to stay at the guest house, place where all the servants were also very polite to him. Just after the first watch, Li made an excuse that he was exhausted by the whole day's boat journey and returned to his room. But he lay in bed sleeplessly, so many worries and so many questions on his mind. He thought over and over again what had happened that day and just could not figure out how the Chongqing yamen had got to know so thoroughly about their actions. He was also wondering about Du Guangyuan's real purpose in treating him as an honored guest. He recalled every moment and every word Du had said when they were together. He found that Du did not mention the murder case except to say that the Chongqing Prefecture had already known the purpose of their trip. And Du kept on telling him about the natural beauty around Chongqing and recommended he stay longer and visit all the scenic spots. What was behind all this?

Suddenly, Li Yanggu realized that they were playing for time, so that they could cover up things in Hezhou. When he reached there, all the loopholes would be patched over and everything would look perfect! Li Yanggu became more worried and decided that he had to leave for Hezhou the following morning no matter what tricks were in store. The earlier he arrived at Hezhou, the less time they would have to hide the evidence.

The following morning, no matter how Du Guangyuan urged him to stay, Li Yanggu insisted on leaving right away. Du Guangyuan understood that he had made up his mind, so he said, "Now that you've decided to leave, it's really impolite to ask you to stay. But some well-known figures in Chongqing have long admired you, and organized a banquet for you at Loquat Mountain. I felt it difficult to refuse such kindness, so I accepted the invitation for you. So, please don't let them down. I'll have your luggage readied tonight so you can leave early tomorrow morning. Is that alright?" Li Yanggu had no choice but to reluctantly accept the invitation. But he told Du Guangyuan repeatedly that he would definitely leave the following morning. Then Du saw Li Yanggu off at the gate of the yamen.

As soon as Li Yanggu returned to his room, he started to reckon the different situations that he might encounter at the dinner table. He believed that banquets with special significance often held lots of danger. But now that it had gone this far, if he was not present at the dinner, they might take it as an excuse to force him to stay for some more days. If so, more time would be wasted and things could become more difficult. "So I'll go if, I must! But I've got to be very careful!" Li told himself. With the decision made, Li Yanggu relaxed. He felt a bit tired and sleepy, so he let himself take a nap. It was a quite long nap. When he awoke, dusk had fallen. The sedan chair sent by Du Guangyuan was already waiting at the gate. Li Yanggu had a quick wash, then told the attendants to wait at the guest house. He told them that if he still didn't show up by the second watch, they should hurry back to Chengdu to get back-up. But until then, they should remain calm, or at least pretend to be. Finishing these words, Li Yanggu left with the sedan chair, uncertain about the coming evening at Loquat Mountain.

It was early summer on the fifteenth day of the fifth lunar month. Trees flourished and flowers were already bursting into luxuriant colors. A half-moon hung in the sky, surrounded by luminous sunset clouds. It was not so common to see such a wonderful moon in Chongqing, a mountainous city. Just as Li's sedan chair was being set on the ground slowly and carefully, Du Guangyuan and several impressive-looking scholars came to greet him. Among the group, there were old men whose hair had completely turned white, along with youngsters about 20 years old. They all looked well educated and behaved very decently. Du warmly introduced each person to Li Yanggu. Li made a deep bow and said: "Yanggu came to Chongqing by chance and had the honor to be invited by you. It's a real pleasure to get together with you all and listen to your advice!" The notables paid their respects in turn with greeting and clustered round Li Yanggu on the way to the dining table. Fourth-rank Magistrate Du began to look like a foil.

Li Yanggu remained in a state of high tension after meeting the notables. He was wondering what kind of dangers were hiding behind the warm and harmonious atmosphere, but he appeared relaxed and joyful. Now and then, he responded to the entreaties to drink a cup or two or said some humorous words which elicited hearty laughter from all the people around the table.

After drinking three rounds, Li Yanggu stood up and addressed the others with his hands folded in front: "I've drunk too much, and I'm leaving tomorrow morning, so please excuse me. I must go now."

The notables were not ready for this. They exchanged glances and then tried to urge him to stay: "It's a rare chance for us to get together with you, Lord Li. And there are many things that we haven't exchanged ideas on. Why not stay a bit longer?"

Du also stood up and said to him, "Seldom do we have such a beautiful moon like tonight! It's not easy for us to gather together from all these different places. How can we part after such a short time? Come, I propose a toast to you!" With these words, he filled a big cup and offered it to Li Yanggu. But Li declined his toast politely, "I usually don't drink much, so please forgive me. If you haven't enjoyed yourselves enough, I'd like to stay longer. You can go on drinking to your hearts' content."

An old gentleman nodded his head in approval, "Now if Master. Li doesn't like to drink, we'd better not force him. The Sichuan dishes here are very famous throughout China. While we are drinking, Master. Li can help himself to some delicious Sichuan food."

Li Yanggu thanked him for his consideration. So he took some food, while singing poems and composing couplets. It was enjoyable. But it was very strange that none of them said anything about the murder case that had happened in Hezhou. And from the atmosphere, there was no sign of any conspiracy at all. "Did I wrong Magistrate Du?" Li Yanggu felt more and more puzzled.

As the evening drew on, the moon appeared even brighter and clearer. The gentlemen did not show any signs of tiredness. But Du Guangyuan proposed it was a good time to end to the dinner. Each of them held Li Yanggu's hands and said goodbye. They seemed distressed at parting. On the way back to the guesthouse, Li Yanggu told the sedan chair carriers to walk slowly. Since Chongqing was in a mountainous area, the roads were quite steep at some points. Though the moon was bright, on both sides of the narrow paths were thick trees and grass. The moonlight was blotted out by the trees and the paths looked very dark.

"'A night with no moon and a strong wind is always dangerous,' as the saying goes. Is Du Guangyuan going to kill me on my way back?" Suddenly Li Yanggu became nervous. He regretted that he had not asked the attendants who knew Kungfu to accompany him. He looked out of the sedan chair and found the dark path quite winding, extending to nowhere. It looked like it was not the same way they had taken him to the banquet earlier. Suddenly, he heard the clip-clop of some horses coming closer. The sound was even louder in the night's silence. Obviously, the horses were chasing the sedan chair. And the carriers seemed to be ready for this. When they heard the horses, they deliberately slowed down their pace.

After they had moved forward another few hundred steps, he heard someone shout at him: "Master Li, wait a minute, please!" Now Li Yanggu almost believed that the Chongqing yamen had conspired to murder him here. When he thought of this as the worst scenario, he calmed down. He asked the carriers to stop and calmly lifted up the curtain of the sedan chair. Then he found that they stopped on a steep slope. Beside the path was a dark valley. He could not see how deep it was. Around them were thick trees and grass. And it was deadly quiet except the hoof sounds made by the approaching horses. "It's really a good place to kill someone!" he thought to himself.

In just a few seconds, the horses arrived. Though in darkness, the knives they were carrying gave off a cold sheen. The soldiers got off the horses and ran to him. Li asked from the sedan chair, "Who are you?"

The soldier walking in front instead of answering his question, asked him "Are you Lord Li Yanggu?"

Li said, "What if I am and what if I'm not?"

The guy looked at him carefully and then said, "It's him. He has a thick beard."

He sounded more like he was talking to himself, rather than talking to the men following him. Li was a little frightened. He told himself that he could not let them kill him so easily. Then he got ready to defend himself. But he was surprised to see all the soldiers bowing to him at the same time and the first one say to him, "Our Magistrate worried that it might be dangerous for you to go back alone. So he sent us to escort you back. But we took the wrong way and got separated from you. Please forgive us for being late." Then Li Yanggu breathed a sigh of relief. He was very grateful to the Magistrate for his thoughtfulness.

"Magistrate Du is really considerate!" said Li Yanggu to the soldiers. Then he asked the carriers to continue. The soldiers gave all the horses to one man and the others protected the sedan chair in the middle. After some more time on mountain roads, they finally came to the main street. The bright moonlight illuminated their way. Li Yanggu felt completely relaxed. But he found that his clothes had already been drenched through with sweat.

It was almost second watch when Li Yanggu returned to the guest house. He changed his clothes and sat down by the window. A wave of sleepiness over came him after his earlier attack of nerves. He felt sleepy, but he did not want to go to bed. His brain was filled with flashbacks of the scene of being stopped by the soldiers. Now he completely believed that Du Guangyuan had bored no malicious intentions toward him at all. He was full of gratitude toward him. He decided he would come to Chongqing again after the case was finished, especially to pay a visit to Magistrate Du. He felt he had to thank him for his hospitality face to face. At this moment, he heard footsteps in the yard. He looked out through the window and saw two stewards supporting an old man walking toward his room under the light of a red lantern. When the lamplight shone upon him, Li Yanggu recognized him as the honest old scholar who had just drunk with him at Loquat Mountain. He hurried to the door to meet him in the manner of a junior greeting a senior. The old man greeted him back modestly and then, holding Yanggu's arm, walked into the room.

Li Yanggu was a little surprised by the old man's

visit, but he hesitated to ask his purpose. The old man himself was very straightforward, directly got to the point: "The saying goes: 'Nobody goes to a temple for nothing.' The reason I'm visiting you at night is that I want to entrust you with a serious matter on behalf of the Magistrate."

Li Yanggu realized immediately that he had come for the murder case in Hezhou. But he pretended to be caught unawares: "I'm only a scholar. What can I do for the Magistrate?"

The old scholar smiled a little and continued, "Lord Li is too modest. You have been ordered by the Viceroy to investigate the murder that happened in Hezhou. Everybody in Sichuan knows about it. Do you intend to hide it from me alone?"

Before Li Yanggu could give any explanation, the old scholar stopped him by stretching out his hand: "In fact, if we look at the murder case again, it is not that difficult at all. The Ju father and son were killed, but the killer ran away. In order to dodge higher authorities, the Hezhou Magistrate arrested an innocent woman and put her in jail as a scapegoat. The Prefectural Magistrates and the Surveillance Commissioners did not look through the case and made a wrong judgment. That's what happened." Li Yanggu did not expect the old scholar to be so direct. With just a few words, he had clearly drawn the outline of the mishandled case. He did not know how to answer him at first.

In fact, the old scholar did not wait for Li Yanggu to make any comment before he continued: "Lord Li, since you've been ordered to clear the case, it seems you should report the full truth, of course. In this way, firstly, the reputation of the honest and upright Viceroy will

285

become more renowned; secondly, Your Lordship will become renowned for his abilities; thirdly, the wronged woman will be cleared. Do you agree with me?" Li Yanggu found his words very reasonable, so he nodded his head to show his consent.

But the scholar gave a cold, slight smile and said, "However, the officials of the Subprefectural Magistrate, the Prefectural Magistrate and the Provincial Surveillance Commissioner are connected with the case; moreover, the Provincial Administration Commissioner and the Provincial Governor are also involved. If the Judgement was reversed, perhaps scores of officials in Sichuan Province would be dismissed from their posts. Think about it, how can this be reversed so easily? Even if you can expose the darker side, how can you seize the killer in such a short period? Without catching the killer, how can the Viceroy prove his judgment and persuade all the officials?"

The old scholar stopped speaking all of a sudden and stared at Li Yanggu. It seemed that he was urging Li Yanggu to think it over, carefully. He waited for a while. And when he found that Li Yanggu did not say anything, he continued, but changed his tone of voice: "Magistrate Du has realized that he made a big mistake in supervising the trial. He kept examining his own conscience. But the case is so complicated. Both the Viceroy and the Governor are watching the progress of it and the Provincial Administration Commissioner and the Provincial Surveillance Commissioner are also involved. Even if Magistrate Du intends to reverse the case, he could never manage it. After thinking it over and over again, the Magistrate considers that it'll be better for all of us if you can mercifully raise your hand high and yield in order to avoid trouble. As long as you uphold the original judgment, all the gossip and chaos in Sichuan will disappear immediately. To protect the officials of Sichuan Province is to protect the Viceroy. From then on, wherever Your Lordship goes, you will have bosom friends there. Magistrate Du has prepared three thousand taels of silver for you. What do you think of it, Lord Li?"

When Li Yanggu heard this, he was at first somewhat taken aback, and then gave out a loud laugh. He covered his ears with both hands and said, "I don't think you drank too much tonight. But how could you speak out loud such foolish words? I've heard about the murder case in Hezhou, but I didn't know any details. This time, I just happen to be passing Chongqing. I did not expect to be misunderstood by your Magistrate. You know, I'm only a small potato in front of the Viceroy. How could he entrust me with such an important task? Well, I'll pretend not to have heard the muddled words you've just said, and I don't want to listen to more. It's pretty late now. I should hurry back to Chengdu tomorrow morning. So please forgive me, I can't accompany you any longer." Finishing these words, Li Yanggu took up his teacup and said goodbye in anger.

The old scholar did not expect that he would be refused so abruptly. He regretted that he had been too straightforward. He wanted to give further explanations, but Li Yanggu stopped him: "Don't worry, Yanggu has been away from politics for a long time. And I have not a bit interest in official affairs in Sichuan. I won't tell anybody the words you said just now!"

The old scholar had to stand up and fold his hands in front of him to make a salute. He said with regret,

"Please don't mind what I said just now. I didn't mean anything by it." Then he called in the two stewards in to support him.

Li Yanggu did not see him out of the room. He said coldly: "Take care!" The old man staggered out of the gate slowly and the three people disappeared.

The next morning, Li Yanggu deliberately got up a bit late. He said to his attendants in a loud voice, "Prepare the luggage. We'll take the morning ship back to Chengdu." Before he left the guest' house, he wrote two letters, one to Prefectural Magistrate Du Guangyuan and the other to the notables in Chongqing. He gave the letters to one of the runners of the guesthouse and asked him to deliver them. He told the runner repeatedly, "I'm going back to Chengdu by ship. Please make sure to pass the two letters to them. Please tell the Magistrate that I'll be back in a few months and pay another visit to him." He asked two persons from the guesthouse to help them move the luggage on to the ship. Then he reluctantly left Chongqing.

The boat sailed downstream toward Chengdu. Unlike the quiet and secret way they came, Li Yanggu stood at the front deck of the boat with his hands folded behind him and enjoyed the view on both sides of the river. The wind blew up his long gown and mussed up his thick beard. Not until the boat had sailed a dozen kilometers away from Chongqing, did he get into the cabin and shave off his beard and change into common peasant dress. He said to the puzzled attendants, "Find a place where the current is gentle and drop me there. You two go directly back to Chengdu and tell the Viceroy that I'm going to Seven-Ravine Bridge. I'll report to him the results of my investigation in one month at the most." Only then did the attendants understand why Li Yanggu had tried to let everybody know that he was leaving for Chengdu.

Li Yanggu walked all the way to Seven-Ravine Bridge after he went ashore. There were in total less than fifty families in the village. But it was considered to be a big village in the suburbs of Hezhou. Li Yanggu was disguised as a merchant collecting mountain produce. He went from door to door to negotiate his "business." The villagers seldom left the mountains where they lived. Though they had some mountain produce in stock, they did not know where to sell them. So they were very happy to find a merchant who had come to them to buy mountain produce. Li Yanggu was not very discriminating about the goods and the prices he offered were pretty good. Therefore, in just one day, he managed to get quite close to the villagers. He chatted with them casually while examining the quality of the goods. It did not take him much trouble to find out the attitude of the villagers. All of them were full of indignation about the injustice against Xiang.

Soon, Li Yanggu got to know the situation at the site of the murder by talking with the people who had been there. From the conversations with Xiang's neighbors, he learned of how Chen Laolun sent the woman matchmaker Sun to the Ju family. By talking with the villagers, he understood that Xiang was a decent woman. Then he went to the Subprefectural town of Hezhou. He investigated privately in teahouses and restaurants. From all kinds of people's talk, he was struck by Chen's sinisterness and ruthlessness. Chen Laolun had fabricated lies against others many times. Li Yanggu also found the matchmaker Sun and elicited from her how

Chen Laolun had begged her to help him marry Xiang's daughter-in-law Zhou. Li Yanggu managed to get acquainted with the chief warden in the Hezhou prison and was told that before Xiang had been put into prison, Chen Laolun had been to the jail three times to interrogate the condemned prisoner, Jin the Sixth. Not long after that, Jin the Sixth had become the "intrigant" of Xiang.

Putting all the information together, Li Yanggu had a clear outline of the case. But who was the murderer? Li Yanggu could find not a single clue. He was very worried and upset. He had been out for quite some time. The Viceroy was awaiting his report. Li Yanggu decided to first go back to Chengdu and report to the Viceroy the injustice that had been done to Xiang. Then he would like to come back to Hezhou again, and concentrate on catching the criminal.

This time, Li Yanggu chose the land route to Chengdu. He had too many worries in his mind, so he could not enjoy the natural scenery on the way. He went so quickly that he covered more than one hundred kilometers within two days.

On the evening of the third day, he came to a small town. The town was not big, but because it was located on the route connecting Chengdu and Chongqing, there were a lot of travelers who used it as a rest-stop. So the town looked crowded and lively. Li Yanggu chose a clean small inn and checked in. After dinner, when he took a walk out on the streets, he found he was very much attracted by the unique style and scenery of this small town. He did not return to the inn until night had fallen. All the rooms were occupied and the wavering candlelight reflected the different figures of the guests against the windows. Some were drinking, while others played chess or gambled with dice. It was too noisy to fall asleep.

Li Yanggu was a little annoyed. He had no choice but to take out a book and start to read. Suddenly, he caught a conversation between two men. It seemed they had been talking for quite some time, but Li Yanggu had not paid much attention to what they were talking about until he heard the topic which was most sensitive to him. One man sounded a bit drunk: "People always say officials in the north are fools. But as I see it, the officials in Sichuan are even more stupid." Hearing this, Li Yanggu put down the book quietly and listened very carefully to their conversation.

The other man, with a Shaanxi accent, asked: "How stupid are the Sichuan officials?"

The drunk man replied, "Have you heard about the killing at Seven-Ravine Bridge?"

"No, never."

"What?! You haven't heard about such a big case? A family at Seven-Ravine Bridge, both the father and son, were killed one night. The Magistrate of Hezhou could not find the killer, so he took the wife as the scapegoat. He judged that she had murdered her husband and son and carelessly closed the case. In fact, the judgment is not at all convincing. But the Magistrate bribed the higher officials. Then, from the Prefectural Magistrate to the Provincial Surveillance Commissioner, they all insisted there was solid evidence to prove the judgment. Now, that woman has been sentenced to be dismembered to death. Heard she's very pretty! What a pity! So you see, how stupid these officials are!"

Hardly after the drunken voice had finished, the

Shaanxi accent continued: "Maybe you are not completely right. How do you know the father and son were not killed by a man who had seduced the wife?"

"I know, I know... of course! I'm sure the woman was wronged!"

"Why? Did you have an affair with the woman?"

"No, no. I don't know her at all, but the guy who killed her husband and son..."

The drunken fellow stopped here all of a sudden. And he did not continue. Li Yanggu could feel his heart thumping rapidly. He never expected that he would encounter an insider here. He stood up, got closer to the window, waiting patiently for the conversation to continue. It seemed that the drunk realized his words might be heard by someone who happened to pass. He did not say anything for quite some time.

The Shaanxi accent became impatient. He urged him eagerly, "We've been like old friends from the beginning. Are you going to keep me guessing the whole night?"

The drunk lowered his voice and answered, "What the hell are you shouting for? I told you the woman was wronged. That's it! I never lie to anyone."

But the man from Shaanxi just would not give up. He mumbled, "Maybe it's just your guess, huh? But you've got to be careful. If the yamen knew this, you'd be arrested for defaming the government."

"Who's defaming the government? They're really a herd of fools. To tell you the truth, I'm the killer!"

"You?"

"Don't believe me? I tell you, that night, when I passed Seven-Ravine Bridge, all the money I had was lost while gambling in Hezhou had made me so frustrated. Suddenly, I found a gate by the roadside was open. So I

292

sneaked into the house. I found a string of money in the sitting room. Then I took the money at once and was about to leave. But just then, an old man awoke—I don't know how I woke him, but anyway, he chased me out and grabbed the bag of money and wouldn't let go. I was afraid that he might cry out for help, so I drew out the ox-horn knife from my waist and stabbed him. The old fellow fell down to the ground without a sound. I was scared! And I turned around and ran. But who would have expected a young man with bare arms to run out from the yard and chase me? I was mad at that time, so I stabbed him in the chest. I didn't know whether he died or not, I just took out the knife and rubbed it on his clothes to clean it. Then I quickly escaped. For the next several months, I wandered in Hubei and Henan. I was afraid of being caught by the yamen. Last month, I heard the case had been closed. So I dared to come back..."

Hearing this, Li Yanggu became very excited. He knew clearly that if he hadn't just happened to run into this murderer, it would have been very difficult to catch such a killer who had killed accidentally and escaped far away after. Now, the criminal was in sight, but he might escape in no time if he was even slightly alerted. Li Yanggu drew a deep breath and calmed himself down. He memorized the room number in which the drunken man was staying and then strode out to the yard. He talked casually with the boy watching the gate for a bit and then left the inn assuming an easy manner. He asked someone for directions to the barracks troop and quickly ran there.

Since the town was located at a very important place, there were more than fifty soldiers garrisoned there. Li

Yanggu took out the letter written by the Viceroy and explained to the chief his identity. The chief obediently conveyed that they would act according to his orders. So Li Yanggu immediately ordered twenty select soldiers to surround the small inn and seize the criminal without any mishap. The chief accepted the order and effectively deployed the soldiers. In less than two hours, the criminal was arrested. Then Li Yanggu ordered several soldiers to escort the criminal to the Viceroy's yamen in ten days. Finally the real murderer was arrested and the case was completely cleared. That night, Li Yanggu had a very deep sleep. He had not had such a good sleep since he had accepted the assignment from the Viceroy.

On the twenty-fourth day of the sixth lunar month in the fourth year of Emperor Xianfeng's reign (1854), the murder case of Hezhou was tried again under the supervision of the Viceroy of Sichuan. When the news spread, people in Chengdu rushed to the Viceroy's yamen to watch the hustle and bustle. They crowded in front of the Viceroy's yamen and blocked the road.

The outer gate was opened just before seven o'clock. The Viceroy, the Provincial Governor, the Provincial Administration Commissioner and the Provincial Surveillance Commissioner entered the courtroom one by one. The Magistrate of Chongqing, Du Guangyuan, and the Magistrate of Hezhou, Rong Yutian, attended the trial as well. They looked nervous and uneasy. All the officers, soldiers and yamen runners wore solemn expression on their faces. And the tiger-head boards with "silence" and "avoidance" written on them added to the extremely awe-inspiring atmosphere in the courtroom.

After Huang Zonghan was seated behind the judge's

294

table, he took a solemn glance at the whole court and then folded his hands toward the jury officials as a salute. He said: "The murder case that happened in Hezhou was nothing special, indeed. But it took the yamens in the province about half a year to try the case. And it seems that the case was getting more and more complicated and difficult to clear. I had heard a lot of complaints about it since it was first tried. But there had been no solid evidence to reveal the truth of the case. I should thank all the fellow countrymen and officials of different levels for their assistance and support. Without their help, the case could not have progressed to the point it has today, where we are holding a joint trial. Please don't just take my opinion as the standard to judge for or against. Speak out about whatever you want to say as long as you're serious. Let us carefully consider the facts from all sides to reach our sole objective: Punish the real criminals so as to satisfy the people. Now it's time to start the trial."

After the Viceroy had issued his order, the accused and witnesses were one by one escorted into the court to be one by one interrogated. Xiang, who had been convicted of murdering her husband and son, was brought into court first. She withdrew her original confession. Next, the "intrigant" Jin the Sixth also revealed the truth about Chen Laolun instigating him to confess that he had been Xiang's intrigant and to insist Xiang was having an affair with him. Viceroy Huang immediately summoned Chen Laolun to court. Chen Laolun realized he had no other way out than to admit that he had conspired to frame Xiang because he was attracted by Zhou's beauty and lured by the money and rank that Rong Yutian had promised to offer him.

Huang Zonghan immediately ordered that Rong Yutian be dismissed from his post and detained him for further interrogation.

Rong Yutian defended himself: "My judgment that Xiang committed murder due to her adulterous behavior not only depended on the testimony of the intrigant Jin the Sixth, but also on the testimony of her daughter-in-law, Zhou." Huang Zonghan right away issued an emergency order to have Zhou brought to court for questioning.

Zhou did not know that the situation had completely changed. So she repeated the same testimony taught by Chen Laolun and testified that her mother-in-law had committed adultery. Huang Zonghan asked her, "Did you personally see your mother-in-law commit the immoral act?"

"Yes, I did," answered Zhou.

"When did you discover it?" Huang continued to ask.

"Two years ago," said Zhou. Huang Zonghan struck the mallet on the table and shouted at Zhou, "If you found out about the affair two years ago, why didn't you say something at that time so that the father and son would not have been killed?" was choked by Zhou in her tracks. The question stopped Zhou in her tracks. She did not know what to do and could not say anything at all.

Huang Zonghan said to the court: "The mother-in-law acted immorally, but the daughter-in-law did not report to the yamen when she knew. How could she be considered pure and innocent? clamp her up!" The soldiers standing on both sides responded "Yes" in loud voices and then lifted Zhou up and threw her on the ground. Before Zhou could turn over, the heavy

296

punishment tool was thrown in front of her.

Zhou was terrified. She continuously begged for mercy from the judge. Huang said to her coldly, "You saw your mother-in-law seduce a man, but did not do anything. This is not a moral woman's behaviour. Do I wrong you when I say you are also immoral?"

Zhou desperately wanted to avoid punishment, so she brooked no delay to clear herself in a shaking voice, "Have mercy, Your Honor! I didn't see my mother-in-law do anything immoral with any man. It was my husband who forced me to say so in court!"

Huang Zonghan turned to Chen Laolun, stared fixedly into his eyes and said to him, "Chen Laolun, do you have anything to say?"

Chen begged while he kept kowtowing on the ground, "I lost my head at that moment. Your Honor, please have mercy on me! Please spare my life!"

Huang Zonghan paid no more heed to Chen Laolun. He turned to the officials sitting on both sides and asked, "What do you think? Is it reasonable enough to correct the injustice agginst Xiang now?"

The Magistrate of Chongqing was so frightened that he shuddered terribly. But the Provincial Surveillance Commissioner looked as if be did not feel any guilt at all. He saluted Huang before he asked, "Now that Xiang is not the murderer, where is the real murderer?"

Huang gave a cold smile and answered, "Your Excellency wants to see the criminal, yes?" He turned to the officer on duty: "Bring him into the court!"

Hearing this, not only was the Provincial Surveillance Commissioner shocked, but also the Provincial Administration Commissioner and the Provincial Governor became secretly very nervous. In a few minutes, the real criminal was escorted into the courtroom. Huang Zonghan struck the table and said to him slowly but in a very stern tone, "Chen Long, confess to the court how you committed murder in Seven-Ravine Bridge!"

The criminal named Chen Long did not dare to deny anything. He described in detail how he had killed the Ju father and son that night. Then Huang Zonghan had the lethal weapon, a bloodstained ox-horn knife, presented to the court. After to Chen Long's confession it had been found in a cave not far from Seven-Ravine Bridge. Chen Long was sentenced to death and was to be executed immediately.

Chen Long was already scared half to death. After the officers dragged him out of the courtroom, Huang Zonghan pointed at the Provincial Surveillance Commissioner and hurled a question at him: "The murder case of Hezhou was so simply and clearly delineated. However, as the Provincial Surveillance Commissioner, you went so far as to take bribes and bend the law. How can you still sit in the judge's seat? Officers! Remove his seat and take off his official cap!"

Several officers promptly pulled the Provincial Surveillance Commissioner out of his seat and took off his official cap before pressing him on to the ground.

Then Huang Zonghan turned to Du Guangyuan, the Magistrate of Chongqing Prefecture: "Du Guangyuan, though you have a fourth rank, you ignored the law, took bribes and fabricated false accusations against a decent woman. You tortured the innocent at will. You even didn't think about pulling back before it was too late. You have roused the people's wrath. Now, I dismiss you from your official post and charge you according to the laws of the country. Do you have anything to say for yourself?"

Du Guangyuan did not say anything. In a panic he got up from his seat and threw himself on the ground. He kowtowed to the Viceroy, asking for punishment for himself.

Huang Zonghan lifted up a writing brush and rapidly finished an order. Soon, the order was announced in the court: "Chen Laolun and Zhou, working in collusion to frame Xiang, are sentenced to be decapitated and will be executed in autumn. The Magistrate of Hezhou, Rong Yutian, decrepit and muddleheaded, for having utter disregard for people's lives, taking bribes and cheating the above governments, is sentenced to capital punishment. The Magistrate of Chongqing Prefecture, Du Guangyuan, for perverting the law by accepting bribes and undermining discipline, is sentenced to exile with the army in Yunnan Province. The Provincial Surveillance Commissioner, Lu Dao'en, for taking bribes, acting to deny of justice and dereliction of duty, is temporarily dismissed from his official post to await further verdict. All the others who fabricated crimes to frame people will be sentenced to exile so long as the charges are proven true. Xiang, a villager of Seven-Ravine Bridge, suffered tortures because she had been defamed. She has proven to be honest and upright. The charges against her were proven false. She is judged not guilty and is now released in the court. Fifty taels of silver from the government will be offered to her as compensation. Xiang Juhua, for having an honorable character shall be given a commendation. The aide of the Viceroy's yamen, Li Yanggu, for shrewdly and efficiently overcoming difficulties in investigating the case and having merit in capturing the criminal, is promoted to be the new Magistrate of Hezhou."

Finally, the murder case taking place in Hezhou was completely cleared. The Viceroy was extolled by the people of Sichuan for his wisdom and astuteness. For a long time, there was a ballad which spread around Chongqing and Hezhou, saying: "Above Hezhou floated a shred of dark cloud, men were killed and adultery was cooked up—done to settle the case, Chen Laolun should be executed." In fact, not long after the final trial of the murder case, Huang Zonghan was promoted to become the Minister of Punishments and transferred to the capital city of Beijing. Among all the people who were sentenced, only Zhou was hanged. Chen Laolun committed suicide in jail. Rong Yutian had his death sentence commuted by the new Viceroy. The former Magistrate of Chongqing Prefecture Du Guangyuan was called back from exile and appointed as a County Magistrate for two terms. It seemed that only commoners received punishment if they broke the law!

图书在版编目(CIP)数据

红丸迷案：中国明清奇案选：英文/刘建业著.
—北京：外文出版社，2001
ISBN 7－119－02050－1

Ⅰ.红… Ⅱ.刘… Ⅲ.法律－案例－汇编－中国－明清时代－英文
Ⅳ.D929.49

中国版本图书馆 CIP 数据核字（1999）第 03608 号

责任编辑　胡开敏
英文编辑　赵　优
封面设计　王　志
插图绘制　李士伋

外文出版社网址：
http://www.flp.com.cn
外文出版社电子信箱：
info@flp.com.cn
sales@flp.com.cn

红丸迷案
——中国明清奇案选
刘建业　著
＊
©外文出版社
外文出版社出版
（中国北京百万庄大街 24 号）
邮政编码 100037
通县大中印刷厂印刷
中国国际图书贸易总公司发行
（中国北京车公庄西路 35 号）
北京邮政信箱第 399 号　邮政编码 100044
2001 年（36 开）第 1 版
2001 年第 1 版第 1 次印刷
（英）
ISBN 7－119－02050－1/I·461（外）
04500（平）
10－E－3199P